Saunders
1984

D0093743

A TIME FOR REMEMBERING

A TIME FOR REMEMBERING

The Story of Ruth Bell Graham

by Patricia Daniels Cornwell

Grason

A ministry of the Billy Graham Association

Box 1240, Minneapolis, MN 55440

Grateful acknowledgment is made for permission to reprint the poems "Let it be twilight," "Perhaps she will land upon That Shore" and "My love has long been yours..." from *sitting by my laughing fire...* by Ruth Bell Graham. Copyright © 1977 by Ruth Bell Graham. Used by permission of Word Books, Publisher, Waco, Texas.

A TIME FOR REMEMBERING. Copyright © 1983 by Patricia Daniels Cornwell. Quotations from Ruth Bell Graham's journals, papers, and personal correspondence. Copyright © 1983 by Ruth Bell Graham. Quotations from William F. Graham Jr.'s correspondence. Copyright © 1983 by William F. Graham, Jr. All rights reserved. Printed in the United States of America. No part of this book may be used or reproduced in any manner whatsoever without written permission except in the case of brief quotations embodied in critical articles and reviews. For information address Harper & Row, Publishers, Inc., 10 East 53rd Street, New York, NY 10022. Published simultaneously in Canada by Fitzhenry & Whiteside, Limited, Toronto.

FIRST EDITION

Designed by Catherine Hopkins

Library of Congress Cataloging in Publication Data
Cornwell, Patricia Daniels.
    A time for remembering.
    Includes index.
    1. Graham, Ruth Bell. 2. Baptists—United States—Biography. 3. Graham, Billy,
    1918–   . I. Title.
BX6495.G666C67 1983   269'.2'0924 [B]   82–48922
ISBN 0-06-061685-7

83 84 85 86 87 10 9 8 7 6 5 4 3 2 1

To
the wise old woman

Let it be twilight
just a little longer . . .
don't turn the lights up
yet;
twilight's a time
for remembering,
twilight's a time
to forget;
a decompression chamber
where the soul
submerged, uptight,
can un-begin
and slowly rise
to night.

Ruth Bell Graham, *sitting by my laughing fire . . .*

Contents

Preface

June 5, 1982
Nickerson Field
Boston University
Boston, Massachusetts

The rain was cold and interminable. It brawled over eaves and blew in billowing sheets through the open stadium, shrouding the girdling lamps in a gossamer of milky light. At one end of the field, glutinous with shoe-sucking mud, was the wooden platform. At the moment it was occupied only by four lines of empty folding chairs, and several tall amplifiers and a baby grand piano enveloped in heavy plastic. Hanks of thick cable snaked across the wet plank floor. The podium was covered with a small, square awning flapping loudly like a wind-ripped flag.

It was 7:00 P.M. For the past hour some thirteen thousand people cocooned in slickers, trench coats, hats, plastic bags and galoshes had trickled through the field house for the 7:30 service. It would not be televised because of the weather. Wide wooden boards bridged puddles leading to the tiers. Rainwater was an inch deep on the seats. Billy Graham had been urged to cancel, but as usual, he had refused, leaving his hotel with plastic-laminated sermon notes and his large-print black leather Bible. Wearing a Greek fisherman's cap, a khaki trench coat, and tinted glasses, he arrived, a flashing blue light attached to the roof of his rental car.

No one seemed to notice the figure who slipped out of the back seat with him and left him at the door, detaching herself like a glider soaring loose from a plane. She skated across the muddy tile floor of the field house, Sheraton trash-can liners over her feet fastened at the ankles with rubber bands. She wore black kid gloves and a fuchsia plastic rain cloak with a matching cap that umbrellaed her from her crown to the tip of her nose. Looking like a psychedelic version of the Morton salt girl, Ruth gave me a wet hug.

In no hurry to file outside to find a seat—there would be plenty to choose from this raw, dreary night—we sat in folding chairs against a cinder block wall, watching the crowd slog by. Outside, propagandists were passing out tracts accusing Billy Graham of being a Communist sympathizer; buildings and buses near the stadium boasted anti-Graham signs and banners; a deranged man less than ten feet from us was asking a security guard in a loud voice if he were Billy Graham disguised as a cop.

Ruth seemed impervious to it all, unaffected by the confusion that seemed to eddy around her husband everywhere he went. She missed little; an amused smile tugged at her lips from time to time as her brain processed images, expressions, snatches of conversation here and there. With dignity, she sat, her styrofoam cup of steaming coffee disappearing beneath her voluminous hat at intervals.

That was the way she liked it, in the middle of the masses and yet invisible. The pathos, the motion around her, interested her. Anonymous, she became animated like a child; she became pensive and reverent—relieved to keep her public self folded up and in her pocket like a dimestore rain bonnet.

"And if people start recognizing me after this book," she once warned me, "I'm going to dye my hair and move to Europe."

The year before the Boston crusade, on a January morning, I telephoned, asking her if I could drive up for a visit. She was in bed with the flu but said for me to come anyway since it seemed I had something very important to discuss. It was a bitterly cold morning and the sky was leaden as I made the two-hour trip from Charlotte, North Carolina, to Montreat, where she lives on the side of a ridge in a house built of century-old logs.

She was alone, split wood smoldering quietly in the fireplace in front of her hand-built bed, where she was propped against several pillows, surrounded by letters, stationery, books, pens, cassette tapes, napkins, Kleenex, and her large black leatherbound King James Bible. She smelled faintly of Rose Milk. A woman of regal loveliness, she is thin but shapely, her features almost flawless, as though chiseled by a loving artist. She is intense but soothing, like the fire on her hearth. Her movements are graceful, her presence hypnotic, even on this day when her bones ached and her eyes were glazed with fever.

"I want to write a book about you," I came straight to the point.

"You want to do what, honey?" she asked, her voice distracted and weary.

"You know, I want to write your biography," I said.

"Well, sure. That's fine," she said with a weak smile. "But I don't think it would be very interesting."

Several days later, she and her husband flew to Mexico and rested for a month. Her health and senses restored, she telephoned me one afternoon at *The Charlotte Observer,* where I was a police reporter.

"Patsy," she said, "*no way* you're going to write a book about me."

I met Ruth through her parents, Nelson and Virginia Bell, whom I grew to love shortly after my mother moved my two brothers and me from Miami to Montreat in 1963, when I was seven. Homesick for my own grandmother, I visited Mrs. Bell several times each month, entering without knocking through the screened-in back porch that led into the warm, fragrant kitchen. Beneath a layer of wax paper on top of her refrigerator there were always cups of homemade custard, generously sprinkled with nutmeg and deliciously moist.

I'd find her in the same place each time, sitting in her favorite chair beside the living room couch, a pink baby blanket over her knees, a battery-powered magnifying glass in her lap.

"Go get a custard," she'd chirp before I'd even sat down. For the next hour she'd spin yarns about her missionary days in China while we played games like Rook or Scrabble.

It was during these visits that I became acquainted with Ruth. She would glide in with dinner for her parents, or perhaps just for a chat. I was struck with her beauty, her gentleness and spontaneous laughter. My next encounters with her came when I was in the local red brick grammar school and would see her car idling out by the endless line of orange buses wrapped around the school. She was there to pick up her younger son Ned. I would conspicuously walk back and forth in front of her car, searching with mock gravity for bus #91, until she spotted me and asked me if I wanted a ride. It was a shame if Ned, much less empathetic than his mother, spotted me first. Once he rolled down his window and said, "You can quit walking around the car 'cause we're going to Asheville."

When I was twenty, Ruth and I began to become friends. In April of 1976 she invited me out to lunch. Invitations to her house, which was two miles from mine, followed. Usually she was alone. Her husband was delivering lectures at major universities and preaching throughout the world. After three decades of international acclaim, his pace was more, not less, frenetic. My earliest memories of him are of his sitting with his family near the back of the Montreat Presbyterian Church on the infrequent Sundays when he was in town. In those days I wasn't aware of who he was, but I surmised, based on all the head-turning and ogling, that he was very important. After the service, people would flock around him to shake his hand, ask him to autograph their Bibles or bulletins, perhaps ask him to pray for them. Once a woman pointed out that the price tag was still dangling from his suit jacket and then asked if she could keep it as a souvenir.

In later years, when I would see him in his own home during my visits with Ruth, I was surprised that he did not seem affected by the adulation and criticism. He just seemed tired. She would attempt to shield him when I or anyone else appeared. "Bill, why don't you go sit up there in the sun and rest while I visit with so-and-so," she would say as he greeted people, a slightly bemused expression in his eyes when she repeated the suggestion two or three times. More often than not, though, he would amble out onto the lawn or into the living room with her and the guests. At home, he didn't look so austere. He usually wore a tennis sweater, jogging shoes, and baggy blue jeans. Sometimes his socks clashed with his shoes or half of his shirt collar was crumpled inside his sweater. His eyes didn't have that steely gleam. They were soft, as though he were far away in thought—and they became softer when they looked at her.

Ruth seemed virtually untouched by the pressures of living in his wake while conducting a significant, though heretofore unpublicized, ministry of her own. Her eyes were vulnerable, much as his were, as though after all the years of being exposed to the public she had not slammed and latched the door to her emotions.

Nonetheless, she has always been a private woman, sensitive to others and fiercely protective of her family. She could not see what good would come of my writing her biography. It was difficult convincing her.

"Ruth," I told her in May of 1981, after she had repeatedly rejected my idea throughout the spring, "I haven't changed my mind."

"I know you haven't," she said, discouraged.

"If you don't let me write this biography, it will be the only selfish thing I've ever known you to do."

"*Boy,* that's really hitting below the belt," she said.

"Not because you'll be denying me the privilege," I added, "but because you'll be rejecting the opportunity to help those who have never met you and never will."

Several days later she telephoned me.

"O.K.," she said.

Acknowledgments

First and foremost I must thank Ruth herself for her assistance in the preparation of this book. I thank her for entrusting me with some two thousand pages of her private letters and diaries—without their artistry and remarkable detail, the fabric of this book would be painfully thin and colorless. I also thank her for the countless hours she spent with me in person and over the telephone, and for letting me excavate for photographs. It is impossible to convey how much her friendship and gentleness throughout all this have meant. It is also impossible to convey how much I appreciate her tenacity in protecting those people in her life who have become, or might have become, characters in this book.

I thank her brother, the Rev. Clayton Bell, of Dallas, Texas, for giving me access to some thirteen hundred letters written by Nelson Bell when he was a medical missionary in China. I thank Virginia Bell Sommerville, of Taejon, Korea, for giving me access to Mrs. Bell's diaries, which were recently discovered in the Bells' basement. I thank Rosa Bell Montgomery for giving me several days of her time in her home in Los Alamos, New Mexico. I thank Mary, Sarah, and Margaret McCue of Mount Sidney, Virginia, for showing me Belvidere and sharing family letters. I am grateful to Irwin S. and Jean Yeaworth of Valley Forge Films for allowing me to view the footage of Ruth's return to China and indulging me in mulled cider and Peking duck while I did so.

I thank Billy Graham's family for their time: his mother Morrow Graham, who died in the fall of 1981; his brother Melvin; and his sisters Jean Graham Ford and Catherine Graham McElroy. I thank the Graham children—GiGi, Anne, Bunny, Franklin, and Ned—for their patience and interviews. I believe this project has been harder on them than anyone else, because Ruth was the only part of their family life that had not been exposed to the public prior to this. I am especially grateful to Bunny for her graciousness and for the amount of time she spent cooperating with me during the book's final stages.

I thank employees of the Billy Graham Evangelistic Association (BGEA) office in Montreat: Evelyn Freeland, Maury Scobee, Karlene Aceto, Sally Wilson, and Stephanie Wills—who are surely sick and tired of hearing my voice over the telephone by now. I thank other BGEA employees and friends of the Grahams: Mrs. Cliff (Billie) Barrows; former public relations director Gerald Beaven; writer/actress Joan Winmill Brown and her husband, Bill Brown, president of World Wide Pictures; writer Colleen Townsend Evans; singer George Beverly Shea; and associate evangelist Grady Wilson.

I am grateful to journalist Dot Jackson for her warm friendship and good advice. Writing can be very lonely. A good friend is a treasure. And I thank Joseph C. Carter, Jr., for his unselfishness and wisdom.

I am grateful to my friends at *The Charlotte Observer* who gave me access to the paper's library and its wealth of clippings. I will never forget that it was the editors there who gave me my first job in journalism.

I thank everyone, and there are too many people to mention, who granted me interviews, shared letters with me, or gave me suggestions. I especially appreciate the contributions of Gay Currie Fox, and of Hampton Talbot (who died in the fall of 1982), for without their vivid recollections much that is in the chapters on China would not be there. I thank with great affection the Rev. Calvin Thielman, Montreat Presbyterian Church, for his time and loyalty.

I am greatly indebted to the scholars who read my manuscript or donated bits of their learning to it: Dr. Mary D. Beaty, Assistant Librarian, Davidson College, Davidson, North Carolina; Dr. John H. Leith, Professor of Theology, Union Theological Seminary, Richmond, Virginia; Dr. Arthur S. Link, Editor, *The Papers of Woodrow Wilson,* Princeton University, Princeton, New Jersey; Eileen Moffett and Dr. Samuel H. Moffett, Professor of Missions and Ecumenics, Princeton Theological Seminary, Princeton, New Jersey; and most of all, my instigator and personal editor, Charles E. Lloyd, Professor Emeritus of English, Davidson College, Davidson, North Carolina.

I thank the following people who took hours from their frenetic schedules to write, telephone, or see me in person: William F. Buckley, Jr., Barbara Bush, June Carter Cash, Julie Nixon Eisenhower, Paul Harvey, William Randolph Hearst, Jr., Senator Jesse Helms, Lady Bird Johnson, Bob Jones, Jr., Dr. Harold Lindsell, Dan Rather, and of course, Billy Graham.

Finally, I offer my warmest thanks to publisher Clayton Carlson, Harper & Row San Francisco; editor Roy M. Carlisle; production manager Tom Dorsaneo; production editor Kathy Reigstad; and editorial assistants Melissa Stoker and Rebecca Laird. I thank my friend and literary agent, Gerard McCauley, who initially took me on (knowing it was a risk) and exhibited nothing but integrity and forbearance throughout. Most of all, I thank my husband and mentor, Dr. Charles L. Cornwell, who had to live with the project for as long as I did.

If I have left anyone out—and of course I have—I offer my sincere apologies.

It would be impossible to footnote every quotation. Therefore, one can assume that all unattributed quotations in the text came from private papers and my interviews with Ruth and others.

In keeping with her wishes, many of the names in the book are fictitious to protect the individuals.

PART I

Before Ruth

NORTH KIANGSU, CHINA, DECEMBER 5, 1916. The Grand Canal meandered through the frozen lowlands like a muddy snake and carried the launch and its barge past dozens of sampans, tugboats, and junks.

Nelson Bell, a twenty-two-year-old medical doctor, buried his chin deeper inside the flipped-up collar of his wool coat, buffering himself from the cold air and the sour smell of dirty feet on the deck outside his glassless window. His wife, Virginia, wrote letters at a small table behind him, glancing up each time he momentarily retreated from the freezing air. Progressing along the Grand Canal, they passed an ancient city surrounded by high gray brick walls. Heads of criminals impaled over the gate stared with dull eyes across the murky water.

Lemuel (which is Hebrew for "belonging to God") Nelson Bell was a witty, intelligent young man with a character as sturdy as his Scotch-grain leather shoes. Handsomely constructed, he had wavy brown hair, even teeth bright as a blade, a square jaw, and a patrician nose. Six feet tall, he was a solid hundred and ninety pounds and looked more like a matinee idol than a missionary. He was in fact a former professional baseball player who had forsaken his ambition because he longed to share the gospel with those who had never heard it. As he stood in his cabin, it was as if the Grand Canal beneath his feet and the faith of his forebears coursing through his veins were moving together, carrying him to his destiny.

He was born July 30, 1894, in the iron-laced Allegheny mountains near Clifton Forge, Virginia, where his father, James Bell, headed the commissariat at the Longdale Mining Company. Nelson Bell's forebears were Scotch Irish immigrants who had begun farming and lumbering some eight hundred acres of fertile land in the Shenandoah

Valley around the early 1700s. He was probably most like his great-great-grandfather John McCue, Jr., whose father had immigrated to America from northern Ireland around 1731. Young McCue, born in 1753, was educated at Liberty Hall (later renamed Washington and Lee University) and set his heart on becoming a Presbyterian minister. This noble ambition was almost deflated by Thomas Jefferson, who upon meeting McCue offered to train him as a lawyer and let him live at Monticello. But McCue refused and set about evangelizing the territory. By 1791 he was ordained and settled in the small parish of Tinkling Springs in Augusta County, Virginia.

A flamboyant man, McCue galloped through the countryside in his two-wheeled gig, his long brown hair streaming back from his high forehead. He spoke his mind from his hogshead pulpit and was subsequently upbraided from time to time at the presbytery meetings he was consistently tardy in attending. During heated arguments he was known to threaten to remove his parson's coat and resort to his fists, and "he could tell comic stories in a manner irresistibly ludicrous," wrote an acquaintance. He died Sunday morning, September 20, 1818, when he was thrown from his horse on his way to preach, leaving behind eleven children. A son, William, one of the county's first physicians, died soon after, and William's widow, Ann Barry McCue, married pioneer John Allen in 1821. Three years later, John Allen and Elisha Rumsey, who also had a wife named Ann, founded a small settlement on the Huron River in southwest Michigan Territory which they christened "Ann's Arbour" (now Ann Arbor, Michigan).

Nelson Bell's maternal great-grandfather, a classmate of John McCue, was the Reverend William Wilson.[1] His daughter Elizabeth married John McCue's grandson Thomas, and they built a plantation in Augusta County which they named Belvidere. The modest, two-story brick house (where Nelson Bell's mother, Ruth Lee "Cora" McCue, was born) was used as a Confederate hospital during the Civil War. In 1864 when Sheridan stormed the grain- and cattle-rich Shenandoah Valley to burn the Confederacy's breadbasket, Eliza-

---

1. William Wilson became of interest to his descendants in 1912 when Staunton-born Woodrow Wilson became the twenty-fifth president of the United States. Family legend has it that he was a descendant of William Wilson, but intensive study of family pedigrees has never been able to verify this claim. Woodrow Wilson's biographer, Arthur S. Link of Princeton University, observes that ". . . when Woodrow Wilson was elected President of the United States, all of his relatives came out of the woodwork." William Wilson and kin were not among them.

beth McCue slipped a gold coin from her shoe and paid the Federal officer in charge to leave the property without burning the barn. Family legend has it that thirty-three years later Elizabeth McCue saw a photograph of this officer: It was the new president of the United States, William McKinley. Her daughter Betty immortalized herself in the valley when another band of Federal soldiers appeared at Belvidere and an officer moved from room to room dropping lighted matches in the closets. Betty followed close behind, stamping them out. When the officer then demanded the brooch she was wearing, she slapped it into his palm, pin first.

"Madam!" the officer exclaimed as he returned the brooch and bowed, "I admire your spunk!"

Elizabeth McCue's daughter Cora was a strong-willed, practical woman who as a child had a bit of a temper. The living room door at Belvidere still bears the scars young Cora gave it when she beat it with the fire tongs after spats with her brother William. In 1882 Cora married distant cousin James Bell, who was as handsome as he was impractical and who had more of a penchant for spinning colorful yarns than for minding his store. Cora handled the family finances, supervised the three children and indulged her interest in world affairs and foreign missions through reading and entertaining furloughed missionaries. A bit of a daredevil, she decided on one occasion when a missionary was visiting to make an impulsive visit to Belvidere. Since her husband had taken the horse-drawn wagon to work, she had no transportation to the foot of the mountain where the train station was. Recalling that there was a handcar at the mine, Cora and the missionary, neither knowing anything about such contraptions, hopped aboard. The track ran past the store and James Bell looked up just in time to see the runaway car streak by, its handle seesawing madly.

"That looks like my wife!" he exclaimed as the car derailed, propelling both Cora and the missionary into a thicket.

When Nelson Bell was six, his mother moved the children to Waynesboro to begin school. Her husband joined them later and began working as a salesman at a local shop. From the start, young Nelson showed that he had inherited the best qualities of his ancestors. He was a devout Christian and unshakably loyal to the Presbyterian tradition of his family. He was a talented athlete, whose intelligence and agility produced maddening spins and intricate strategies on the tennis court or baseball field. As he matured, his fondness for baseball grew into a passion, and by age sixteen he was the captain of his high school's champion team. He quickly distinguished himself as a pitcher with his own version of the knuckleball. Holding the ball firmly in his fingertips, he'd stand ramrod straight, his eyes hidden by the shadow of his cap as he slid them left to right, checking the bases. Slowly, he'd cock his body like a catapult and snap forward, sending the unspinning ball floating toward the plate where it either jumped over or dived under the befuddled player's bat. In every cheering crowd, his fiancée, a willowy, gray-eyed blonde named Virginia Leftwich, was watching, her milky complexion flushed beneath a sweeping hat.

Virginia, born April 12, 1892, in Richmond, was the oldest of four children—two boys and two girls. Her father, Douglas Lee Leftwich, was a traveling salesman and expert cabinetmaker with a magnificent baritone voice. Shortly after Virginia's birth, her family moved to Charlottesville, then to Waynesboro, where she lived five blocks from the Bells' three-story house.

Her ancestors included high-ranking military officers, scholars, and physicians. She was descended from William Wertenbaker, whom Thomas Jefferson had appointed in 1826 to head the library of the University of Virginia. Her uncle was the prominent Princeton University historian Thomas Jefferson Wertenbaker. Her relative Charles Christian Wertenbaker, a novelist and foreign editor for *Time*, would scandalize the family: When he was told in 1954 that he had incurable cancer, rather than suffer the physical and mental ravages of the disease, Wertenbaker slashed his wrists in his home off the Bay of Biscay in southern France and calmly watched himself bleed to death while his wife, Lael Tucker, dripped morphine into his wounds to dull the pain. She then published several accounts of her husband's suicide.

Though Virginia Leftwich and Nelson Bell had been acquainted as children, it wasn't until high school that they fell in love. Fragile in body, she was stubborn and valorous in spirit, with a sensitivity to stress that would make pain an integral part of her life. After graduation, Nelson entered Washington and Lee University while she studied nursing in Richmond. He had intended to study law, but his plans were dramatically altered by a seemingly insignificant event. On a winter's evening in 1911 when the air was sharp and stars shone like pin pricks in a black curtain, Nelson and a friend strolled across campus spinning their career plans as young men do. Abruptly, his companion slowed his pace and turned his shadowy face to him. "Nelson," he asked, "did you ever think of becoming a medical missionary?" As the two silhouettes paused on the frosty grass, their words emerging in smoky puffs, Nelson knew without equivocation that come morning he would switch from law to pre-medical. He had been caught in the wake of the Student Volunteer Movement for Foreign Missions, launched by American evangelist Dwight L. Moody in 1886. Since that time, thousands of America's most intelligent and attractive young men and women had enlisted to achieve "the evangelization of the world in this generation."[2]

Nelson had heard his mother's missionary friends tell of their experiences in China, a land of mystery on the dark side of the world, polarized by squalor and opulence, where few Westerners had trod, save importers of opium or Christianity. He would go there, he decided. But a small white cowhide sphere would almost scotch his plans. In 1913, while a student at the Medical College of Virginia in Richmond, he signed a baseball contract with the professional Virginia League after it was agreed that he wouldn't have to play on Sundays. Two years later the team was sold to the Baltimore Orioles. To play in the major leagues had been a dream he had kept in a pocket of his heart since childhood. For weeks his conscience and ambition waged a silent struggle; the former finally overruled the latter, and he resigned from the league. In May of 1916 the executive secretary of the Southern Presbyterian Foreign Mission Committee cabled him, asking if he could leave for China immediately. One of the two American doctors at the Tsingkiang General Hospital in North Kiangsu had died after only a few months' service. Nelson and Virginia agreed to accept the offer, with the stipulation that their departure be delayed three months to give him an opportunity to serve at least a brief residency.

Forsaking her Baptist heritage, she became a Presbyterian; he received his medical license, and on June 30, 1916, they were married. They began their lives together in the coalfields of West Virginia where he served his residency, and in early November they hauled their few belongings to Seattle, Washington, and sailed to the Far East. Two of the dozen Southern Presbyterians to join the China

---

2. Kenneth Scott Latourette, *A History of Christianity,* vol. 2 (New York: Harper & Row, 1975), p. 1019.

mission field that year, they docked in Shanghai's International Settlement after nineteen days of turbulent waters and gut-wrenching seasickness. They were met by Jimmy and Sophie Graham, veteran missionaries who would become two of the Bells' closest friends.[3]

"Poor Virginia Bell," one missionary woman muttered to another as they eyed the slender blonde standing on the quay beside a small mountain of boxes and trunks, "she won't last a year."

Dressed in tailored woolens, hats and gloves, the Bells gripped the sides of the rickshaw and squinted in the late morning sun. With tins of cheese, a Virginia ham, bolts of cloth, and medicines secured with ropes on all sides, the couple bounced through the crowded streets to the train depot, looking like animated anachronisms in an Oriental fairy tale. From Shanghai the train clattered slowly a hundred and fifty miles northwest to Chinkiang, where a ferry carried them across the muddy Yangtze River to the Grand Canal. On December 5, they boarded the launch that took them the remaining one hundred and twenty-five miles north to Tsingkiang. Traveling that distance along the Grand Canal would take as long as two weeks in the future when the water was low or choked with ice. But this time, their sail lasted a brief forty-eight hours. There had been little sleep for them the night before in the dark, dank cabin below the deck full of Chinese who had chattered like magpies until dawn. Wretched on their slivers of sleeping-shelves, they had spent the noisy, black hours stretching out and tucking in their legs as they vacillated between being cramped to being cold.

Disembarking at the Tsingkiang quay, they were surrounded by bartering rickshaw coolies tugging at their baggage while the shrill music of foreign tongues cascaded over them. Women nursing infants eyed them with mild suspicion while others squatted on the shore washing rice in the filthy water.

The one hundred and seventy bed Tsiangkiang General Hospital had been built two years earlier by Dr. James Baker Woods, a medical missionary in China since 1894. It rested on a six-acre tract of land less than a mile from the canal and, like every other settlement and city in China, it was surrounded by a gray brick wall. Absalom Sydenstricker, father of Nobel prize winning novelist Pearl Buck, had founded the mission station in 1887. Beyond the north wall of the compound were the bleak fields where peanuts and sweet potatoes

---

3. Jimmy and Sophie Graham are not related to Billy Graham.

had been harvested two months earlier. In every direction, the expanse of bleak earth was interrupted by thousands of tan, conical grave mounds, kept clear of grass and weeds by filial caretakers who feared the wrath of the ancestors they worshiped. In this land of too many people and too little food thousands of cultivatable acres were sown with no crops but bones and veneration.

During the summers in Kiangsu, temperatures rose to 106 degrees and monsoon rains poured from the heavens until the Grand Canal rose from its bed like a watery beast and coiled over the earth, devouring the peasants' mud dwellings. Fields flowed together into lakes as the farmers fled in crude boats and rafts or climbed the few trees, clinging to branches like tattered birds. As brightly colored paper and pottery idols washed away with their livelihoods, the people wondered what they had done to arouse the malevolent spirits. When the land was dry, winds roared through the Gobi Desert, sweeping billowing sheets of yellow dust through Inner Mongolia, over the Great Wall and fifteen hundred miles south into Kiangsu, where grit blotted the sun and seeped under doors and through window frames and every other crevice. And the people's gods turned furies, ranging the earth to unleash all manner of terrors—hailstorms, droughts and black clouds of locusts to prey upon the grainfields.

It was during these times of tragedy that the Chinese turned to the missionaries and clung to them, seeking refuge in their compounds and begging food for their starving children. Forgetting their prejudices and resentment, many swallowed the foreigners' religion along with their medicines. "God is not an idol," the Westerners explained to a people who had more gods than they could count. "There is only one true living God who loves you and sent His Son to die as a sacrifice for your sins," they'd say to the ragged prisoners they would bring bread and bandages to in the wretched prisons, where the whistling of the guards to announce an execution was as constant as the wind. Some Chinese understood and believed what the missionaries told them. Others did not; they wondered what this Jesus had done to anger His Father so.

To the Chinese, the foreigners were a curious people with hair and eyes the colors of the wheat, sky, soil, and grass. The men had teeth like mules and the women had feet as big as boats. They came from a cradle in the West where the sun, they said, rose while it set in China, and set while it rose some twelve hours later. The missionaries in north Kiangsu called themselves Southern Presbyterians, and the ones in the southern portion of the province called themselves Northern Presbyterians. The superstitious Chinese people, who reckoned themselves to be already one year old at birth, decided that these strange people must be at least one hundred years old when they were delivered from their mothers' wombs. To many Chinese, the missionaries were *yang kuei tse,* or foreign devils, who had been disgorged from East India Company ships along with the opium traders during Queen Victoria's reign. The people of God and traders of "foreign mud," as the drug was called, fell under the same anathema. Like the men who forced opium down China's throat, the missionaries, many Chinese believed, were ambassadors of a wicked imperialism and were devoid of respect for Chinese government and culture.

Politically, the Bells could not have entered China at a more unstable time. In 1911, the Manchu dynasty, which had become increasingly corrupt since it came to power in 1644, had been overthrown. The Chinese had turned to the West for hope, believing that they too could enjoy the West's power and advanced technology if China became a democracy. Thus, the Republic of China was born, founded by Western-educated Sun Yat-sen. His successor Yüan Shih-k'ai had appointed chieftains or warlords to govern the eighteen provinces, believing that he could exercise central control over them and their armies. Instead, "official bandits," as the peasants called the soldiers, had roved about raping, pillaging, and murdering while the warlords fought among themselves for power. Wealthy landlords fled the countryside for the safety of city walls, leaving irrigation and flood control systems unattended. The fruits of democracy were marauding, flooding, and droughts. For the peasant once oppressed by the empress dowager, the new republic embodied a more formidable randomness and terror. For some intellectuals, it was time to study other foreign ideologies, such as Marxism.

What the official bandits left behind, the dirt bandits crept in like rodents to devour. They were even more dangerous, for they were civilians who moved about incognito, often tilling the soil by day and raiding their neighbors by night. They had a penchant for kidnapping children and selling them into slavery or child prostitution. Ransom was usually the objective, and notes would arrive in small bundles along with a severed ear or finger. Another ear or finger would follow if payment was delayed. Though missionaries were not immune, they made it known that they would not pay ransoms under any circumstances.

A Time for Remembering

Final disillusionment with the West came with the Treaty of Versailles in 1919, when the West gave Japan former German concessions in China's mountainous Shantung peninsula. It was a gift that was not the West's to make, and it symbolized to the Chinese that the West perceived China as inferior, unworthy of the rights that other nations enjoyed. Less than a year later the Comintern sent three members of the Bolshevik party to China. Within months the official Chinese Communist Party had been organized.

In describing the political and economic scene in China, the missionaries used one word repeatedly in their letters and diaries: "chaotic." Each night rifles crackled in the countryside beyond the Bells' compound wall, breaking the smooth silence like firecrackers. In the hospital, Nelson did not always know whether he was treating a bandit or a guileless peasant (he once recognized his bandages on a criminal's head impaled over the city gate). One never knew when Chinese sentiments would turn antiforeign, as they had in the 1900 Boxer Rebellion, when churches were burned and Christian missionaries and their Chinese converts murdered. And yet, life and death, the Bells believed, were as much a part of God's providence as their traveling to China had been.

2

A Second Little Nuisance

Ruth was a very normal child but above the average in spirituality. I'd say she was rather deep in her feelings. She was a very thoughtful little girl, and she was pretty, with curly hair and big hazel eyes.

Margaret Sells, former missionary to China

In late spring, 1920, wheat and barley fields in the north Kiangsu lowlands burgeoned with the most promise in forty years. Chinese peasants in shapeless gray-blue trousers worked silently as the earth warmed to imminent summer. The collectors of night soil wove through the crowded streets of Tsingkiang, their stinking buckets swinging from *bien dans* across their shoulders as they headed to replenish the fields.

The Tsingkiang General Hospital was filled with Chinese suffering from cholera, tuberculosis, and venereal disease. Doctors treated burns and knife and gunshot wounds inflicted by bandits who frequently tortured their victims into revealing where the family money was hidden. The majority of gunshot wounds, however, were the result of domestic brawls. Ever since the fall of the Manchu dynasty nine years earlier, Chinese men had been cutting off their queues. Squabbles that had been settled by the painful yanking of the long braids now, it seemed, found more violent expression. There were the usual cases of attempted suicide, caused when Chinese lost face or hope and swallowed match heads or arsenic. Children were carried into the hospital, their scalps eaten to the bone from home treatments of arsenic for "that heavenly thing" as the Chinese called malaria. Doctors removed long needles from torsos and faces—other home remedies for meningitis and kala-azar (black fever).

Most Chinese did not trust the Western doctors: They were monsters who made medicines from dead Chinese babies' eyes and bones; they were alchemists who changed Chinese marrow and other bodily elements into gold. Often the superstitious natives did not visit the hospital until it was their last hope. Then tumors weighing ten to forty pounds were removed. One day a one-hundred-eighty-three-pound woman arrived at the hospital gate, pushing her tumescent belly ahead of her in a wheelbarrow. After Nelson Bell had removed the tumor, she weighed ninety pounds. Untreated broken bones that had healed at bizarre angles were rebroken and set. A local peasant finally resorted to treatment after his broken ankle fused, leaving his foot pointing backward.

By 1920, Dr. Bell was the superintendent of the growing hospital. He was known for his compassion, humor, and long hours. Often he performed as many as nine operations in the morning alone, leaning over a sea of white in the glow of a low, tin-hooded lamp while nurses wiped the sweat from his face with towels. At meals as the children were growing up, he frequently teased his wife and children by describing that day's procedures in graphic, gory detail. A highly skilled surgeon, he was versatile enough to remove cataracts or fill a tooth; he could amputate a leg and then fashion a prosthesis from a beam of wood. He frequently made housecalls fifty miles into the countryside, his black Harley-Davidson motorcycle (with sidecar) bumping over the rutted, six-foot-wide dirt roads. He sometimes gave his own blood to patients, because the Chinese would not donate theirs, not even for money. Blood, the Chinese would explain, "is handed down from our ancestors. He who loses it in this world will not have it in the world to come. Who would willingly spill or waste a drop of it?"

But what was most important to him was souls, and he would later say that the hospital existed "primarily for the preaching of the Gospel." Ambulatory patients were required to attend daily chapel. There was a full-time evangelist on the hospital staff to work with the male patients and a Bible teacher to work with the women. And to Dr. Bell, the spiritual gifts were more significant than athletic or surgical skills. There was a slip of paper under the glass covering his rolltop desk. On it he had scribbled the fruits of the Spirit, a reminder that this was his true ambition: "Love, Joy, Peace, Longsuffering, Gentleness, Goodness, Faithfulness, Meekness, Self-Control." And, recalled a former missionary, "I never knew a man whose life so beautifully manifested those characteristics."

He was also renowned for his courage. Once two hundred corrupt militiamen began looting the nearby home owned by the Grahams, then on furlough in the United States. When a houseboy rushed to the operating room and told Dr. Bell, he ran to the scene, kicked down the locked gate and chased off the mob single-handedly. Then he followed the thieves to their camp and retrieved a stolen bicycle. On another occasion, while he was traveling by barge, a Chinese man who could not swim fell into the Grand Canal. Dr. Bell dived into the muddy water after him while the other passengers watched in amazement, not understanding why this foreigner would risk his life for a coolie. In an environment where the most formidable mental enemy was the feeling of futility, his colleagues knew him as a man who was never tormented by discouragement. To many Chinese, he was "Chong Ai Hua," or "the Bell who is lover of the Chinese people."

On Thursday, June 10, 1920, Dr. Bell bolted upstairs to his bedroom in the gray brick Chinese house on the compound. He rolled up his sleeves, scrubbed his hands and filled a pan with steaming water. His heart thudded harder than it normally did when he delivered a baby. This was different. It was his own. No one recalls what time she arrived, but it is certain that it was the year of the monkey, which Asian astrologers claimed spawned multi-talented, adventuresome, and witty people. Ruth McCue Bell, named for her paternal grandmother, would fulfill those prophecies.

She began life rather unceremoniously. Because she was a girl, none of her parents' Chinese friends passed out red-dyed eggs or ignited strands of firecrackers in celebration. Now, they thought, "Chong Ai Hua" had two little nuisances, Rosa Wertenbaker having been born two years earlier. Ruth wouldn't even have an official birth certificate, for the record of her birth was registered in the Nanking consulate, which would be destroyed by fire in 1927.

In 1922, the Bells built a two-story gray brick house on the compound to accommodate their growing family. It had a corrugated red tin roof, a two-level porch, and three dormer windows, and it was less than a hundred yards from the hospital operating room where Dr.

Bell began work at 8:30 each morning, after breakfast and family devotions. The Bells, like most missionaries, were determined to westernize their children, who would one day leave for American colleges, husbands, and homes. Ruth's parents also worked to make what could have been Spartan living conditions comfortable. After the hospital acquired a generator, Dr. Bell equipped the house with electric lights and a refrigerator; later he installed a telephone system in missionary homes within a mile radius of his compound, more than a decade before lines would connect Shanghai to the smaller cities.

One of the biggest inconveniences, and one that could not be remedied, was the absence of indoor plumbing. The bathrooms consisted of two cubbyholes—one off the upstairs porch and the other off the kitchen. Each contained a square wooden box with a hole in the middle and a five-gallon bucket underneath, emptied daily by a collector of night soil. Though there was a well on the compound, the water was too hard and contaminated to use for drinking or cooking. So each day, water was carried from the Grand Canal and emptied into large earthen jars called *gongs,* which stood outside the kitchen door. Half a cup of crystal alum was poured into each, and the murky water was stirred with a long stick until the impurities sedimented. Though most of it was used for cooking, some became drinking water after it was boiled in a large kettle in the kitchen and then filtered twice through cotton in Dr. Bell's homemade galvanized tin water cooler in the pantry. What was left in the *gongs* was heated each week and carried to an upstairs bedroom for bathing. If it was winter, the water was poured into a tub set before a tin trash burner, stoked with soybean stalks and bits of trash until it thawed a narrow margin of air. Usually, Rosa would take her bath first and young Ruth would follow, slipping gingerly into the tepid water and spending the next few minutes rotating in the tub as the fire scorched the side closest to it and the icy air froze the other. After a brisk scrubbing, Ruth scrambled into her flannel gown and crawled into bed with a hot water bottle. Other than the trash burners, there was no heat in the bedrooms. Downstairs, the fireplace and the kitchen stove were heated with the fifteen tons of Shantung coal Dr. Bell purchased for forty-five dollars each winter.

Mrs. Bell began furnishing their new home with the half-dozen Empire maple, oak, and mahogany pieces her father had lovingly crafted for her not long before she married. Other items were made by a local Chinese carpenter. The living room was in shades of blue with Mandarin rugs on the polished hardwood floors. A coal grate was in one corner, an upright piano stood between two windows, and flowered paper covered the walls. Their mother schooled the children in the strictest of manners—dress-clothes at dinner and no elbows on the table. Tardiness at morning devotions meant no sugar on one's porridge. Sassing was unthinkable. Along with Chinese food, the Bells ate Southern fare like fried chicken, biscuits, and apple pie. Tomatoes, lettuce, asparagus, and other vegetables were grown in the small garden behind the house, which she shared with the other missionaries. Mrs. Bell turned her bleak patch of earth into an oasis, shaded by mulberries, Chinese elms, locusts, and fruit trees, which rustled like starchy petticoats with each movement of the wind. Chrysanthemums, geraniums, lilacs, irises, and roses bordered the porch and the compound wall.

Like most missionaries, the Bells hired Chinese helpers and paid each of them two American dollars from the Bells' combined seventy-five-dollar monthly salary, an amount that tripled when converted to Chinese currency. The wages and working conditions were superior to those endured by other Chinese peasants. The cook was the head servant, and without his prowess at bartering in the marketplace, Mrs. Bell would have had to contend with merchants tripling their prices the minute her foreign face appeared. She taught him to prepare American dishes, though some of his early attempts at making biscuits, for example, were disastrous. She supervised him closely to ensure that he washed all vegetables in boiled water and practiced other sanitary measures. Others did the laundry and cleaning, and in the gatehouse lived Liu Er, an affable sentry of sorts who monitored all who entered and left the compound. He also carried the water from the Grand Canal each day.

The family's most important servant and the one dearest to Ruth was her amah (nanny) Wang Nai Nai, who lived in a small room in the Bells' house. She had been a procuress of "little flowers," or child prostitutes, before missionary Sophie Graham had converted her to Christianity. Barely five feet tall, Wang Nai Nai weighed ninety-six pounds in her thickly padded winter clothes. Her face was broad and flat, and deep, cheerful wrinkles radiated from her small dark eyes. Her thinning gray-streaked hair was always in a bun and because she was of peasant stock, her feet were unbound. Though she doted on Ruth, Wang Nai Nai was sometimes less than affectionate with Rosa. To the superstitious Chinese, it was a shame for the first child to have been born a girl instead of a boy.

Though servants freed the missionaries for the tasks they had traveled more than seven thousand miles to do, they weren't the luxury one might suppose. They bickered among themselves, and they needed constant and close supervision. On two occasions, the amah forgot to wash Ruth's hands before bed and the child awoke screaming and stained with blood after a rat bit her finger. Scorpions scuttled into laundry baskets, and bedbugs and lice stowed away on freshly laundered linen and clothing. The house would soon have been infested had Mrs. Bell not stood guard at the door to inspect each article the servants carried in from the hospital laundry.

Despite all precautions, illness was virtually accepted as the norm. Scarcely a month passed without one of the Bells contracting flu, a cold, a viral infection or unexplainable low fever. Mrs. Bell was plagued by daily headaches that rammed through her temples like a white-hot iron and sent her blindly retreating to her bedroom, where she lay with the curtains drawn until the throbbing and ringing in her ears subsided. Home treatments of narcotics and soaking her feet in hot mustard water offered little relief. Though their cause would never be known, it was suspected that her headaches were malarial and triggered by stress. The threat of death by disease was very real to the missionaries, and foreign graves were plenteous. In December of 1924, the Bells were given their first son, whom they named Nelson, Jr. Ten months later he died of amoebic dysentery. His mother slipped his small corpse into a fresh white baby dress and lined his coffin with white linen. He was buried in the brick-walled foreign cemetery in Tsingkiang, where many other American children who had never seen their homeland had been laid before him. Forming a dark knot beneath the bleak winter sky, the missionaries surrounded the tiny raw grave and sang the Doxology. "Praise God from Whom all blessings flow . . ." Ruth's voice, jerky as a bow misguided across a violin, sounded at hip level as she stood beside her parents, her round face swallowed by a coarse woolen cap.

Dying for Christ was part of the Christian tradition Ruth was nurtured in. She was familiar with the believers who had been persecuted and murdered during the Boxer Rebellion, and with other stories of Christians who had suffered for the glory of God. The martyrs were among Ruth's heroes. To become a martyr was to weave one's story into the fabric of Christian legend; it was the highest and noblest expression of love for God.

It is virtually impossible to describe a child's concept of the Creator, except to say that children tend to see Him with more clarity than adults do. Perhaps this is because young minds often have an unquestioning faith in the truth found in symbols. And to little Ruth, God was an all-powerful, Heavenly father. She so dearly loved Him for His loving her that at the end of each day, just before she sank into a heavy sleep, she would kneel beside her bed and pray that He would let her die for Him. Rosa, meanwhile, was the pragmatist; she countered her sister's prayer with one of her own: "Please, God, don't listen to her!"

The difference between the sisters' prayers was significant. Ruth was imaginative and tended to romanticize. To her, the coda rendered by a bullet or long knife was appealing. Rosa was more scientific. She often fantasized about being kidnapped by a band of bloodthirsty bandits and carried off to the black hillside, where she would proceed to convert the barbarians around their campfire. Dying was not part of her reverie—it was wholly impractical, not to mention unpleasant.

Ruth was indeed an unusually spiritual child, but behind her brown curls and innocent eyes lurked a devilish little imp that prodded her into chasing Rosa around the yard with dead bugs and, on one occasion, a pair of scissors. Their spats were like small typhoons, with their two tiny bodies virtually disappearing into a whirling cloud of flailing feet, fists and tangled hair. They shrieked and pummeled with such ferocity that the servants used to circle round and place bets.

Fights in the Bell household, however, were the exception rather than the rule. Tense moments were usually defused by Dr. Bell's sense of humor. He wasn't the stereotyped Calvinist who disapproved of fun; instead he believed equally in working hard and in playing hard. In the yard he built a fifteen-by-twenty-foot brick swimming pool, which held five thousand gallons of well water. Not only was it a source of pleasure, but it enabled the family to endure the unbearably hot summers. Unlike most missionaries, who left the lowlands from June to August and vacationed in the mountains of Kuling or in Japan, the Bells stayed at the hospital compound, working as usual and taking frequent dips in the cool water. Dr. Bell also helped build a clay tennis court on the compound, and he and his missionary colleagues made a golf course by sinking soup cans into the lawn. His most curious creation was a corn popper he built from a trench mortar. When the pressure reached one hundred and eighty pounds, the trigger was pulled and popped kernels exploded into a cheesecloth bag. Liu Er, the gateman, was placed in charge of this contraption, and the first time he pulled the trigger the blast knocked him and his chair over backward.

Rosa and Ruth's playmates were Hampton and William Talbot, sons of missionaries who lived half a mile from their house, and Sandy Yates, whose missionary parents lived in nearby Huaian. During the school year Sandy lived with the Bells. Several afternoons each week these friends convened in one of the yards, where they played kick-the-can, croquet, and tag and capered in the sandpile, on the swing, on the monkey bars and in the tree house Dr. Bell had built high in the arms of a mulberry tree. Ruth's pastimes included playing with dolls, hanging over the edge of the tree house until her brain swam in her head like an egg yolk, and balancing along the six-inch-wide top of the compound wall. Like most children, she was curious. One afternoon she decided to investigate a large nest high in the tallest mulberry tree in the yard. Without a thought she shinnied up the trunk and discovered a brood of buzzard fledglings. Scarcely had she peered into their cavernous maws when the parents returned and began dive-bombing her. Balancing along the top of the wall the next day, she was smashed on the top of her head by one of the putrid, grudge-bearing birds.

Ruth's greatest indulgence was her pets: She had a menagerie, including canaries, pigeons, ducks, turtles and a goat. Her favorite ward was Tar Baby, a black mongrel quite attached to Ruth but notorious for grabbing Chinese women by their bound feet and dragging them off the walk. Ruth was perpetually rescuing guinea pigs from the hospital laboratory, picking up lost baby ducks, and discovering flea-infested kittens, which she would carry home and bathe in Lysol. In an early diary entry she wrote: "I found a baby mouse today, but it bit me and died."

When one of these pitiable creatures, whether mouse or bird, died, she would assemble Hampton, William, Sandy, and Rosa and hold an elaborate funeral complete with hymns and eulogies. The deceased was then buried in Ruth's animal cemetery near the sandpile. She was so tenderhearted that she had a habit of picking up any dead animal she stumbled upon whether it was a pet or not. Her mother put an end to this when she noticed a rank smell coming from a closet one day and discovered a dead bird Ruth had stuffed in a sweater pocket and forgotten.

In 1927, the Bells' world was temporarily disrupted when war broke out between the Communists and the Kuomintang (Nationalists). Eight years earlier the parties had formed the first united front since the fall of the Manchu dynasty. Chiang Kai-shek had succeeded in unifying China, bringing many of the warlords under control and establishing himself in Nanking, the capital of the Republic. But in the spring of 1927, he turned on the Communists and ordered the assassinations of party members and labor organizers, thus precipitating a bloody civil war which would last until the late thirties. The inland missions lay in the path of marching troops, and the missionaries kept their ears to their radios, listening for instructions from the American consul in Shanghai. In late spring, the orders crackled repeatedly: "S.P.M. missionaries in Taichow, Tsingkiang . . . be on the banks of the Yangtze River tomorrow morning. The USS . . . #245 will pick you up." The Bells sailed to the United States and settled in Waynesboro for several months, where a third daughter, Virginia, was born. From Waynesboro they moved to Holden, West Virginia, where Dr. Bell headed the surgical department at a local hospital. A year later the family moved to Houston, Texas, where he served as a lay minister at First Presbyterian Church.

China reopened to missionaries in 1928 and the family set sail on the SS *President Cleveland,* arriving in Tsingkiang on December 15 to discover that soldiers had ransacked the hospital, making sport of smashing expensive pieces of equipment such as the X-ray machine. They had stolen doorknobs, locks, electrical fixtures and blankets, and they had slashed the luxurious window screens which kept flies and other insects out of the wards. Various groups of soldiers had occupied the Bells' home but had found little to steal—shortly after the evacuation, Chinese friends had hidden the Bells' belongings in the attic, removed the staircase and then plastered over the entrance. Soldiers puzzled over this strange American-style home that appeared to have an attic but no way to get to it. They periodically questioned Liu Er.

"I have worked here many years," he would blandly reply, "and never heard anything about an attic."

Other missionaries were not so fortunate. Addison and Katherine Talbot discovered that all of their belongings had either been stolen or destroyed. The soldiers uprooted rosebushes and shrubbery in search of buried valuables, until the once opulent yard looked as though a giant mole had gone on a burrowing spree.

After several weeks of repolishing floors and whitewashing walls, the Bells' home was restored. Once again it was filled with the smells of baking bread and bubbling molasses candy and the sounds of the family singing the hymns Mrs. Bell played on the piano. Dr. Bell continued his hospital duties, and his wife worked in the women's clinic, recording names and symptoms before the patients saw a doctor. She taught her daughters to read and write, and when the occasional "missionary barrel" of secondhand clothing was shipped over from the United States, she rummaged through it with gusto and then set about ripping and reshaping the fusty garments into dresses and suits.

In this setting Ruth had begun to define her world. Family was a buffer, a refuge. Beyond it there was nothing but the suffering and death on the other side of the compound wall. And in this setting she had also begun to define her tastes. She admired the delicate beauty of the Orientals with their almond eyes, ebony hair and gracefulness. She felt awkward and unattractive in comparison. Beauty meant fresh flowers and ancient edifices, which either sprang from the earth or seemed to. She admired the rich red lacquers made of pigs' blood, the leathers, silks, satins and ornate calligraphy. Wood was rare and was therefore old and worn smooth from countless feet mincing across it or fingers resting along the contours of armrests. She would have been content to remain happily safe in her imaginative, warm little world, but the realities beyond the wall would begin to intrude.

3

A Crumbling of the Wall

I wish I could draw an adequate word picture of it; mobs
around on the bank looking with all their eyes to see every
move of these queer foreign creatures; cursing going on in a
continuous stream, "foreign devil," "imperialism," "down
with the church," and all the other slogans that the
Bolshevists (backed up by our old enemy Satan) have put
into the mouths and minds of these who will not come to the
light because their works are evil.

Nelson Bell, April 10, 1930

It was the summer of 1930, the year of the horse, which in
Chinese mythology symbolizes wisdom. In Tsingkiang's marketplace
the pungent odor of ripe, raw meats and vegetables mingled with the
savory smells of frying fish and cabbage, and garlic. Merchants
hawked wares, and donkeys burdened with sacks of rice, pottery, and
reeds clattered skittishly in the choked, narrow street. Peasants
moved in a noisy throng, while beggars crusty with filth and disease
watched slyly from the borders, like black birds along a fence, waiting
for their next chance to extort a coin.

Nelson Bell had removed the isinglass flaps from his tiny black
Austin Healey before driving his family to town. The foreign car and
its foreign devil driver crept ahead in a series of stops and starts—an
ideal target for the wispy Chinese boy just yards from the driver's
open window. He launched a mouthful of spittle just as the car
lurched forward, and Ruth, perched innocently behind Dr. Bell, was
splatted on her rosy right cheek. Horrified, she watched her father

jam on the brake and bolt from the car like a rabbit. Slick as a sidewinder, the lad wove through the crowd with his Western nemesis springing after him. Snatching his young antagonist in midflight, he cuffed his bottom soundly—it was one of the rare moments when a missionary experienced justice, small though it was.

Misfortunes, injustices, even tragedies had struck the missionaries prior to 1930. But a flurry of shocks, seemingly random in their cruelty, would blow through the Bells' world as never before. And Ruth, now ten, was old enough to understand each one in all its harsh detail.

The first tragedy during this period struck Gay and Ed Currie. It was their second loss—several years earlier their three-year-old daughter Lucy Calvin had died of botulism after wandering into the pantry and eating contaminated string beans. Two of the Bells' dearest friends, the Curries were missionaries in Haichow, a hundred miles north of Tsingkiang. She was a school teacher. He was a robust preacher, affectionately dubbed "The Wrestling Parson" during World War I, when he'd challenge servicemen to the mat, stipulating that losers accompany him to the next church service. The morning of November 24, 1930, the servants left the Curries' three-year-old son John Randolph unattended and he fell headlong into a cauldron of boiling water. Moments later the scalded child died in his mother's arms. The Christians' response was again one of acceptance. "So swiftly did his little spirit return unto God who gave it," missionary Jack Vinson wrote at the time, "it seems as tho' he were only running on eager, impetuous, hasty feet, at the Saviour's call and springing into His waiting arms. . . . It's well with the lad. He is safe forever in Jesus' keeping."

In 1931 death would visit a young missionary couple who had arrived in Tsingkiang shortly after the Bells. He was a clergyman, attractive and gentle. She was a handsome woman with porcelain skin, dark eyes and long black hair. For ten years they lived on the compound with the Bells, spending many evenings together talking and reading aloud, playing such games as Rook and Twenty Questions, or listening to the grainy music of the Victrola. On the day of Ruth's birth the couple had held hands on the Bells' living room sofa, waiting until the first strangled cry rang through the house. In 1927, they were transferred a hundred miles south to Taichow. The dialect was different and they had to make new friends. The wife, rationing her energy between four young children and the countless Chinese around her whose souls she longed to reach, sank deeper into the oblivion of exhaustion. In the fall of 1931 she was in the clutches of a nervous breakdown, but there was no professional help for missionaries so far from home. Her one glimmer of hope, which she often spoke of wistfully as she sat on her husband's lap, was that they were to be furloughed the following summer—for the first time in seven years. One day the small, bright opening in her black wall of despair closed forever when a cable arrived from the Southern Presbyterian Executive Committee. Not only did its message unjustly upbraid missionary wives for not working hard enough, but it informed all fieldworkers that salaries were to be cut and that all furloughs would have to be delayed another year because of the depression in America and a subsequent shortage of funds in the mission board's treasury. On October 26, at three o'clock in the morning, while her husband slept, she crept out to the frosty yard and cut her own throat.

Missionaries did not publicize suicides—to take one's own life was a senseless tragedy, not a martyrdom. Dr. Bell, however, was unusually candid, for not only did he discuss the sad event with his family, but he wrote the Executive Committee a blistering letter in response to their insensitive one.

The next tragedy struck Jack Vinson, one of the field's most respected and popular missionaries. Just days after the exhausted young wife's suicide, bandits raided the city of Yang Gia Gi, and Vinson traveled there to check on members of his flock. The marauding band captured him along with three hundred Chinese. Still weak from a recent appendectomy, he could not keep up with the other prisoners, so one of the bandits menacingly poked him with the barrel of a rifle. "If you shoot me," Vinson replied calmly, "I'll go straight to Heaven." He was murdered along with thirty-five Chinese. When Ed Currie retrieved the corpse, he found it deposited on a makeshift bier inside a Buddhist temple. As he moved the body to wrap it in grass matting, the head rolled off.

In America wreaths might be hung from doors and periods of mourning observed; here life for the missionaries went on without pause no matter who died or how. God, they believed, took care of the dead. It was the missionaries' job to care for the living.

Ruth was shaken by the deaths, but, taking her cue from her parents, she accepted them as God's will. She would, however, have a more difficult time accepting one of life's less dramatic intrusions. In 1930, Dr. Bell decided it was time to expose his daughters to more advanced schooling than they had been receiving in their mother's bedroom each morning. Prior to Ruth's tenth birthday, lessons in hygiene, spelling, arithmetic, reading and geography had come from secondhand textbooks and dog-eared *National Geographic* magazines mailed from friends in the United States. On June 8, 1930, the Bells set out for Shanghai to meet Lucy Fletcher, a young schoolteacher hired by the Foreign Mission Board in Nashville, Tennessee, to teach the missionary children. Ruth and her family sailed the hundred and twenty-five miles south to Chinkiang on a launch infested with bedbugs, mosquitoes, fleas, and rats no amount of repellent could deter. With the children nestled close, the Bells warily eyed the armed soldiers loitering about the deck, "waiting for the first bullet to be shot," Dr. Bell recounted to his mother, "preparing to hit the deck on cue."

From Chinkiang they traveled by train to Shanghai, where Lucy Fletcher's steamer was berthed, and received word from the American consulate that all women and children were to evacuate north Kiangsu because the fall of the central government was imminent. Typically, Dr. Bell ignored the warning. He was well informed about the political situation in China but, like many of his colleagues, he was not willing to admit that a Communist victory was possible. "Communism," he acknowledged that summer, "is certainly growing and becoming more bold." But as for a takeover and the subsequent withdrawal of the missionaries, "Christ," he believed, "will surely return before that disaster." Nor would he or many of his colleagues realize how menacing the Communists could be to Westerners until 1935, when Red soldiers on the Long March forced missionaries John and Betty Stam up a hill two hundred miles north of Tsingkiang, stripped them of their padded outer garments, and cut their throats.

The threat of the government's impending fall passed quickly and the Bells and the new teacher traveled back to Tsingkiang. Lucy Fletcher, an attractive, dark-haired woman in her late twenties, moved into a bedroom just below Ruth's, much to the child's dismay. Initially, Ruth resented this new source of authority, and she found Lucy's high-strung personality grating. She would hate school—she just knew it. But her fears were soon dissolved by Lucy's warm, sisterly attentions. She became a confidante and mentor who read her *Borden of Yale, Huckleberry Finn*, and other classics. She introduced her to the poetry of Edith Gilling Cherry[1] and, more importantly, to the works of Amy Carmichael, who from then on would influence Ruth more than any other writer. A skilled Bible teacher, Lucy instilled in Ruth a love and respect for the Scripture. Her methods were rather rigorous: Her examination on Genesis, for example, required her pupils to summarize the contents of all fifty chapters. Lucy also offered five dollars to any student who could flawlessly recite from memory the Sermon on the Mount. (After weeks of struggle, Ruth recited the three chapters making only one error—she collected four dollars and fifty cents.)

The advent of school filled Ruth's life with new adventure, for it took her beyond her childhood boundaries. Each morning, shortly after eight o'clock, she, Rosa, Sandy Yates, and Lucy left the compound for the mile walk along the ancient twenty-foot-high mud wall. After centuries of erosion the wall was mounded and pitted by the wind, with battlements protruding at intervals like worn teeth in an old man's gums. It bordered the suburbs and below it was a moat that had healed together, leaving shallow puddles of scummy water. It was a popular spot for the disposing of dead infants, and the setting caused Ruth's sensitivity to recoil within her. Two pariah dogs the Bell children had named "Gorgon" and "Mussolini" ranged among the grave mounds north of the wall, waiting for the small corpses occasionally seen face down in the brackish moat water, just yards from peasants rinsing their rice or nightsoil buckets. Local superstition dictated that if a child died before cutting his teeth he could not be buried lest evil spirits return to take a brother or sister. Corpses were usually shoved through the small orifices in the brick hutch-shaped baby tombs, or they were abandoned on grave mounds or in the moat. Sometimes parents left sick or deformed infants in these hellish places before they were dead.

As Ruth and Sandy walked with Lucy through the cold early morning air on October 17, 1932, they were halted midway on the wall by a peasant woman's cries of "Alive! Alive!" She motioned toward the moat where a baby boy lay in the mud at the edge of the water. Ruth recorded the event in a letter to Rosa, then away at high school in Korea:

"I scrambled down to where it lay and saw it breathe, then give a tiny cry, so I ran for Dr. Woods and then came back and Miss

---

1. In later years, Edith Gilling Cherry's poem "Gates of Splendor" was set to music. The result was the hymn "We Rest On Thee."

[Fletcher] went to hurry things up while I stood and fanned off the huge green flies that had settled on it. . . . Its eyes were opened and filled with pus so that all you could see was yellow. A few rags lying by were all it had and its tiny naked body was blue from cold."

The infant was bathed and fed in the mission hospital; two days later, he died.

By age twelve, Ruth had ceased any coveting of martyrdom and was now dreaming about becoming a missionary. She admired their goodness and courage, but the one thing in the world that moved her most was kindness. And they were kind, not only to her but to those around them who were suffering. She decided she would become a spinster missionary to the nomads in Tibet. It was a rather bleak future she cast, unfitting for a girl whose mind was filled with bright, imaginative particles just beginning to coalesce. Virtually every day at dusk, she would slip away to her tiny attic bedroom, her favorite nook in the house, with a doorway so low that she had to stoop to enter. Inside was a small window facing west with the city's worn earthen ramparts stretching across the earth like a scar. Grave mounds erupted from the fields like lesions, creating a barren vista broken infrequently by lone herdsmen grazing sheep and goats. As night fell, she would watch the shadows rolling like a giant dark wave over the wall, across the fields, and beyond the evergreen-bordered priests' graves. The setting sun bled crimson over the roofs of a village on the horizon in its glorious attempt to push back the edge of darkness.

Ruth began demonstrating a germinal imagination strongly tinged with gothic elements and absurd humor. She sketched cartoon figures and fantasy creatures, and she painted flowers, landscapes, and religious scenes. Nature took on special meaning, and life of all kinds became symbolic of greater truths.

Her pragmatic father took a dim view of these budding abilities. "Ruth," he wrote to his mother, "has real artistic talent. For a long time we knew she was clever with drawing but recently she shows remarkable talent. . . . But it has never been a talent I have especially desired for a child of mine." He failed to see how his daughter's creativity would aid her in Christian service. Mrs. Bell, however, was more sympathetic to Ruth's romantic and sentimental nature because those traits were indigenous to Leftwich blood. Probably it was from her mother's ancestors that Ruth also inherited her hypersensitivity. She was a cuddly, dependent child who, when she was thirteen, dreaded the thought of leaving home for the first time.

Rosa had left home in 1932 for Pyeng Yang Foreign School, fifteen hundred miles from Tsingkiang, in what would later become Pyongyang, North Korea. It would have been far more convenient had the Bells sent their children to the Shanghai American School, as many of the other missionaries did. But they preferred the curriculum of Pyeng Yang, a Christian school of a hundred and forty students, where academics were rigorous and the Bible was acknowledged as the authoritative word of God.

Ruth's dread of leaving home was augmented by the awkward stage she had entered. As a teenager she was plump and gap-toothed, and she wore glasses. She fastened her long hair in a barrette, and the round, black frames hiding her eyes looked like something a prankster might have penciled in. Her dowdy appearance might have been ignored had she been a scholar. But she was no more a bookworm than was her German shepherd, Prinz, and she had not been from the first moment Mrs. Bell had begun tutoring her in the bedroom and accused her of being "somewhat scatter-brained." In fact, Ruth was quite intelligent, though it was probably true that she had more marbles in her creative pocket than she had in her mathematical one. And they did tend to bounce about, clatter and roll to all corners, as her voracious curiosity rapidly shifted from one topic to another. In short, her intelligence was more intuitive than analytical, and her lack of academic prowess didn't make the notion of leaving home for Pyeng Yang any more pleasant. It probably wasn't coincidental that two weeks before she was to set sail from China she was stricken with a high, tenacious fever.

On September 2, the Bells and Lucy Fletcher accompanied Rosa, Ruth, Hampton, William, and missionary friend Sophie Montgomery to Shanghai, where they spent the night in the missionary home at Number Four Quinsan Road. The Victorian brick building, which was in the city's International Settlement, was a boarding house run by Edith Spurling and her assistant—two English spinsters. Missionaries often stayed there while traveling through the city. That hot, sticky night, Ruth lay awake on top of her tangled sheets, tears trickling into her ears and hair and forming cool wet spots on her pillow, as she begged God to let her die before morning. This time she wasn't asking to be a martyr. She just wanted an escape. And, as usual, God did not give in.

Early the next day the Bell girls, Sophie, and the Talbot boys boarded the *Nagasaki Maru,* and from the rail Ruth watched her parents diminish into tiny specks on the receding quay as the ship sailed down the Huangpu River to the East China Sea. Hours later they crossed into the Yellow Sea where a typhoon swept up the steamer as though it were a toy, buffeting its sides with fifty-foot waves. From water-streaked portholes they watched the heaving waves crash over the lugsails of a junk a hundred yards away. Seasickness dulled Ruth's fear of the storm and the inchoate ache of separation. When the water was once again still, she too retreated into silence as her mind buried itself in sadness like a clam in the gray sand left by the surf. The typhoon was a harbinger of the emotional turbulence she would experience during the next three months of homesickness.

In Nagasaki the young travelers boarded a train. Merchants hawked outside their car, advertising "Bento! Bento!" until Ruth and her companions opened their windows and exchanged coins for wooden boxes containing chopsticks, white rice, and Japanese pickles. The moon was round and low like a ripe fruit, its luminance settling over the landscape like pollen. The train lumbered a hundred miles northeast toward the Sea of Japan, which had begun seeping inland, forming misty bays flecked with shadowy fishing boats. They disembarked in Moji, where half-naked men with boa constrictors coiled around them followed musicians in a parade, their laughing faces wavering in torchlight as the city celebrated its harvest festival. Boarding a ferry in Shimonoseki, the young party sailed across the Straits of Korea to Pusan, where they boarded another train. Muted, straw-roofed Korean villages and jagged mountains streamed past Ruth's window until she drew the curtain around her sleeping-shelf and finally surrendered to unconsciousness.

Each night that fall she buried her head beneath her pillow so her two roommates would not hear her cry herself to sleep in the Spartan gray brick dormitory. She wrote her parents three times a week, begging them to let her come home. The epistles ranged from the pathetic to the desperate—a six-foot-long Japanese scroll filled with Ruth's ornate script and morose ponderings. Word of her unhappiness reached the school's administration. One day she was summoned to the office of headmaster R. O. "Pops" Reiner.[2] He motioned for her to be seated and asked if it were true that she was homesick.

---

2. A decade later, Reiner would be captured by the Japanese, strung up by his thumbs, and given the water torture.

"Yes, sir," she replied shyly. "And I've lost weight too."

"How much did you weigh when you arrived here?" he asked, studying her thoughtfully.

"One hundred and thirty-three pounds, sir."

"I see," he said. "And how much do you weigh now?"

"One hundred and twenty-nine pounds, sir."

"I see," he said; his eyes twinkled behind his glasses, but he was too kind to laugh. The unhappy letters home continued, and finally, on October 13, Nelson wrote Mabel Axworthy, the young spinster in charge of the primary grades:

> [Ruth's] letters have not been typical of a normal homesickness as much as a feeling aggravated by introspection and failure to get out with the other children properly. . . . We feel she has been staying in her room too much; not only has she written these long letters to us, but she has also written long letters to other members of the station. They are really exceptional in their descriptive character, but they take time she should be spending either in study, or in play. . . . We feel Ruth has a slight tendency to revel in the sad side of things, letting her religion (which is exceedingly real and precious to her) take a slightly morbid turn.

Ruth's concept of eternity was so real and wonderful to her that she tended to let her mind drift toward it when she was homesick, tired or inundated with unpleasantness. "Some people," her father frequently remarked, "are so Heavenly minded that they're no earthly good." From time to time, young Ruth was one of those people. One day, as she and a friend were ironing, she exclaimed, "Oh, just think, the end of the world may come soon and then we will be so happy!" The friend, somewhat weary of Ruth's fantasizing about Heaven, blurted, "Oh, you Bell girls surely are stuck on the end of the world!"

When she received Dr. Bell's letter, Miss Axworthy asked Ruth to "mother" the eighth graders. Soon she was so busy looking after them that she forgot herself—a remedy that would become habit, and one she would frequently prescribe to others in the future. Her homesickness subsided and her wish for the end of the world was, once again, tucked back into its mental cupboard. But this did not mean that she wanted to stay in school. In December she opened her final offensive by announcing to her father that she had "been praying" and was convinced that it was God's will for her to come home.

"Well," he replied firmly, a slight smile tugging at the corners of his lips, "your mother and I have been praying too and that's not the answer we got."

Finally surrendering to her fate, she found, before long, that she was actually enjoying herself. One year she was elected class president, and she became the cartoonist/poet for *The Kulsi*, the school yearbook. A prankster, she was not above stuffing a pair of hose and shoes and placing them halfway under the dorm mother's bed, rubbing shoe polish on the back of doorknobs, modeling snakes out of clay and leaving them coiled in shadowy corners—to mention just a few of her ignoble deeds.

After her junior year, the Bells furloughed to the United States and rented a stone house in Montreat, North Carolina, eighteen miles east of Asheville. Rosa, who had contracted tuberculosis the year before and dropped out of Pyeng Yang, began treatments at a nearby sanatorium. Meanwhile she and Ruth finished their senior years of high school at Montreat, graduating in the spring of 1936. Rosa left for Wheaton College, twenty-five miles west of Chicago, and Ruth, barely sixteen, returned to Korea for a year of postgraduate study because her parents believed she was too young for college.

4

War

I pray constantly that God will help us bear the testimony and witness we should. A faith and confidence exhibited only in times of peace does not amount to much.

Nelson Bell, 1937

Throughout the sweltering summer of 1937 Virginia Bell sewed six hours daily. The stacks of print skirts and dresses grew. So did the threat of war.

Since the late nineteenth century the Chinese had been embittered by Japan's expansion into Manchuria, the northernmost region of China, comprising three provinces and more than half a million miles of farmland, forests, and mountains rich in coal, iron ore, gold, lead, and copper. By the early thirties, Japan's incursions were rapidly escalating. In March, 1932, its Kwantung Army completed the occupation of Manchuria, creating the puppet state of Manchukuo, which it proceeded to build into an industrial and military base for Japan's expansion into Asia. The aggression would culminate in the bombing of Pearl Harbor. On July 7, 1937, her soldiers attacked Chinese troops at the Marco Polo Bridge near Peking, thus beginning the occupation of northern China. In the summer of 1937, Chinese Communists and Nationalists ended their own civil war and united against Japan in an attempt to bring an end to this violation of Chinese territory.

According to the lunar calendar, fall arrived on August 8. The cloud-spotted, deep blue sky shone like Ming porcelain. The sun was hot but a steady breeze cooled the compound, rustling like a light rain through the mulberry and weeping willow trees. Mrs. Bell was now forty-four, her hair was graying, and her figure had become matronly. Her lips were thinner, as though the strain of her work and the agony of her daily headaches were beginning to show in her face. She had spent the summer working on a new wardrobe for Ruth, who was to board the *Empress of Asia* on August 19, sail to Vancouver, and then travel by train to Wheaton, Illinois, where she would begin her freshman year of college. Rosa was spending the summer in Waynesboro with her grandmother—Grandfather Bell had died the March before. She reveled in being away from home and had written cheery letters to her family about college life. If her observations were supposed to encourage Ruth, they didn't.

"Ruth," her mother wrote, "is a precious child and still a child and going home will be hard for her. It is certainly the one hard thing missionaries have to do—have their children so far away during these important years." Missionaries could never be sure how their children would fare once they left the compounds for America, where they would fall in love and choose careers. In the West evil was more difficult to define than it was in the Orient, where the fruits of sin were repulsive, frequently culminating in the horrors of infanticide, spiritism, and banditry. As they had done when they chose a high school, the Bells had picked a college where the Bible was respected as the authoritative word of God and the world was held in abeyance. Dancing, smoking, drinking alcoholic beverages, as well as other vices, were forbidden. Ruth was not interested in going to college, for she had already planned her future: She would devote her life to carrying the gospel of Jesus Christ to the arid Himalayan mountains of Tibet, or the "Roof of the Globe," as it is called; she would never marry; all she would need in life was a working knowledge of Tibetan and the Bible—and she certainly didn't need to sail halfway around the world for that. Her parents simply smiled at such talk.

At seventeen, Ruth had shed her adolescent awkwardness. The gap between her front teeth had disappeared along with her chubbiness and her glasses. At five foot five, she was slender, though shapely, and graceful. Her nose was flawlessly chiseled, her forehead, broad and high. Like the sea, her eyes changed depth and shade with every shadow and light, until it was troublesome determining what color they were: When she laughed, which was often, they were light brown flecked with gold; in more somber moods they hinted of amber or rust. Though she would not weep or lose her temper in front of others, the fluidity of her eyes usually gave her away. Rarely premeditating an action or analyzing it afterward, she lived by her intuition, acting upon impulse more often than reason. Unusually kind, it was her impulse to fill the voids in other people's lives and rarely to think about her own. She seemed unconscious of these merits, just as she did not seem to notice the fawning attentions of her young male acquaintances. To be sure, Ruth appeared anything *but* a spinster missionary in the making.

While Ruth and her mother made the final preparations for college, Dr. Bell prepared for war. He stockpiled a six-months' supply of kerosene, fuel oil, and gasoline. Sugar, flour, and vegetables were plentiful, but the family would have to do without butter. Thirteen-by-eighteen-foot American flags were painted on the roofs of the hospital and their home, and the Stars and Stripes run up the flagpole. Ordinarily the missionaries did not flaunt their foreignness, but Dr. Bell was determined that there would be no "accidental" bombings of the mission compound. The family's boxy RCA-Victor radio became their focus, and throughout each day Dr. Bell slipped on the headphones and fidgeted with dials as he attempted to fish news from the deep static.

On Friday, August 13, the day Ruth's baggage was to be sent ahead of her by launch to Chinkiang, Chiang Kai-shek sent his best German-trained units to Shanghai where Japanese were garrisoned. The ensuing battle was savage. Chinese dignity and hostility were no match for Japanese weapons, and before the day was spent the city fell. Reinforcements of airplanes and pilots were assigned to the small airfield near the Tsingkiang mission. By the thousands, Chinese began fleeing the larger cities, seeking asylum in the less important ones or in the countryside. Launches drifted offshore, their pilots afraid to berth lest refugees inundate them. Ruth's father canceled her travel plans, made new ones and then canceled again. "She is jubilant over the prospect of staying," Mrs. Bell wrote the next day. "There is nothing left for *us* to *decide*. It is just impossible to go. We feel like we are on a holiday. . . . We are pretty well blocked-in, but feel we are as safe here as anywhere."

While Chinese planes raided the Japanese forces in Shanghai, a typhoon roared inland from the Yellow Sea. Bewildered Chinese huddled in doorways and alleys as both nature and man ravaged them. Inland, the missionaries and Chinese Christians registered no fear—on a Sunday morning while the Bells sat in church, the bell outside began clanging madly, announcing an air raid. All three hundred and fifty members of the congregation remained seated, and the service continued. In villages where foreigners were already having to evacuate, some missionaries took the fourth commandment literally and refused to flee on Sundays.

On August 14, as Mrs. Bell sat in the living room monitoring the radio, the U.S. consul began urging all foreigners to leave the inland cities. More than two hundred Europeans, and several Americans and missionaries, had been killed days before when a Chinese plane accidentally bombed a Chinese settlement in Shanghai. On Monday, August 16, the Japanese raided Nanking twice and bombed Yang-chow, a hundred miles south of Tsingkiang. The local Chinese panicked. In anticipation of air raids they dug deep trenches and furtively ran after planes, their knuckles white as they clutched low-caliber rifles. Often, they only harmed themselves when ditches collapsed and weapons misfired. The fighting drew closer, and on Tuesday, August 17, three Japanese planes attacked the Tsingkiang airfield while the Bells were eating supper. Two bombs landed near the runway but did little damage; a third landed in an open field and killed a cow; and the fourth bomb did not explode. The Chinese were terrified by this travesty of war, and dozens lobbed their belongings over the Tsingkiang compound wall, begging for asylum inside the hospital and other mission buildings. And "every time we leave the compound," Mrs. Bell wrote, "they think we're evacuating. Just our being here means a lot to their peace of mind."

On August 19, white ensigns fluttered from tugs as they pulled crowded barges down the Huangpu to waiting steamers. It was the day Ruth would have sailed from China had it been a different world. Nine hundred refugees jammed the *Empress of Asia,* and it left Shanghai without her. "Prospects for college that fall," she wrote, "faded gloriously out of sight." Her relief, however, was to be short-lived.

On September 1, the American ambassador urged the Bells and colleagues Jimmy and Sophie Graham to leave immediately for the United States. Sophie, who with her husband had been on the China mission field for forty-three years, had recently suffered a stroke that had left her partly paralyzed. But neither infirmity nor danger would prod them to heed the ambassador's warning. The Bells were of the same mind: "We don't feel any urge from the Lord," Mrs. Bell wrote at the time. Five days later the Bells received a wire from the American consul general: "Urgent: Americans advised make plans proceed Haichow from where evacuation about September 20 will be by Naval vessel probably to Shanghai telegraph immediately Consulate Shanghai or Embassy. . . ."

The next day, Dr. Bell wired back: "Message received please wire whether later evacuation possible. Auto roads Haichow under water [Sophie] Graham invalid travel difficult, local conditions normal. Can you assure us that in complying with your telegram we will proceed either Shanghai Tsingtao? Some have financial and mission responsibilities which make this imperative. How much baggage permitted each individual?"

On September 8, a voice crackled over the radio, its words directed at the "stubborn missionaries and leaders." Its message: "Foreigners have been invited for the last time to leave."

The Bells finally began packing their belongings and storing boxes in the attic. On September 17, at dawn, they piled baggage on the porch and Ruth stood sentry, eyeing the dozen rickshaw coolies milling in the yard. Inside the bare house voices united as the Bells and the servants sang "God Be with You till We Meet Again." Jimmy and Sophie Graham soon arrived to make the journey with them. The group planned to travel north on the Grand Canal by launch, transfer to a houseboat in Sutsien and take a train to Haichow where an American destroyer would be waiting. From there they were to sail a hundred and ten miles to Tsingtao, a European-style port city four hundred miles north of Shanghai. Japan had too many commercial and industrial interests in Tsingtao to bomb it, and numerous missionaries had already sought refuge there.

The coolies loaded the rickshaws, picked up the poles and trotted along the narrow street to the canal, their powerful calf muscles knotting like fists with each slap of their bare feet. Houseboats, barges, and sampans crowded the muddy water, and women washed clothing while their children bathed with the ducks and geese. Chinese friends had gathered on the shore to say good-bye and help them board. Ruth stared out of her glassless cabin window at the constant stream of half-naked coolies flowing in and out of the small water gate in the ancient city wall to her left. They dipped their buckets into the canal and retreated, their full loads swinging perilously on their *bien dans.* High above the city's tiled roofs buzzards glided, forming lazy black V's in the clear sky. With a sharp blast of a whistle, the barge eased forward. A warm breeze washed through the cabin, and the group of friends on the shore disappeared around the bend.

At two o'clock the next morning, they transferred to the houseboat, owned and piloted by a Chinese family who lived on the aft deck. The bow was cluttered with spare oars, pots, shoes, and other miscellaneous items, either wedged into the thatch of the passengers' shelter or fastened to the boat. A low-burning oil lantern gently bobbed from a post. Ruth unrolled her blanket and settled on the dusty wooden floor between her sister Virginia and Sophie Graham's servant girl, Gwei Yin. A soft wind puffed the boat up river while she lay half-asleep, listening to the groaning wood and the water lipping against the sides. Several hours later at dawn, she watched the sun ooze like an egg yolk through the willows lining the shores.

Saturday afternoon, September 18, they docked one mile from the Longhai Railroad, ten minutes after the departure of the 2:20 train that the Bells and Grahams were scheduled to be on. From a mud hut telegraph office in the tiny village of Yuin Ho, Dr. Bell sent a wire and was instructed to spend another night in the houseboat and advance to Haichow in the morning. Another band of withdrawing missionaries would wait for them there. The next morning, the Bells and Grahams were at the station by 8:30, but this time, it was the train that was late, following an air raid. They finally boarded at 10:30. Less than ten miles from Haichow they were again delayed when a warning was sounded that twelve Japanese bombers, returning from a raid in Hsuchowfu, were approaching. Passengers dived from the cars and hid in fields as the ominous droning sounded in the distance. The missionaries sat quietly in their cars, heads bowed, while the gray sea of clouds high above them slowly, heavily, settled over the track, shrouding the creaking locomotive and those cringing in the fields. Momentarily, the bombers roared blindly overhead and were gone. "The Lord," Mrs. Bell recorded, "is not unmindful of his own."

American consular authorities had alerted the Japanese to the missionaries' evacuation and had been assured of cooperation. Obviously, Japan's idea of working with the Americans wasn't exactly what the Americans had in mind. While the small party of missionaries in Haichow were crouched in a dugout, wondering where the train was, the city was being shaken by the severest bombings of the war. Dr. Bell did not believe the attacks were coincidental. "That demonstration in Haichow Sunday," he wrote his mother, "was evidently put on for our benefit. . . . Lovely 'cooperation,' wasn't it?" The train arrived late that afternoon and at 8:00 P.M. the missionaries boarded a tug in the Haichow harbor, embarking upon the four-mile sail to the destroyer. A full moon hung in the clear sky and followed them out to sea. Ruth stood on deck watching the illuminated ship in the distance while thousands of invisible Chinese eyes watched the tug from military posts in the black crags on either side of the bay.

Cutting the engines, the pilot steered the tug alongside the destroyer and a narrow wooden footway was secured between them with rope. The sea jerked the two vessels together and apart like a berserk accordionist, slamming the gangplank against the tug as the ships rolled together, opening a maw of black churning water as they rolled apart. Chinese seamen lifted Sophie Graham and perilously approached the straining plank while sailors in loose white uniforms stretched over the destroyer's side, reaching for her. Faces were constricted and gray; garments, drenched with spray, clung to the backs and shoulders braced beneath the dead weight: Like a daguerreotype, the men and the missionary poised at the brink of a cruel, roiling sea. Then suddenly, inexplicably, all became quiet; the turbulence died and the plank steadied "as if an immense hand had stilled the water and held the ropes," Ruth recorded. Sophie Graham was passed from one set of strong hands to another. The moment she was safely aboard the destroyer, the waves and the wind unleashed their fury again. Prayerfully, the other missionaries struggled over.

Aboard ship Filipinos in white gowns served the missionaries coffee and sandwiches, and officers relinquished their quarters to them. They had traveled less than a mile when nine Japanese warships materialized from the darkness, their external lights extinguished. The dark, silent hulks circled the American destroyer like fish shadows around a lure. Then they slowly scattered, their curiosity or desire to intimidate satisfied. The Yellow Sea was as smooth as a millpond and the ship plowed ahead at thirty knots, reaching Tsingtao at 1:30 A.M. Because women and children were not allowed to spend the night aboard, naval boats intercepted the small party and carried them ashore. By 3:00 A.M. the Bells had settled into friends' cottages on the Kiaochow Bay. They had arrived with their radio, bedding, summer clothing, and table silver.

From Tsingtao, travel to the United States was possible. Dr. Bell booked Ruth on the USS *Chaumont* to sail October 22 to Kōbe, Japan. From there she would sail to Seattle aboard the SS *President*

McKinley. "My, but it is *hard* to see her leave," her mother wrote. "She is timid and would far rather stay here." The Friday morning of her departure, Ruth and Elizabeth McLaughlin (a missionary friend traveling with her) were up by five-thirty and on the quay by seven. They paid a steward five dollars for embarcation and hugged their families good-bye. It would take six days to cross the Yellow Sea and sweep around the tip of South Korea toward Kōbe. Though Ruth did not want to leave, she was comforted that her family was safe in Tsingtao. She could not know that in less than three weeks, while she was yet aboard ship, they would return to Tsingkiang, unable to stay away from their friends and responsibilities any longer. They found conditions much worse than they had left them. Emboldened Japanese pilots had begun firing machine guns at the hospital to frighten the staff, and the bombings had become closer and more frequent. It was as though the brief evacuation had served no other purpose than to get Ruth out of China. As the cold sea waters tumbled together, healing the gash left by the *Chaumont,* the passageway between Ruth and her birthplace was sealed. She would not return until half a century later.

Shortly before reaching Kōbe, she drew up a most peculiar list for a confirmed old maid:

If I marry:
He must be so tall that when he is on his knees, as one has said, he reaches all the way to Heaven.
His shoulders must be broad enough to bear the burden of a family.
His lips must be strong enough to smile, firm enough to say no, and tender enough to kiss.
Love must be so deep that it takes its stand in Christ and so wide that it takes the whole lost world in.
He must be active enough to save souls.
He must be big enough to be gentle and great enough to be thoughtful.
His arms must be strong enough to carry a little child.

In Japan, she boarded the SS *President McKinley* and settled into steerage, just behind a massive propeller where the ship's metal hull was the only buffer between her and the fathomless sea. During her nineteen-day passage, two people would jump overboard. The first suicide made a strong impression on her.

Early into the voyage, on a cold evening shortly before midnight, a young American wrapped in a heavy overcoat sat on deck smoking. Having suffered from a mental disorder in Bangkok, he was being accompanied home by the medical attendant seated beside him. He watched the tip incandesce like a coal as he studied the cigarette lightly clamped between two fingers of his cupped hand. Aimlessly, he stood, dropped the butt to crush it beneath his heel, and before his aide could gasp, he had hurled himself over the rail, disappearing like a dream into the ravenous waves. Minutes later, the ship's engines abruptly died, and with the cessation of the guttural throbbing around Ruth's berth, she awakened. Sitting up, she peered through the porthole, shivering in the raw air seeping around its rim. Beyond, the dark water and starless sky bled together like black ink. A long needle of light pricked the water's surface as a lifeboat filled with twelve sailors searched for the man who had vanished in the churning wake just minutes earlier. A sense of foreboding settled over her as she watched their progress. The atmosphere became sinister.

Fifteen feet below her "lay a long rope curling and twisting in the water like some phantom snake," she recorded at the time. "A chill crept down my spine." She slipped her coat over her gown and she hurried to the deck where a small group of passengers had clustered along the rail. They watched the lifeboat rise and fall while "a wind laughed through the mast tops," she wrote. "Laughed to see man battle with the elements over one small human body. Laughed at his helplessness." Her aroused imagination teased her eyes. Several times she thought she saw a body or parts of a body bobbing in the wake; she thought she heard muffled human cries of distress rising above the wind and the wash. After a fruitless search, the lifeboat was hoisted aboard, and Ruth, chilled by the dank, salty air, returned to her bunk.

When she viewed events through her faith, nature became symbolic of eternal truths. It was a tool used by God to reveal His glory and love: The blanket of clouds shielded the train from the vision of the Japanese pilots; the sea became still when the sailors carried Sophie Graham over the gangplank. Her description of the suicide, in contrast, portrays a savageness in nature and reduces man to a faceless pawn in a random universe. To her, that was the world without God, without the meaning implied by His existence and subsequent participation in human lives. Separation from God was the heathenism outside the compound wall—it was the Hell of being alone in the universe with oneself. Without the Creator, all creation was heartless; the world was formless, a void, with darkness upon the face of the deep.

PART II

5

An Innocent Abroad

There was a certain other-worldliness about her.

Harold Lindsell

It began like the opening scene in a grainy, grade-B movie: *Slow Boat to Wheaton,* or *Missionary Girl Grows Up,* it could be titled. The young, innocent heroine stands in the Chicago train station, a solitary stillness in the din of shuffling shoe leather, human babble, hissing decompressed air, and clanking steel. Bundled in a black wool coat, she's surrounded by battered bags and trunks containing the sum of her worldly goods: a miscellaneous assortment of homemade garments, three scarves she had made herself (one pink, one blue, and one white), a small collection of her favorite books, and her dog-eared King James Bible. Then, she enters the Wheaton College campus in her size seven saddle shoes (the ones that bleed chalky white polish every time it rains), her eyes full of wonder, her dignity slightly wounded by the freshman orange and green "dink" planted on her head, her composure lost in curiosity, fear and naiveté. Alas, she has been in this strange new world no more than a month when in rides the villain.

Several male upperclassmen, who collectively embodied this scoundrel, were to blame for the ignominious event that was about to occur. Vying for her attention since she had arrived, these young men had, on two occasions, whisked her into Chicago for dinners and ice shows. She was the sole freshman on these double dates, and on both occasions her escorts chose to ignore a tiresome detail—her 10:30 curfew. Both times, it was after midnight when she was deposited in front of the tightly locked Williston Hall, which served as the student cafeteria and a women's dormitory. A peculiar chunk of Gothic Revivalism, it was built of rusty red brick studded with tiny rectangular windows and towered over the sloping lawn, its roof cutting darkly into the night like a dragon's back. Ruth's first-floor room was the last one on the west end, just close enough to the ground for her to rustle behind the boxwoods and, with a boost from her date, crawl over the sill. She managed this feat quite nicely the first time. The second would do her in.

On that ill-fated Friday night, well after 10:30, one of Ruth's friends dropped by her room for a visit and found she wasn't there—or anywhere, it seemed. Riffling through the sign-out book in the lobby, she next discovered Ruth had left no clue as to her whereabouts. A verbal alarm rang through the corridors, finally reaching the ears of the elderly dorm mother, the same woman who weeks earlier had portentously advised one of Ruth's dates, "She's so heavenly looking she won't last long on this earth." Scowling through her pince-nez, she periodically scanned the floors. Sometime after midnight, Ruth squirmed through her window and moments later calmly emerged in the hallway, toothbrush in hand, heading toward the bathroom. She was quickly intercepted.

"Where have you been and how did you get in?" the dorm mother demanded.

"I've been on a date and I climbed through my window," Ruth replied innocently, her honesty fortunately stopping short of adding "just like I did last time."

She was expeditiously given an appointment with the dean of students.

Ruth lived by a strict but simple moral code. During her childhood she had never been handed a book of regulations containing dozens of petty sins which might serve as footnotes to the Decalogue. The original ten were enough. She had also just come from a world where air raid bells, Japanese bombers and bandits were one's major concern. This new threat labeled curfew failed to impress her. She had never even bothered to peruse the Wheaton College handbook. Had she done so she might have discovered what one of her more responsible dates, Harold Lindsell, would later affirm: "Now, there were two things you didn't do at Wheaton College, and one of them was you didn't climb through a window." Ruth did not like to burden people with her concerns, and she liked it even less when people wanted to be burdened with them. She maneuvered in her own small sphere, her scanner picking up everything except the air traffic control channel: Circuitous or not, her routes and timetables were her own. This attitude wasn't always appreciated by her well-meaning friends, who were often thwarted in their efforts to advise her. Her independence was even less appreciated by administrators, as she was soon to find during her session with Dr. Wallace Emerson, a psychology professor and the dean of students.

His office was in Blanchard Hall, an imposing limestone fortress, trussed with ivy and appended with towers and battlements. In his chambers, next to the president's office on the second floor, he sat behind a sturdy oak desk facing a wall of books; his wire spectacles were perched on his nose; a thin mustache and goatee framed his unsmiling mouth. She demurely seated herself at a prudent distance.

"Anybody has the right to think anything he wants to of you," he said icily.

She looked squarely at him during the ensuing avalanche of stony words, her throat tight and the tears she refused to cry pounding behind her nose and eyes. Because she would not break, he assumed she didn't care and he admonished her for what seemed to Ruth an eternity. Finally, he was silent, his face impassive as he looked at the young woman whose seeming indifference baffled him.

"You have disgraced the school," he said without emotion. "You have disgraced your parents. You have disgraced yourself. You can choose between expulsion for a semester or an indefinite campusing."

Returning to China was impossible and she had no intention of moving to Waynesboro. What would she say to Grandmother Bell: "Can I live with you for several months because I've been kicked out of school?"

"I prefer to be campused, sir," Ruth remarked in a steady voice.

He nodded and released her. Hurrying to the infirmary where Rosa was in bed with pleurisy, she shut the door and wilted. Between great sobs she related the story to her sister until a visitor's knocks sent her fleeing into the closet lest anyone see her momentary lapse of self-control. Ruth, who had never let a young man hold her hand, much less kiss her, had never imagined prior to this that she could appear to be something she wasn't—promiscuous. She felt dirty, and she felt the victim of injustice, for the men who were responsible for returning her to campus after curfew had gone unpunished. Worst of all, the thought that she had disgraced her parents filled her with despair, for that was something that, as she said, "I would rather die than do."

Being campused meant that she was no longer allowed to date or to leave the school grounds. The restrictions were perhaps more troublesome for Harold Lindsell, a lanky, brown-eyed blond, than they were for Ruth, for he was more than mildly interested in her. Lindsell was an attractive twenty-four-year-old senior with a fondness for well-cut pinstripe and doublebreasted suits. He was considered the campus gentleman-scholar, and he was by chance well acquainted with Rosa, who had told him all about her younger sister. Since September, he had eagerly watched for her. On the November afternoon when he had first seen the new female student in the cafeteria, there had been no doubt who she was. Without delay he had headed for the infirmary, where he knew if he visited Rosa long enough he was bound to meet her sister. More than an hour later, and still wearing his camel's hair coat (as if to imply he could stay only a minute), he rose from his wooden chair and was introduced to Ruth. Days later, he telephoned her and asked if she would accompany him to the Friday night Literary Society meeting. Literary societies were Wheaton's version of sororities and fraternities. Seeming a bit flustered over the telephone—and rightly so, for he was seven years her senior and she already had a date—she accepted. On a brisk Friday night in November he had escorted her to the meeting. "I thought she acted a little strange," Lindsell later mused. "It turned out I'd sat her next to the boy who'd asked her out to the same thing."

After Ruth was campused, Lindsell seized the moment like a champion. He escorted her to her classes, enrolled in one of her sketching courses though he wasn't remotely artistic, and became her confidant. His attention flattered her and rebuilt her recently shattered self-esteem. He became her mentor—something she was woefully in need of. Ruth was unabashedly ignorant of American verbal gymnastics, such as innuendo and double meanings. Her parents had never discussed sex with her (she later claimed that she had "learned the facts of life from the Bible"). Her speech rivaled Mrs. Malaprop's and her naiveté was as pure as distilled water. On one occasion, Lindsell asked what her family ate for Thanksgiving dinner in China. "Bastards," she replied, meaning bustards. Later, when she attended her first American wedding, Lindsell was an usher and offered her his arm at the door. "Oh, *Harold!*" she laughed as she shoved it away.

By the spring of 1938 the Wheaton faculty realized that Ruth's infractions were committed out of ignorance, not wickedness. They lifted her sentence, much to the relief of the Bells, who had remained steadfast in their trust of her. By this time, communication between them and their daughters in America was erratic. The Japanese were censoring mail in Shanghai, and letters sometimes took more than two months to reach the mission station. Throughout northern and central China the land was rent with zigzagged trenches. Soldiers had seized railroads, burned villages, and smashed bridges. Tanks lumbered over washboard-rutted roads, white smoke puffing from their machine guns as they hit ill-equipped Chinese infantrymen. The Bells' son Clayton and daughter Virginia were virtually the only American missionary children left in the interior. Their parents firmly believed that nothing would happen to them without God's sanction.

Flags with the Rising Sun floated over cities around Tsingkiang. Japanese planes, their racks loaded with bombs, sheared the hospital's red tin roof, snapping the American flag to attention with their wake. The lobbies, outpatient clinics and some three hundred and fifty beds overflowed with Chinese who had been torn by bullets and shrapnel and crushed by falling roofs. Many people were armless or legless, charred and punctured by rock and wooden splinters. And Japanese anti-American sentiments were becoming overt. Nelson Bell had thus far placated local platoon leaders by inviting them on personal tours of the hospital facilities, serving them tea and sweets, indicating with an almost Oriental deference that inside the compound he, not they, was in command. Such courtesies, he knew, could work but so long. Many of his colleagues were receiving the treatment that he felt sure was soon to come his way. "The destruction of life and property [is] sweeping over us," he wrote. "The list of Americans who have had their faces jabbed and slapped by the Japanese is a long one and getting longer. The homes, schools and hospitals of American missions which have been looted and destroyed by Japanese already run into the hundreds."

While conditions in China worsened, Ruth began fighting a battle of her own. In the spring of 1938 she was visited by a student from the University of Chicago who had attended high school in Korea with her. He had since abandoned his Christian faith and he challenged her to do likewise. "It could be the best thing that ever happened to you," he suggested. It would, he urged, be her liberation. The seduction of the intellect began slowly as the doubts sifted through her brain and began to coalesce. It was as though a tremor rolled from the top of her head to the base of her spine, shaking her loose from her spiritual moorings.

She didn't doubt the existence of a Supreme Creator, a Universal

Truth, a supernatural unifying force. The earth was too ordered, she realized. But what about the Bible? How could she be so sure that its words were true? What if Jesus Christ was nothing more than a brilliant philosopher—a Socrates of sorts?

"He was either God or a liar or crazy," Ruth announced to Lindsell one day.

He suggested that she accompany him to the home of a certain saintly Bible professor. "Perhaps he could pray with you," he added hopefully.

"I don't want prayers," Ruth replied. "I want proof."

For weeks they debated—she armed with skepticism, he with the Bible. "How do you account for the sin and sickness in the world?" she would ask. "How do you know what the Bible says is true? Is there any proof?" She argued with her friends, with anyone who would let her into the conversation, until her classmates fairly gulped when they saw her glide their way. What they didn't understand was that Ruth wasn't arguing to win. She was arguing to lose.

"I can't be sure that God loves me, for who am I amongst so many?" she said to Lindsell' one afternoon, toward the end of summer. "I don't feel loved or cherished. I'm not even sure He's aware of my existence."

He patiently and systematically presented the facts of his faith. Then, finally, he added simply, "But Ruth, there is still the leap of faith."

She knew that what he said was true. If God could be measured, then He would be too small; if He could be proven, then He would be too simple. Her finite mind had been attempting to capture His image in its tiny, dark box; her dim eyes had tried to illuminate the mysteries of the world; her fingers had ventured to touch her own intangible soul. It wasn't God who was too small, it was she. And without faith, the bridge between the two of them vanished.

Her faith had never been severely tested before this. Now, it was stronger. She still did not have all the answers, but she found she didn't need them. The Presence she had sensed since birth was yet there, like warmth she couldn't see, like music she couldn't touch, like love she couldn't prove.

At the end of the summer she visited her grandmother and invited Lindsell for a weekend. He wanted to marry her. But she had only just turned eighteen; she was too young, she told him kindly. In truth, she didn't plan to marry *anyone,* not in three years, not in thirty— never. Of course, it was entirely possible that Ruth had yet to meet a formidable opponent. Thus far her world had been populated with charming, attentive young gentlemen. In short, what she needed was a man who was as independent, stubborn, and mystifying as she was. Far away, in the rural South, such a person did exist.

6

Billy Frank

My love has long been yours . . .
since on that day
when we first met;
I will never quite forget
how you just paused
and smiled a bit,
then calmly helped yourself to it.

Ruth Bell Graham[1]

It was early fall, 1940. Maples flamed in red and gold on the Wheaton campus, light winds tossing their leaves and spiraling them groundward to darken and die like cooling embers. The October sun burned obliquely, a dazzling white face peering through clean blue glass, illumining all with its unblinking gaze. The air was tart with the smell of autumn, sharpened pencils, acrid inks, and the pungency of woolens warming in summer's waning heat. Bodies felt suddenly weightless, momentarily unattached as the leaves, as they wafted between seasons, as yet unburdened by the winter and the work ahead.

At that moment the world was opulent and infinite, and Billy Graham felt peacefully buoyant as he slouched in the orange pickup truck, hot light breaking through the windshield and over his trousers. His sleeves were pushed to his elbows and his long slender legs ended abruptly in a pair of scuffed brogans. Beside him, Johnny

---

1. *sitting by my laughing fire* . . . (Waco, Texas: Word Books, 1977), p. 54.

Streater squinted in the white glare, his fingers loosely curled around the wheel, his head slightly tilted as they chatted. Streater, a senior, was a twenty-five-year-old Floridian with short-cropped curly brown hair and dark twinkling eyes. Four years earlier he had bought the truck, girdled its metal flatbed with wooden planks, and painted "Wheaton College Student Trucking Service" in large blue letters on the doors. His new assistant was a twenty-one-year-old North Carolinian with a resonant voice and a refined Southern accent. He had graduated from Florida Bible Institute in Tampa that past spring and had arrived at Wheaton the month before, chagrined to find he was once again a lowly freshman. Streater had met him weeks earlier and had liked him at once, for there was a poignant boyishness about Billy, a gentility and decency that drew people. And before Streater thought twice about it, he had asked him to be his partner, offering him a whopping fifty cents an hour to help haul furniture, luggage and other impedimenta for the students and local residents.

Billy was six feet two inches of raw scaffolding topped by a mane of wavy, dark blond hair. He had perpetually dark circles under his eyes, but his face was a striking concentration of strong features that seemed to have been forged or chiseled rather than molded: His brow was high and intelligent, his nose and jaw strong; his deep-set eyes were as blue as a Siamese cat's.

Within a week of his arrival at Wheaton his classmates had dubbed him "Preacher," for he was an ordained Baptist minister. He had barnstormed in Florida for the past three years, holding revival services and proclaiming the Good News from street corners and barroom doorways. In the process he had forsaken his Presbyterian heritage, not in response to urgings of heart, but to deacons who threatened to cancel the revival services he was holding at a small Baptist church unless he agreed to be immersed. Without struggle or fanfare, he was baptized in a nearby lake. Though he sometimes doubted his call to the ministry and his effectiveness, he never questioned his insatiable desire to reach lost souls. It was an obsession, and time after time he would find himself pacing in front of a crowd, preaching from the supple black leather Bible gripped in his left hand.

William Franklin Graham, Jr., was born November 7, 1918, on a dairy farm outside Charlotte, North Carolina. False news reports declared that World War I had ended at 11 o'clock that morning. Four days later the war indeed ended, and Billy Frank, as his family called him, began his boyhood on a two-hundred-acre tract in the piedmont where days began hours before dawn and ended soon after dark. His world was earthy and immutable, punctuated by the pleasant sounds of warm milk drumming into pails and bottles thick with cream clattering in the delivery truck as it bumped along the loamy red dirt roads. Nature was cyclical, moving like a shadow across a sundial, from life to death, from death to life—its early stirrings felt in the thaw of March, its waning in October.

Spring and autumn were intoxicating, the months in between, dreary. By late June, the lemony perfume of the magnolias and the fragrance of the apple blossoms were gone; jaded by fecundity and heat, nature was reduced to the tawdriness of fat sunflowers and orange daylilies swaying from spindly stems along the roadsides. Steamy and monotonous, summers droned like the lethargic beetles hovering over the yard by day and the cacophonous cicadas at night. Winters were bleak, the raw days rarely culminating in the enchantment of snow, the trees bare silhouettes against the lawn and fields.

Perennially, there was the rapacious kudzu that transformed majestic oaks and pines into leafy dinosaurs reared on massive hindquarters, waiting to devour little boys who wandered too far from their fragrant kitchens or fusty barns. The cadence was constant—men were born on the land and died there just as their fathers before them. There seemed to be no question that Billy Frank would maintain the rhythm and become a farmer like the five generations of Graham men before him.

There is confusion about just who Billy Graham's early forebears were. Candidates include Sir "John with the bright sword" Graham of Kilbride, Scotland, who was noted for his bravery, and John Graham of Claverhouse, Viscount Dundee, notorious for his persecution of the Scottish Covenanters during the reign of Charles II. With more certainty it can be said that Billy Graham's direct ancestors emigrated from Ireland in 1772 and settled on a thousand acres along the Catawba River at the North and South Carolina line.

His grandfather William Crook Graham, born in the fall of 1840, was an opinionated Democrat with a temper and a fierce loyalty to the Confederacy. After he died in his armchair in 1910 he was lauded as the "Bravest Confederate in Mecklenburg," a suspect accolade in light of his company muster roll, which indicated that he was absent without leave on at least two occasions. Whether from patriotism or bounty bonds, Private Graham served for the duration of the Civil War in the Sixth Regiment of the South Carolina Volunteers. He suffered typhoid fever and a grievous leg wound. He was eventually taken captive by an enemy troop. Like his ancestors, he was devoted to the land, and after the war he returned to his farm in the Sharon township. In 1870 he married Mollie McCall and they raised eleven children in a log house on the center of their property. Their ninth child, born in June of 1888, was named William Franklin.

As a young man Frank Graham was a solid six-foot-two and handsome. He was fond of fat cigars and fine clothing, and he was a raconteur, known throughout the county for his jokes and colorful yarns. Though he lacked formal education, he was considered one of the shrewdest horse traders in the piedmont. A man of integrity, his handshake was as binding as a signed contract. He was kind, dutiful, and frugal, but his religion was rooted in works rather than grace until 1906, when he attended a revival at a local Methodist church. For nine evenings he attended the services and spent the late night rides home in his horse-drawn wagon unraveling what the evangelist had woven into his consciousness. On the tenth night no amount of tugging or picking would eradicate the message. As the steadily clopping hooves carried him back to the farm, he realized he had been converted.

Four years later, when Frank was twenty-two, he drove his sporty buggy to Lakewood Park west of Charlotte where couples drifted in rowboats or took languid strolls on Saturday nights and Sunday afternoons. Not long after he'd tethered his horse he noticed a slender young woman with fine strong features and pinned-up dark blonde hair. Her name was Morrow Coffey and she was eighteen. She eyed him obliquely—not for the first time, for she had seen him riding through the county and had long wanted to meet him. Before the Saturday evening had ended, the two had been introduced and the gentleman who had accompanied Morrow to the park found himself quite alone. Frank treated her to her first roller coaster ride and then drove her home.

Morrow had grown up just outside Charlotte, her forebears having settled in the Carolinas at the end of the eighteenth century. Her father was Benjamin Morrow Coffey, a dark, sharp-featured man who in his youth, as Morrow recalled the legend, had "penetrating brown eyes that could look right through you." When he was nineteen, he enlisted in the Eleventh Regiment of the Confederate Army, and on an early March morning he left home. Slipping him a New Testament and kissing him farewell, his mother stood at the edge of the yard, watching his back, his easy stride, watching him recede until there was nothing but the horizon. Throughout the war he carried the small leatherbound book in his breast pocket; his last vision of his mother's watching him leave home for war hung in his mind like an icon. On July 1, 1863, the opening day of the Battle of Gettysburg, he fell near a rill along Seminary Ridge, a bullet lodged below his left knee. As he lay upon the blood-soaked earth, acrid smoke and flames around him, a shell burst nearby and blinded his right eye. After a four-hour wait, he was carried from the field, loaded into a dray along with other wounded, and carried to a hospital. Awaking later from a whiskey-induced sleep, he discovered his sawed-off leg in a tub beside his bed. In early 1864 Coffey returned to his home and married his childhood sweetheart, Lucinda Robinson. With a wooden leg and a mule, he began farming. When his third daughter was born, he abandoned his hope of having a son and named the girl Morrow, after himself.

Morrow grew up in the thousand-member Steele Creek Presbyterian Church. By the time she met Frank Graham she was a conservative, no-nonsense believer. She set the tone for their lives together when on their wedding night in 1916 she unpacked her Bible first thing and began what would become their family tradition of daily devotions. From that point on, she set about to cure her card-playing, cigar-smoking husband of his worldliness.

The Grahams lived in a two-story, white clapboard house, with a sloping porch. It stood on a patch of dirt which at present harbors the IBM Building in one of Charlotte's prime business districts. Their first child, a daughter, died shortly after birth. Billy was born a year later, followed by two sisters and a brother. His mother was determined to raise them in a Christian atmosphere, but in the early years, the Graham home, like the Coffeys', was more Church-oriented than it was spiritual; their faith, like their affections, was inhibited. Young Billy's was a religion of ritual, of moral regulations, blessings at mealtimes, and church on Sunday morning. As a boy, he crackled with nervous energy like a long thin wire; he chewed his fingernails and had a mild stutter. Impetuously magnanimous, he had a proclivity for exaggeration and for lavishing both friend and foe with kind words and generous favors. The athletic field was the one spot where he could vent the electrical storm within him, and each day he loosed it on the basketball court or baseball field. "When we were teenagers we didn't know what 'hyper' meant," his brother Melvin recalled. "When I think back, he was probably hyper." Billy's mother often said in exasperation that she "wanted the doctor to give him something to calm him down."

When Billy was ten, his family moved into a sturdy brick house on a barren rise not far from the place of his birth. By age twelve, he was head and shoulders taller than the other boys and thin as a reed, weighing a meager hundred and sixty pounds. He had corn-colored hair and wide blue eyes, and an intensity that often caused people to think there was something unusual, if not important, about him. As a teenager, when he wasn't working on the farm or playing baseball, he was riding with pretty girls around the county in a friend's convertible. Depending on whom Billy was interested in—and he dated a different girl "about every week," claimed his sister Catherine—it was common to see him holding a young lady's hand in the sunshine, her hair whipping in the wind. In fact, he was rather much the local heartbreaker. As Catherine later recalled, "He was just *so* good looking, and the girls were just crazy about him."

Young Billy was not spiritual in the least. God was like a flower pressed between the pages of a book—to be briefly sentimentalized when chanced upon in the A.R.P. Presbyterian Church he attended each Sunday. Academics, like his religion, were largely ignored, understandably so, for he had little time to study. Each morning he and Melvin rose at 2:30 to begin their chores, a schedule so habitual that Melvin would momentarily blink awake at that hour for the rest of his days. Tumbling out of the house into the immaterial world of shadows and silence, they would amble along a narrow path, then through the alfalfa field, finally reaching the barn. Billy, who always had an aversion to milk, claimed he lost his taste for it when one of the cows planted a crusty hoof into his bucket. Uncle Clyde Graham, who lived across the road, owned a bottling machine. After the boys delivered their quota, it was poured into glass bottles which were fitted with cardboard stoppers and stamped Graham Brothers Dairy.

After a rigorous scrubbing and a hearty breakfast, Billy went to school. He was not an exemplary student and one day one of his teachers visited his mother to tell her so. Perhaps in an effort to frighten her into motion, the woman paused at the front door on her way out and declared, "Billy Frank will never amount to a thing."

In the spring of 1934, when Billy was fifteen, a revival, held seven miles from his house, would initiate a change in him. Lawyers, doctors, farmers—the wealthy and the poor—turned out in droves. They bumped along the rutted roads in their trucks and glided from their fine city dwellings in their shiny sedans, while he ensconced himself in the cool solitude of his red brick home, ignoring what he judged to be a raw lumber tabernacle full of mummery and emotionalism. He had heard about Mordecai Ham, a fiery Baptist minister who had been preaching there for three weeks. He had been brought to Charlotte by Albert Sidney Johnson, the prominent minister of the First Presbyterian Church. But he had gotten such a drubbing in the newspapers that Billy's own church had refused to acknowledge his existence. One afternoon one of his father's assistants, Albert McMakin, announced he would attend that evening's service, and urged Billy to go along. To please him, he agreed. Bathed and already perspiring in the warm night air, they climbed into the man's car and roared to the tabernacle.

It was jammed. Wives wearing dark linen suits, voile dresses, and straw hats sat beside dapper businessmen. Women in blousy cotton dresses sat primly, husbands ramrod straight beside them as though an undertaker had stuffed them into their shiny Sunday suits. The faces of the farmers were tanned like belting leather, whited in a band across the brow from the shade of their hats; their flesh glowed from soapy scrubbings, but the slivered moons of dirt beneath broad, furrowed nails remained. The airless atmosphere was heavy with moist heat and toilet water. Young Billy shrank into the back and peered over slicked-down hair and hats. Ham was intelligent and articulate, and unabashed in his hatred of sin. Billy listened with fascination, and from that moment on he couldn't stay away.

Night after night Mordecai Ham warned about hell, fornication and liquor, his eyes snapping, his bone-white hair falling across his moist brow. Unnerved and convicted, Billy ducked and dodged whenever the preacher's accusing finger seemed pointed his way. Then one night the fear slid from him and the minister's voice became strange, distant, as though another Voice were speaking through him. An incipient yearning stirred deep within, filling him unutterably and irresistibly. Sawdust shifted beneath his shoes as he walked forward to surrender himself to Christ.

Revivals came and went like the seasons. For some of the local folk, equilibrium was restored a week after the tent had been folded and the evangelist had moved on to another town. For others, their walk to the altar had changed their lives. Though superficially Billy was the same Billy Frank his friends had always known, inside, his soul was embattled, waged in a struggle he could not ignore. To him, God was a force to be tangled with. How much simpler it would have been had God been that-great-something-out-there looking down on him; but no, He was a powerful and persistent presence. For the next eighteen months, Billy was torn between Christ and worldliness. When the weather was warm, he would lope through the woods behind his house, jumping over two deep gullies, heading for a creek where he sat on a boulder in the sun. There he spent uninterrupted hours reading his Bible and praying, mulling over how to live his new-found faith.

In the fall of 1936, he left home for the mountains of Cleveland, Tennessee, where his parents had enrolled him in the recently found-ed Bob Jones College. He would last one semester. After the open, sunny world of the farm, Bob Jones College impressed Billy as a windowless, darkened room where the emphasis was upon sin, "Thou Shalt Nots," and the eradication of worldliness. Griping was forbidden and signs posted in the barrack-style dormitories reminded the students they had better mind their attitudes as well as their tongues. Athletic competitions with other colleges were nonexistent; holding hands and kissing were felonious. His spirit withered. Then a tenacious bout with the flu robbed him of his physical strength.

In early January, Billy sat in Dr. Bob Jones's office, nervously in-forming the man that he was leaving, bailing out. In turn he was flayed for his lack of Christian integrity, for his blighted character. With the urgency Jones so often employed when promising the face-less unbelievers an eternal fiery Hell, he promised him a lifetime of failure. Billy had side-stepped the aura of God's will because he had darted from the shadow of Bob Jones; at the tender age of nineteen, he was a lost man.

In February of 1937, Billy transferred to the Florida Bible Institute in Tampa. Buoyed by the sunshine and cheery atmosphere, he thrived. He began preaching in empty buildings or on a cypress stump in a nearby swamp where no one could hear him attempt to erase the remnants of his nervous stutter. He preached anywhere he was invited, practicing each sermon as many as twenty-five times before feeling confident enough to deliver it. He condemned sin and warned of damnation, possessing a power that from the beginning drew people. Local reporters strayed into his services, making such observations as: "Young Graham does not mince words when he tells church members that they are headed for the same hell as the bootlegger and racketeer unless they get right and live right."[2] Posted around Tampa were his homemade handbills: "Have you heard the young man with a burning message?"[3]

During his first year at Florida Bible Institute he fell in love with an attractive, dark-haired young woman. In 1938, he asked her to marry him. She accepted, only to reject him the following year because she was in love with someone else. It was a sharp blow, and Billy begged God to change what had happened, to somehow reverse the inclinations of her heart or of his. But prayer, he discovered, was not a wish-book filled with slick promises of happiness and plenty; he learned that God often did not give him what he wanted because He'd rather give him what he should have. In his greatest hour of dejection, he gave what was left of himself to all that he conceived of God.

He graduated in 1940 and left Tampa with a new earnestness about his Christian call. He promised himself he would never kiss a woman again until he knew she was "the one," as he put it, who was to be his wife. In fact, he would ignore women in general, as much as he could, and focus his energy on his work, on his preaching.

By the fall of 1940, Billy's social fast was about to be broken. Ever since he had met Johnny Streater he had been hearing about a striking young woman named Ruth Bell.

"She's beautiful," Johnny Streater said one afternoon as the truck bounced through the Wheaton streets. "She's the second nicest girl on campus, the nicest being my girl, of course."

Streater and his fiancée, Carol Lane, were studying Chinese and planned to go to China as missionaries after graduation. It was not surprising that they had become acquainted with Ruth. Streater was an eager matchmaker, and often as he and Billy made their rounds in the truck, Streater would vividly describe Ruth's physical and spiritual merits, on one day building up to the hyperbolic clincher: "She's *so* spiritual that she gets up at four o'clock each morning to read her Bible and pray." Though Ruth did have devotions first thing in the

---

2. Untitled personal scrapbook, Collection 15, Archives of the Billy Graham Center, Wheaton, Illinois.
3. Untitled personal scrapbook, Collection 15, Archives of the Billy Graham Center, Wheaton, Illinois.

morning, in truth, she was usually staggering out of bed that early to study Greek, a course she would later describe as her "academic Waterloo."

"I want you to meet her," Streater concluded.

"Well then," Billy said, "let's go!"

His opportunity came in November when he and Streater strolled from the library to Williston Hall for lunch and discovered Ruth in the hallway chatting with friends. Streater introduced them. Ruth smiled, slightly startled by his intense blue eyes. He acknowledged her with a courteous reserve that masked his sudden rush of interest—"I fell in love right that minute," he later said. Even so, he managed to hide his feelings so well that it would be some time before Ruth was aware of them. Indeed, in later years she would never quite recall the first time she met Billy, but she thought it might have been when he and Streater were playing chess on a table beside a windowsill.

Billy expeditiously wrote his mother and told her he had found the woman he would one day marry—he loved Ruth because she looked just like her. Morrow, knowing blarney when she saw it, burned the letter years later for fear Ruth might discover it and be insulted.

After several weeks, Billy finally mustered sufficient courage to ask Ruth for a date. It was early December and he, Streater, and several friends were studying in Frost Library when they noticed Ruth sitting at an empty table on the other side of the room.

"Go ask her! Go ask her!" the men urged, as they jogged him to his feet.

Quietly, he walked across the painfully silent library, slipped into the chair beside her, and asked her to accompany him to the school's presentation of Handel's *Messiah*. She accepted and watched his retreating back with interest.

The day of the concert a steady snow fluttered against the windowpanes of the beige frame house at 304 North Main Street, four blocks off campus. Ruth and seven other coeds lived upstairs in tidy rooms furnished with honey maple desks, dressers, and beds covered with firm new mattresses. Her room was directly to the right after climbing the stairs; its two windows overlooked a Baptist church and the boyhood home of Harold "Red" Grange, the highly acclaimed Chicago Bears running back. Downstairs lived the elderly maiden sisters Julia and Cornelia Scott, who had become more than a bit fond of Ruth after learning that she was the mysterious do-gooder who had been sneaking out before light on snowy mornings to shovel the walks cornering the house. She filled the women's world with unexpected pleasures, leaving them stockings bulging with nuts, sweets and trinkets at Christmas and keeping humor circulating through the house.

It was a minor matter for Ruth to pick just the right dress to wear on her first date with Billy Graham: She had only one "good" dress—a plain black wool sheath that she had made herself.

"Which dress shall I wear?" she asked her roommate with mock seriousness, "my black one or my black one?"

"Neither," she replied. "For a change, why don't you wear your black one?"

Ruth pinned up her hair, slid into her one pair of pumps and looped her strand of dimestore pearls around her neck. He arrived at the front door, spruce in a blue tweed suit he had bought for fifteen dollars at a Maxwell Street bazaar in Chicago.

Billy was unlike anyone Ruth had ever met. Weeks earlier she had overheard him praying with a group of students and had marveled. He wasn't unctuous or pietistic, nor did his words emerge in the smooth reverential tone of a Christian elder statesman; he was earnest, quietly confident, and personal. Clearly, he spoke as one who knew God, and knew Him well. He was a man who seemed to comprehend the amplitude of God's might and authority—seemed to comprehend it so thoroughly, in fact, that it had become part of him. Ruth sensed this and recorded in her journal at the time:

> [Bill] has been an inspiration. Sleeping almost none, [giving] all the time, so dead in earnest, all else falls in line with the longing to make Christ known in all His saving power. Filled with the Spirit, humble, thoughtful, unpretentious, courteous. And the verse stands out vividly, "Neither count I my life dear unto myself. . . .
> No reserve. Just [giving]. Desiring only to be well-pleasing to Him.

But what interested Ruth was that as Billy escorted her through the milky, snowy air, leading her over the frosted walk to the concert, he seemed completely unaware of his uniqueness, his poignancy, his gift.

In his mind he was the uncertain freshman who longed to win souls to Christ and win Ruth Bell for himself: He felt inadequate to do either. To Ruth, he was the cool, self-assured gentleman who, much to her fascination, was neither obsequious nor flirtatious. Indeed, because he kept his emotions tightly cloaked, he came within an inch of politely ignoring her. She pondered this as they sat side by side in the triumphant flow of Handel's *Messiah*, never imagining that at that moment he was, as he recalled years later, "a bundle of nerves" inside a bargain-basement suit.

Late that night, she entered her room. The windowpanes were cold and clear. Beyond the arborvitae flanking the porch, the lawn and the elm-bordered street were roundly insulated with snow. The world was mute, as though life had been blanked out, so obliterated and noiseless that the only sound was the faint static of existence. She knelt on the carpet beside her bed and prayed, "God, if You let me serve You with that man I'd consider it the greatest privilege in my life."

For the next month Ruth and Billy ignored each other. Convinced that his friend was hopelessly in love, Johnny Streater finally warned him, "Whoa boy, you'd better slow down!" And he obeyed, even though it took the sum of his self-control to do so. As it turned out, his concept of "slowing down" led him to avoid Ruth altogether. Her thoughts, meanwhile, had again focused on the mission field and her belief that she was destined for it. She spent Christmas alone in the Scotts' house to find out how much aloneness she could endure. "It was," she wrote her parents, "a bit of a test as to whether or not that part would be too hard in the field, should the Lord place me in pioneer work alone." Next, she decided that surviving aloneness wasn't enough. What she really needed to aid her on the mission field was to learn how to fly an airplane. She informed her mother of this in a cheery note, assuring her that "it isn't as dangerous as driving."

Their second date came some six weeks after the first, in February of 1941, when Ruth decided to invite Billy to her house party—one week before the event, two months after her friends had secured their dates. Reluctant to ask a man out, she had procrastinated until the last possible moment and agreed to cooperate only after her housemates had sufficiently harassed her. "Why don't you write him?" one of the women suggested, "then he'll have more time to think up a good excuse not to come." She did just that and he quickly accepted. Their next date came a week after the party when he invited her to attend a church service with him. Afterward, he parked his 1937 green Plymouth at the curb, walked her to the door and hesitated.

"There's something I'd like you to make a matter of definite prayer," he began as they stood on the porch, their breath vaporizing in the cold, brittle air. "I have been taking you out because I am more than interested in you and have been since the day Johnny Streater introduced us last fall. But I know you have been called to the mission field and I'm not definite."

Billy had been surrounded by would-be missionaries ever since his arrival at Wheaton. But he had never felt pulled in that direction—until recently, he told her. "And not all because of you either," he added quickly, "though I have wondered if the Lord has been speak-. ing to me through you." Many years later he would admit that he had been so in love with her that he was tempted to consider spending his life in the arid mountains of Tibet if that was the only way he could be with her.

Ruth, however, had no idea what he was thinking or why he was standing on her porch on a bitterly cold night talking about the mission field. Baffled, she watched his car disappear in a swirl of smoking exhaust. She didn't see him again for several days and when they finally passed each other, he seemed preoccupied, almost indifferent. Ruth could only assume that he was reacting to her. "The strange creature waits till I begin wondering if he's changed his mind," she complained to her parents, "then he asks me out."

Her security was further weakened when the wife of professor Mortimer B. Lane (Streater's future father-in-law) dropped by to warn her about him. Ruth was in bed, miserable with a cold, when "Mummy Lane," as the students affectionately called her, appeared with a quart of freshly squeezed orange juice and a list of the young ladies Billy had dated and then dropped over the years. "Ruth," she concluded, "I don't want to see you hurt." Opening her *Daily Light* that night, Ruth read, "Meddle not with them given to change." She and her roommate collapsed in a spasm of laughter.

That winter she began describing Billy in letters to her parents:
"He must be six-three or four. Has blond wavy hair. Is very slender. All of which is quite immaterial. His great earnestness is what most deeply impresses those who know him. He is undoubtedly a man of one purpose, and his fearlessness in preaching the Gospel must be a joy to the Lord. More about that later. I know if I went on it would begin to sound allegorical. And why all the detail anyway?"

A pattern began. She would describe Billy, then drop the subject only to re-introduce it, sometimes in the next paragraph. It was as though two voices were speaking: her reason, which claimed that he was just another date, and her emotions, which could not let him go:

"Despite Bill's fearlessness and sometimes sternness, he is just as thoughtful and gentle as one would want a man to be. Maybe it's the South in him. . . . At any rate, he really makes you feel perfectly natural and looked-after without being showy or obnoxious. Sounds like I'm in love, doesn't it? Don't get worried. I'm not." Again, she announced that she was changing the subject, only to resume telling them about him in the next sentence, reminiscing about a date on a recent snowy evening: "You know—funny how the little things pop up in the memory. His way of going about things, his self-control. . . the way he put both hands on the wheel and squared his shoulders when he began, the strength and keenness of his profile when the streetlight fell thru the snow sifting on the windshield and lit up his face. I wasn't watching him directly, but one sees a lot out of the corner of one's eye. Oh, I shouldn't be writing all this. You'll think me a romantic nit-wit."

Ruth's college career was briefly interrupted in March of 1941, after doctors performed what they thought was a routine appendectomy on Rosa and discovered that she had tubercular peritonitis. She began convalescing in the private home in Wheaton where she had been living. Ruth dropped out of school to take care of her, eager for the chance to look after the sister who for so many years had looked after her. Ever since Ruth had left home for Korea, Rosa had demonstrated an almost motherly concern for her. During Ruth's first winter in Wheaton, Rosa had noticed her sister shivering in her thin cloth overcoat and had promptly taken her to Marshall Field's in Chicago. Using her own meager savings, she had bought Ruth a heavy beige wool coat, one that was much warmer, much more handsome than anything Rosa would ever have bought for herself.

Though weak from her illness, Rosa was still hearty enough to employ her match-making skills. She urged Ruth to fall in love with Billy. The local consensus was the same: He and Ruth were suited for one another, and half the campus, it seemed, was "praying for the relationship." Ruth was praying for it too, but sometimes she wasn't sure whether she should petition for a win or a loss. In his enigmatic manner, Billy expended considerable energy ignoring her. Then he would materialize from the vacuum and ask a question like this one: "Do you think I'm asking you out too much? Because I don't want to embarrass you by taking you out too frequently."

Ruth, whose keen intuition told her that Billy was being overcautious, would never have dared to broadside him with her suspicions. The game was played on, reaching its culmination later that spring when he said to her, "I haven't tried to win you, Ruth. I haven't asked you to fall in love with me. I haven't sent you candy and flowers and lovely gifts. I have asked the Lord, if you are the one, to win you for me. If not, to keep you from falling in love with me."

After that remark, Ruth decided to start dating other men. The ensuing flurry of dates had predictable results:

"Either you date just me or you can date everybody *but* me!" Billy announced.

In a collective answer to a myriad of prayers, Ruth and Billy were registered a "couple" in the eyes of their peers. He became domineering, quizzing her about how much sleep she had gotten, whether she had exercised, whether she had eaten properly. She was known to be whimsical about meals, and if he discovered she hadn't eaten lunch, off he'd march her downtown to buy her hot chocolate and a sandwich. Then, chin propped on folded hands, he'd grin at her from across the table while he forced her to eat every crumb. On double dates he had the annoying habit of changing her order from iced tea to milk. As he watched after his woman in the manner of his ancestors, he harbored the notion that she had surrendered her career plans. That was his gravest miscalculation, and it almost cost him the war.

"I think being an old maid missionary," Ruth informed him one day, "is the highest call there is."

"Woman was created to be a wife and mother," he countered.

"There are exceptions," she said matter-of-factly, "and I believe I'm one of them."

"If that's the case," he announced, "we will just call a halt, during which time you should search the Scriptures and pray until you find out just what is God's place for woman in this life. And when you find out and are willing to accept God's place, you can let me know."

For a week, when she wasn't in class she was in her bedroom, praying and scouring the Bible for direction. When she could stand her exile not a moment longer, she sent for him and dubiously acquiesced. Her concession, however, would prove to be more of a détente than a surrender.

In the rural world of Billy's youth, as in most of the world, the woman's life revolved around her husband's; suppressed, she developed the facility of asserting herself invisibly. Morrow Graham was gentle and submissive, living eighty-nine years without ever owning a driver's license because her husband did not think women should drive. Yet it was she who kept the books for the dairy farm and ran the household. Ruth, in contrast, was accustomed to strong-willed, outspoken women like her mother. Billy's authoritativeness galled her. It also intrigued her, as she later recalled, and made her feel "cared for and safe."

"He isn't awfully easy to love because of his sternness and unwavering stand on certain issues," she wrote her parents on June 2, 1941. "Many a night I have come in almost hating the man because I wanted my way in some little thing that was either unwise or foolish or something, and he wouldn't give in even if it meant losing my love. . . . Then, tho' I'd be so mad I'd have to get down and pray for victory, Bill would just look down at me and say, as only Bill can say, 'Ruth, you know it's because I love you.' And I'd feel myself slipping."

In early June, the interminable winter had finally been burned from the earth, leaving it clean and emerald. Gone with it was the routine of daily walks to class, faces nettled by snowy blasts, minds adroop from long nights of study. Summer vacation was upon them. Students, hauling battered trunks and suitcases, straggled from dormitories to waiting cars, joyous at reprieve and pained at good-byes. Billy's Plymouth was packed for Florida, where he was to hold youth revival services for several weeks. Before leaving, he asked Ruth to marry him. She paused, then replied that she could not answer him. He headed south, his heart heavy, as he dreaded the finality in that tiny "no."

If she said yes, she would have to relinquish what she had for years believed to be God's will for her life. Giving up that was in many ways synonymous with giving up her identity, for she believed she had been born to serve God, not a man. Rosa, however, encouraged her to accept his proposal.

"But what about my wanting to be an old maid missionary to Tibet?" Ruth asked her.

"There's no place in the Bible that says, 'Blessed are the old maids,'" she replied.

7

The Ring

It was so very good of God
to let my dreams come true,
to note a young girl's cherished hopes
then lead her right to you.
Ruth Bell Graham

From the war-torn cities of China came the cries for mercy, *"K'o lien! K'o lien!"* Starving peasants wandered aimlessly amid collapsed buildings and rubble-covered streets, their eyes vacant, the stench of death clinging to the earth like ground fog. They pummeled tree bark and skimmed slime off ponds for food; there were rumors of cannibalism. The climate was restive and ready for propagandizing and organizing in the name of change; so it was that the Communists continued to undermine the Nationalist regime.

In Tsingkiang, the missionaries were imperiled, and their work was overwhelming. Occupying Japanese soldiers were becoming overtly resentful of what they conceived of as the Americans' influence over local Chinese; they were embittered by the United States government's willingness to sell fighter planes to China. It didn't surprise Nelson Bell when the American consul entreated him to flee. First he refused: He could not abandon the people when they needed him now more than ever. He soon reconsidered when he learned that his wife was suffering from malaria and a kidney infection and that Rosa had been admitted to Zace Sanatorium in Winfield, Illinois, with both lungs tubercular.

In May, the Bells sailed home. A month later Germany would attack Russia, scotching Soviet military aid to China and speeding the economy's downward spiral. In August, Japanese would capture the remaining Tsingkiang missionaries and, without explanation, imprison them in the attic of the Bells' house for a month. Many of their colleagues had already been sent to concentration camps to face starvation, torture, disease and death.

Ruth was elated over her parents' return; at last they were safe and at last they would meet Billy Graham. She wrote them June 2 while they were yet aboard ship, failing to mention that he had asked her to marry him. Her feelings toward him and matrimony were still ambivalent: "He has his faults," she explained to them in the letter, "and some people do object to his fearless, uncompromising presentation of the Gospel. But that was the first thing about him that commanded my attention and later my admiration—as I grew to know him better, my trust. And now—but, then I'm going easy on that."

Her letters and diaries are filled with a tangle of emotions that range from proclamations of her love for him to declarations of her independence. She still greeted the notion of marriage with reservations, and her skittishness made her wonder about the nature of love: She had always heard it filled one with ecstasy and a sense of abandonment. In truth, Ruth wasn't struggling with a clash of hearts, but a clash of wills.

The Bells arrived at Wheaton July 4 for a brief visit with Ruth and Rosa. Then they traveled to the Mayo Clinic in Rochester, Minnesota, for thorough medical examinations. Dr. Bell purchased a car and drove his wife, daughter Virginia, and son Clayton to Waynesboro where they would live with his mother for a month. Ruth remained at Wheaton with Rosa. Billy, meanwhile, was preaching at the Christian and Missionary Alliance Church in Tampa and daily checking for a letter from Ruth. One morning, a thick envelope postmarked July 6 arrived. It bore her familiar unique script, and he sequestered himself in his manse bedroom before eagerly ripping it open. He felt a rush of joy as he read the words: God, she believed, would have her say yes to his proposal of marriage.

Though Ruth's ambivalence had not disappeared, she believed the relationship was "of the Lord," she explained to her parents in a letter July 7, after telling them what she had done. "I almost stand in awe of him and yet I'm not afraid of him. To be with Bill in this type work won't be easy. There will be little financial backing, lots of obstacles and criticism, and no earthly glory whatsoever. But somehow I need Bill. I don't know what I'd do if, for some reason, he should suddenly go out of my life. And Bill needs someone to understand him, someone who would be willing to take the quiet place of praying for him. . . . I knew I wouldn't have peace till I yielded my will to the Lord and decided to marry Bill. I must admit I have had real peace since doing so."

In late July, Ruth rode the train to Waynesboro and Billy drove northwest in his Plymouth, preparing to meet the Bells for the first time. The Blue Ridge rolled like a hazy frozen ocean to his left, wrapping closer with each mile, lifting him, finally setting him down in the Shenandoah Valley. Old gnarled apple trees with hard green fruit flanked the whitewashed fences on the roadsides; beyond rolled velvety pastureland freckled with white-faced cows. On July 30, a hot, cloudless Wednesday, he nosed through Waynesboro and parked at Grandmother Bell's house, discovering that there was no room for him there. Dreading the unexpected drain on his already thin wallet, he registered at the nearby Hotel Wayne. That night at dinner he found to his delight that the reception was warmer than he had even hoped. He thawed in the steady flow of the Bells' humor. By dessert, the two men had struck up a friendship that would lead to Dr. Bell's being Billy's closest advisor for the next thirty-three years. The next morning, Billy checked out of his hotel (discovering that Dr. Bell had paid the three-dollar room charge). He and Ruth's family left for Washington, D.C., where Dr. Bell had an appointment with Far Eastern officials at the State Department. (He planned to warn them that the Japanese intended to attack the United States. Friday morning he braved the capital and was politely ignored; some months later the Japanese would bomb Pearl Harbor.)

Saturday Billy left for Charlotte, relaxed of mind and soul, for the Bells had accepted him. Ruth would join him in several weeks to meet his family, which by now was more than a little curious about her. For months, Morrow Graham had urged her son to bring home a snapshot of this young woman who was alleged to look like her. Melvin, not privy to that description and knowing only that she was from China, expected her to have straight black hair and Asian features. His sisters didn't strenuously exercise their imaginations over the matter at all because they assumed she "was probably just another one of Billy Frank's girlfriends," as Jeannie later explained.

At the brink of summer Billy had finally coerced Ruth into relinquishing a photograph, something she never did gracefully—or honestly, for that matter. There were few things in life she disliked more than having a lens leering in her face and its owner coaxing her in a cloying voice to "say cheese." It wasn't unusual for her to enlist her sense of humor just before the shutter clicked (resulting in any number of comical facial contortions). Nor was it unusual for her to surgically remove herself with scissors, leaving gaping holes in yearbooks and group portraits. Not knowing what he was up against, he patiently waited while she rummaged through her belongings to fulfill his request. Explaining innocently that it was "all I could find," she handed him a snapshot taken when she was a twelve-year-old frump, her long hair pulled back and fastened with a barrette. Demurely holding a hollyhock at her waist, she looked like a parody of a cemetery monument. His first morning home his family passed the picture around the table—in silence.

"Well," his mother said, clearing her throat, "she doesn't look like that now, does she?"

No, she was soon to find, Ruth didn't look like that at all. On a Saturday afternoon in August, Billy ushered Ruth into his home. Dressed smartly in a navy suit, a flower in her lapel, she entered the sunroom where Morrow Graham sat regally beside a crystal bowl of white petunias. "Oh," Billy's mother recalled thinking with pleasure, "she's beautiful."

During the week that followed, ten-year-old Jeannie roared Ruth around the countryside in a black pickup truck, instructing her in the art of driving, which culminated in Ruth's backing through a hedge in front of the house. Evenings were spent on a hard pew inside Sharon Presbyterian Church where Billy was preaching each night that week. What she witnessed was the opening scene of her life with him, the reel of film snapping into place and beginning to spin.

On Saturday night after the service they had retreated to the fish pond behind the house, where the air was warm and fragrant with the smell of newmown grass. Their romantic moment was abruptly ended when a man named Herbert began pounding on the front door, pleading to see Billy. An alcoholic who had known Billy since childhood, he had attended that night's service and resisted the altar call. After downing several stiff drinks, he found himself staggering to the Graham farm, unable to stand his misery any longer; he was weeping when Billy led him into the parlor and gently shut the door. He had tried to stop drinking in the past, but each time he stayed away from the bottle for several days, one of his friends would hand him a glass and off he'd go on another binge. His wife and children feared him. Throughout his angry, drunken years, something beyond him—he figured it was God—had followed him quietly and relentlessly like the moon over a traveler's shoulder. He was tired of running.

Ruth and Billy's mother sat in the family room, pretending not to notice the man's loud sobbing and wild talking. Then Billy invited them to pray with them. Quietly, Ruth listened to the cascade of self-mortification pouring from the man. "I had never heard a broken-down sinner pleading for forgiveness," she wrote at the time. She would spend the rest of her life hearing just that.

On Sunday, after dinner, Billy led Ruth through woods and pasture to the red-banked Sugar Creek where he had spent so many hours in his youth basking in the warmth and peace he craved. It was his sanctuary, the place for his most private self, and he was sharing it with her. They perched on a boulder, the shallow water running sluggishly below their feet, the sun working highlights into their hair. And they entreated God to save his childhood friends, to redeem people like Herbert. "As I listened while he prayed," Ruth recorded, "I realized a little bit the burden weighing on his heart." They lingered until the sun burned obliquely through the trees and long shadows unrolled from the trunks.

That night's service was somewhat disconcerting. Billy's delivery was too fast, his gestures so exaggerated that he looked like a caricature of himself. It was a bit much for a staunch Presbyterian whose idea of worship was a dignified delivery and a quiet reverence in the congregation. As the organist began playing the familiar hymns for the altar call, Ruth closed her eyes and, almost apologetically, asked God to overlook the frailties of man and touch the hearts of at least one or two of the people around her. A quiet creaking fluttered down the row of pews as more than forty stood. In a steady stream they moved forward, eyes fixed on the bare wood beneath their feet, tissues dabbing away tears. She watched with disbelief, filled with awe as she eyed Billy, standing at the end of the aisle, head bowed, hands folded beneath his chin. He did not wear the pietistic look of a spiritual salesman who had just delivered a slick pitch. No. His power was in the message he had faithfully presented; he was the instrument, not the musician. She saw that then.

On their way home, he was quiet, disappointed that the high school friend he had prayed for most had remained firmly planted in his seat during the altar call. She too was silent, knowing that there were and would be times when he was distant, absorbed, almost unaware of her existence.

Monday, Ruth rode the bus to Montreat, where her parents were buying a house. They drove to Waynesboro the first week in September, leaving Ruth to stay in a rustic summer cabin in Black Mountain with her friend Gay Currie, who had grown up in China with her. They invited Billy to spend the day. On September 5, while he was making the two-hour drive, Gay blacked out Ruth's front teeth, unfastened her long hair, and helped her select a home-made, flower-printed dress (that was at least two sizes too big). Kicking off her shoes, she set out to meet her beau, her bare feet patting along the country road winding downtown. She didn't know that Billy, dressed in white from collar to shoes, had a surprise for her too. Tucked inside a pocket was a yellow-gold engagement ring, purchased with every penny of the sixty-five dollar love offering he had received from Sharon Presbyterian Church.

Thick red dust billowed from the car's back tires as it lumbered up the grade, driving right past the "snaggle-toothed" mountain girl, as he later described her, staring at him from the roadside. Suddenly recognizing the quizzical face in his rearview mirror, he crunched to a halt and backed up. A bit unsettled by this unexpected scene in his romantic drama, he mutely opened the car door for her. Then he began to laugh.

The unpainted pine–board cabin was located in an isolated mountainous tract, wild with huckleberry bushes, mountain laurels, and rhododendrons. A slender stream whispered through the side yard, and a thick rope swing dangled from a tree. They sat on the porch in the white sunshine, staring sleepily at the vista as they talked. The Black Mountains slumbered in the distance, their contours taking on human shapes as shadows moved across them during the waning afternoon. Blighted chestnut trees jutted from slopes and ridges like broken feathers, as though a tribe of giant Cherokee Indians had reclined in various positions around the Swannanoa Valley a millennium ago and had turned to earth.

Near dusk, they drove fifteen miles west to the top of Sunset Mountain, famous for its panoramic view of Asheville and for Beaucatcher Tunnel, which had been blasted through years earlier. As the molten sun set on one side of the ridge and the milkglass moon rose on the other, he gave her the ring.[1]

Ruth's exuberance would quickly fade when her life was temporarily interrupted that fall, suspending her in an idle solitude—a fertile

---

1. Several days later, Ruth's ten-year-old brother Clayton eyed the ring and innocently asked, "Is it a diamond or a grindstone?"

soil for anxiety. About the time Billy had given her the ring, her health had begun a slow spiral toward exhaustion. Listless and fatigued, she often slept until noon in the house her parents were renting in Montreat while their new home on Assembly Drive was being renovated. Fearing that Ruth had a touch of malaria, they forbade her to return to Wheaton for the first semester. They decided to send her with Rosa to the Southwestern Presbyterian Sanatorium in Albuquerque, New Mexico. On November 6, the Bells tucked her into a train bound for Wheaton to meet Rosa at Zace Sanatorium. Together they boarded the train for Albuquerque.

The Southwestern Presbyterian Sanatorium was a cluster of gray stucco buildings with red slate roofs. It was located on sparkling green grounds, interwoven with tidy gravel drives and stately Lombardy poplars. Rosa was restricted to the infirmary, and her sister moved into a building nearby. There Ruth spent the days in her glassed-in sunporch, absorbing the clean hot light and the majestic view. To the east, the Sandia and Manzano mountains rose eleven thousand feet; extinct volcanoes puckered to the north. She luxuriated in it all, curing like fruit in the sun until she felt weightless, absolved of all responsibility. "It rained yesterday and a cold wind was blasting," she wrote her parents. "It blew all the clouds away last night and morning found us in a crisp cold world of dazzling sunshine and snow-capped mountains. The air is so clean and fresh—like on board ship. I am feeling on top of the world." Such a respite, she added, "is a blessing. It makes people stop rushing around and gives them time to stop and to begin really enjoying life."

It's not surprising that she would, at this moment of detachment, entertain second thoughts about the engagement. Doubts settled in with tenacity and Billy was not there to chase them away. She wrote him a crushing letter, telling him she did not think she was in love with him and that marriage was, perhaps, unwise. Miserable, he could do nothing but wait until Ruth returned to Wheaton.

In December, she returned to Montreat, believing that she was leaving her sister to die, for there was no hope for her recovery. Doctors had already performed a phrenicectomy on one lung, permanently collapsing it, and were giving her weekly treatments to induce pneumothorax, or a temporary collapse, of the other to rest it. But in February, she announced that she would refuse further treatment. God would heal her, she decided. As a physician, her father realized that the consequences of Rosa's actions might be death; but as her father and a man of great faith, he did not want to interfere with her act of Christian commitment. "Make sure you're being led of God," he told her, "and use your own head." Then, despite the doctors' emphatic warnings that she would hemorrhage to death, he instructed them to comply with his daughter's wishes. All treatments were stopped. Prying herself out of bed each day, Rosa began visiting and helping other patients until her strength was spent. With each attempt, her determination and energy increased. Eventually she was walking a mile into town daily, where she would force down an ice cream soda at the drug store before returning to the sanatorium. By the fall of 1942, her lungs had expanded, her X-rays confirming that she had been completely cured. "Only God could have done this," one of the doctors marveled to Dr. Bell.

When Ruth returned to Wheaton in January of 1942, Billy asked if she wished to give him back the ring. She hesitated, depressed by the finality of the gesture, unsettled by the image of him vanishing from her life. No, she answered, her words edged in frustration. The problem, she explained, was that she still believed she was meant to be a missionary.

"Listen," he said, "do you or do you not think the Lord brought us together?"

"Yes," she had to confess.

"Then," he said firmly, "I'll do the leading and you'll do the following."

And, as Ruth would later remark, with a twinkle in her eye, "I've been following him ever since."

Ruth could live with following as long as she wasn't tethered like a nanny goat. And sometimes that was just how she felt. She almost slapped his ring back into his palm one afternoon during a disagreement over church affiliations. Already an ordained Baptist minister, Billy had no interest in returning to the Presbyterian church, a change that would involve three years of seminary after college if he wished to become a Presbyterian minister. Since he had left the Presbyterian church, he assumed that Ruth should do the same. The remark that almost cost him the engagement was his comment, as they were riding in the car one afternoon, that "Dr. Bell couldn't possibly be a man of God and remain in the Southern Presbyterian Church."

They disagreed about other matters, too, like Ruth's health habits, which had never been good and were now even worse. By March, she had lost ten pounds and was suffering from insomnia. Having never felt the slightest impulse to do anything more rigorous than walking, she marveled at Billy's daily regimen of wrestling, jogging, and calisthenics. Billy did his best to help her mend her ways:

"Saturday night," Ruth wrote at the time, "he presented me with a bag of grapefruit and oranges and a box of [vitamin] pills . . . and the order to go upstairs and clothe myself warmly. Then he marched me up to the end of Howard St. where houses are nil and he started in. And I mean he started in. Sixty times he made me jump, feet apart & clap my hands over my head & sixty times he made me hold my arms out and touch first right hand to left foot, then left hand to right foot. Plus other of his pet calisthenics. There was no pleading for mercy and no teasing him out of the notion."

But in the main, Billy's lectures on the merits of good diet, sufficient sleep, and exercise "went in one ear and out the other," as Ruth described it. (Ironically, despite her disdain for strenuous exercise, she would forever maintain an enviable figure.)

Billy worried about Ruth because it was his nature to worry about most things, a trait indigenous to Graham blood and one that would always amuse his family. His pessimism would prompt his own children to nickname him "Puddleglum," after the valorous though pessimistic Marsh-Wiggle in C. S. Lewis's fairy tale *The Silver Chair.*

The Monday after Ruth's strenuous and unprecedented exercise session, she felt ninety years old and spavined.

"It's good for you!" Billy said cheerfully when she complained.

"Well, you needn't have started the exercising off with such ferocity," she retorted.

"If you'd been exercising all along like you were supposed to," he said, "you wouldn't have gotten sore."

In the fall of their senior year Billy opened a savings account and began tucking away dollars for their future. They would be married, Ruth decided, Friday, August 13, 1943.[2] But Billy didn't yet know how he would support a wife. He had applied for an Army chaplaincy after the Japanese had bombed Pearl Harbor but had been told to wait until he graduated from college; then he would need either a seminary degree or one year as a pastor followed by a preparation

---

2. Coincidentally, on Friday, August 13, 1937, Shanghai had fallen to the Japanese, thus delaying Ruth's departure for college; and on August 13, 1910, Nelson Bell had asked Virginia Leftwich to marry him.

course for the chaplaincy offered at Harvard University. He had also considered enrolling at the University of Chicago to earn his master's degree in anthropology, his college major. Meanwhile, numerous churches were offering him jobs.

One morning in chapel, in the fall of 1942, providence intervened. A Christian businessman named Robert Van Kampen gave his testimony and afterward noticed the lank blond who happened to be sitting in the front row. On a whim he wandered over to chat.

"What do you want to be when you finish school?" Van Kampen asked.

"A preacher of the gospel," Billy replied.

Van Kampen booked him for the following Sunday at the small Western Springs Baptist Church, located in a middle–class suburb fifteen miles from Wheaton. It had one hundred members and no minister. Each Sunday a different layman would meet with the congregation in the basement of the unfinished building. The pews were rows of flap-bottomed seats purchased from a defunct movie theater, the walls were brick, and the floor was cement. A coal furnace grumbled from one corner. Billy accepted the invitation, began preaching there regularly, and was offered the job of pastor. If he took it, he would begin after graduation and his salary would be forty-five dollars a week, one third of which would pay the rent of a small, furnished apartment in nearby Hinsdale. In early January, 1943, he accepted the offer, stipulating that if the Army accepted him he would be released from the church immediately. He sealed the deal with a handshake without ever having consulted Ruth. She was incredulous that he had not even asked her opinion. And she was concerned, for she believed his call was to evangelism, not to the parish.

The spring of their senior year Ruth saw previews of what was to come. President of the Student Christian Council and a respected speaker, he was chosen by Dr. V. Rymond Edman (who was en route to taking over the presidency of the college) to replace him as the preacher at the Wheaton Tabernacle, which was attended by both faculty and students. Billy was also in demand at churches throughout the state. She spent most of her weekends, even the senior grand finales, alone. "I'm a rotten sport about his leaving," she wrote home. "It's no fun. I never thought about this side of it. What is it going to be like after we're married? I probably won't see as much of him then as I do now."

8

"That Hustling Baptist Preacher"

Now that I love you
and see with eyes
by love enlightened
and made wise,
I wonder how
men look at you
who do not see you
as I do?
They see (they must)
the fire and steel,
the driving force
I also feel.
But
do they ever,
ever see
that gentler side
revealed to me?

Ruth Bell Graham

Shortly before 8:00 P.M., Friday, August 13, 1943, the setting sun glowed like a dying ember and long shadows crossed the stone walkway leading to the arched door of the Montreat Presbyterian Church. Inside, clematis poured from windowsills and the altar, mountain laurel woven into chicken wire banked the stone platform, white candles sputtered quietly. Two hundred and fifty guests, mainly missionary friends, waited in the uncushioned wooden pews while Ruth stood just outside the sanctuary, elegant in her homemade gown of white satin and her long veil of point d'esprit; her white satin cap was shaped like a dogwood blossom and quilted in pearls. Carrying a bouquet of painted daisies and tuberoses, the bride moved slowly down the aisle toward the tall young man in white jacket and black trousers who would soon be her husband.

Repeating the vows they had written themselves and memorized, they were married by the Reverend John Minder, a friend from Billy's Florida Bible Institute days, and the Reverend Kerr Taylor, a former missionary in China. Sophie Graham's daughter played the organ and Chinese friend Andrew Yang sang a solo. Rosa was the maid of honor; Ruth's sister Virginia and childhood friend Sandy Yates were bridesmaids; Billy's sister Jeannie (who would later marry Billy's future associate evangelist Leighton Ford) was the junior bridesmaid. A wartime wedding, its participants had made up in imagination what they lacked in funds: Ruth's childhood missionary friend Gay Currie had decorated the sanctuary, scouring the coves for its wealth of foliage; the bridesmaids' dresses were secondhand (two of them worn in Johnny Streater and Carol Lane's wedding); Ruth's mother had made the bouquets.

Since Billy and his brother Melvin had always been close, Billy had asked him to be the best man. The groomsmen were evangelist Jimmy Johnson (a Wheaton classmate of Billy's), and Grady Wilson and Roy Gustafson, who would one day be important members of the Billy Graham Evangelistic Association; Ruth's brother Clayton (who would one day be a prominent Presbyterian minister) was the junior groomsman. It was more than a marriage of two people; it was the wedding of two entirely different backgrounds, as symbolized by the men who performed the ceremony and the people who participated in it. It was also a union of permanence, its vows so sacred that Ruth would never remove, for even a moment, the thin gold band that Billy slipped on her finger.

After the ceremony and a late reception, the Grahams drove northeast toward Blowing Rock for the honeymoon. As is often the case with a honeymoon and the beginning of a marriage, things were less than perfect. By Thursday, the seventy-five dollars Billy had saved for the trip was depleted. They returned to Charlotte and then Montreat to visit their parents before nosing the Plymouth into the seven hundred and fifty mile drive to Hinsdale, Illinois. En route, a cold front roared in and Ruth caught a chill. By the time they parked in front of their apartment at 214 S. Clay Street, she had a high fever. Billy was scheduled to preach in Elmira, Ohio, that weekend and did not think he should cancel. Uneasy about leaving a sick wife, he checked her into the best local hospital he could find before he left. His telegram and box of candy did not mollify her. He was aptly though inadvertently punished: When the collection plate was being passed he dropped in one of the two bills he had in his wallet. To his dismay, he realized he'd pulled out the twenty dollar bill instead of the five. Since his intention was to tithe only five, Ruth told him with gleeful vindication when he returned home, "that's all God gave you credit for."

This slot of second priority would take some getting used to. She soon learned that he would rarely cancel a preaching engagement regardless of how ill either one of them was: Years later, he slipped in the bathtub and cracked three ribs hours before he was to address students at Oxford University, but he mounted the podium as usual, without benefit of pain pills, for he did not want to cloud his mind. Frequently victimized by pneumonia, he would, nonetheless, spend much of his life standing bareheaded in rain-swept stadiums. In retrospect, Ruth would not have changed him: "I'd rather have a little of Bill," she often said, "than a lot of any other man."

As a young minister, Billy received numerous invitations to preach throughout the Midwest. Rarely could they afford for Ruth to go with him. The separations were wretched. "Before I was married," she wrote her mother in March of 1944, "I worried because I didn't miss him more. Now I worry because I can't miss him less." Unbeknown to him, many times just after he had walked out the door for a trip, she would crawl into bed with a severe headache or an upset stomach. Then, when the pain had passed, she would tend again to household chores, cleaning the white wicker furniture, the small kitchen, and throw rugs. She spent hours studying her Bible and thumbing through magazines and newspapers in search of sermon illustrations, an avocation she would enjoy from then on.

Many of Billy's better book and sermon illustrations can be attributed to her perusals. And it was at this time that she discovered the authors who were to become her favorites: George MacDonald, G. K. Chesterton, Alexander Whyte, and F. W. Boreham. It became habit for her to scour secondhand bookstores, a list of the out-of-print books she sought tucked in her wallet. In later years her bookshelves

A Time for Remembering

would be full of her finds, including first editions signed by the author. Reluctant to let her husband outgrow her intellectually, she developed the habit of reading biographies, histories, novels, books about art and foreign countries. Billy's appreciation of her intelligence and learning was something he often proudly mentioned to friends and family.

It was during these times of aloneness in the small house, in the strange town, that she began to gather her energies and talents into a core of independence.

It was as if her emotional extremities began to draw in, like a hermit crab inside a shell. Ironically, the result was not a reclusiveness insensitive to fellow human beings. Instead, by degrees, she was strengthened, energized by a solid spiritual and psychological power cell. It was her profound faith, her relationship with God, that would stay her through the most trying times. From it she derived her ability to survive and rescue.

The first phase of their marriage was peppered with the usual adjustments and oversights. He draped his wet towels over the top of the bathroom door. She depended on serendipity instead of recipes for her cooking, and the results—like a yellowish batch of pickled peach jello—were not always palatable. Nor did he appreciate her quick tongue.

"I have never taken your advice," he told her bluntly one day, "and I don't intend to begin now."

"*I'd* be ashamed to admit," she replied, "that I had married a woman whose advice I couldn't take."

Like many new husbands, he wasn't always a paragon of sensitivity. One day several of Billy's bachelor friends visited unannounced and suggested that they all go into Chicago.

"That would be fine," Ruth said happily, eager to escape the monotony of the apartment. "I have some shopping I can do. I'll go get my coat."

"No," Billy said. "We guys just want to be alone. No women today."

No amount of begging would change his mind. Through tears she watched the car drive away, and she prayed, "God, if You'll forgive me for marrying him, I'll never do it again."

Billy did not intend to be unkind. He was simply acting like many other new husbands, inexperienced in the art of making a new bride happy and secure. When he realized how much he had hurt her, he was full of tender apologies. Ruth's method was not to nag, but simply quietly to let him know her feelings. The desired results were usually forthcoming. In fact, from the beginning, she understood him better than his deacons did.

His travels irritated certain pillars of the church who wanted the minister to be at their beck and call around the clock. At first, no one dared utter a syllable against him, for he was doing the church far too much good. By early 1944, attendance had doubled and tithing had increased so dramatically that they had redeemed their mortgaged sanctuary, ceremoniously burning the contract in a pie pan. Then Billy became a local celebrity when a well-known radio broadcaster named Torrey Johnson invited him to take over "Songs in the Night," a forty-five-minute program of preaching and singing. It was broadcast live from the church each Sunday night at 10:15. Billy persuaded gospel singer George Beverly Shea to assist and immediately the show was a success. Ruth's job was to sit near her husband during the broadcasts, just beyond the eerie glow of the colored light bulbs around his table, and pass him notes during the hymns to give him suggestions for his next remark. "All she'd have to do," Shea recalled, "was write a sentence down and he could keep on going."

Soon the show was being broadcast twice each Sunday, and the town of Western Springs dubbed him "That Hustling Baptist Preacher." The speaking invitations multiplied and some of the deacons began to grumble, one finally suggesting that if Billy did not discontinue his travels, the church should cut his salary.

He had received numerous job offers, from both churches and radio stations, and though he did not intend to accept any of them, "he enjoys hanging that over the deacons' heads once in a while when they get out of hand," Ruth wrote her parents. "If they think they can run Bill, they've got another think coming." He was also plagued by several parishioners who were the resident troublemakers. Like magpies, they formed a black knot in the congregation, generating a cackle of criticism about the minister and his non-Baptist wife, swooping in to snatch up the slightest sliver of glittery gossip or detail. They fell soundly into John Calvin's category of those determined to take offense, and in keeping with good Calvinistic tradition, Billy offended them mightily.

"Some of you need to confess the sin of trouble making," he announced during an evening service as he stared unabashedly at the guilty flock. "A person tries to build a testimony for God in this town and all you do is tear it down. You had better confess before God has to remove some people. As for me, I'm here to [do] this job for God and with His help, I'll get it done regardless."

Despite the problems, Ruth wrote, "God is blessing and when a man gets saved it makes everything seem worthwhile."

Billy had twice applied for an Army chaplaincy and had both times been refused because he was underweight. But in August 1944 he was accepted. Had he followed this course he would likely have been assigned to a base where he would have spent the remainder of the war behind a desk; still three pounds underweight, he would not have been sent overseas. Then illness intervened and changed the course of his life. First, he began experiencing stress-related paralysis of the throat. Then in early October he contracted a dangerous strain of mumps in both sides of his neck. Though a doctor visited him daily, there were no antibiotics available. Ruth camped at his bedside, feeding him strained baby foods and liquids. Several times his temperature climbed so high that he became delirious. One night, burning up, he began describing angels on the ceiling. "Can't you see them?" he asked. Ruth, desperate with the fear that he was dying, knelt beside the bed. Her prayers were tears. When he finally emerged from his sickbed six weeks later, he was white as a corpse and weighed one hundred and thirty pounds.

One morning a hundred-dollar check arrived from a woman who had heard Billy on the radio. "Please go down to Florida and take a vacation," her note read. The money could not have come at a better time; the Grahams drove to Miami. They rented a small room on Seventy-ninth Street, several miles from the ocean, not knowing that Torrey Johnson was vacationing in a hotel three blocks away. When Johnson discovered that Billy was staying nearby, he invited him to go fishing. While reeling in "at least a score of big fish," as Billy recalled, Johnson asked him to become a full-time evangelist for Youth for Christ. He would be responsible for organizing rallies, or crusades, as they were later called, and new Youth for Christ chapters throughout the United States and Canada. After discussing it with Ruth, he accepted the offer. He resigned his position at Western Springs, then his Army commission, believing he could reach more servicemen through his rallies than he could from behind a desk. The members of his congregation were not surprised by his decision; they had sensed it was only a matter of time before he would leave. Neither their church nor any church could contain him, for he paced about like a caged tiger. "I don't think Billy would ever have made a very good pastor," observed Myrna White, a former parishioner. "I don't think he's the type who would be happy settling down in one place." Robert Van Kampen realized that it was time for his protégé to pack when he found fourteen preaching invitations in the church mailbox one morning. "Our church is too small," Van Kampen recalled thinking. "God has given him a special gift—he's going to be another Billy Sunday or Dwight L. Moody."

Now married to an evangelist, Ruth knew that the separations could only become more frequent, so she reasoned that if she couldn't be with him, she should at least be allowed to live where she would be happiest. Early in 1945 they packed the car, drove south to Montreat and moved into an upstairs bedroom in her parents' house. For the next year Billy would travel to virtually every large city in the United States, thanks to a wealthy man from Kenosha, Wisconsin, who had given him and Johnson airline credit cards. There was not sufficient money to buy Ruth airline tickets; unless Billy drove to his rallies, she stayed in Montreat.

In the summer of 1945, Ruth joyfully prepared for the birth of their first child. Finding a plain straw bassinet, she painted it blue and lined it with quilted blue satin. Then she trimmed it with yards of her wedding veil. On September 21, while Billy was away, Ruth gave birth to their first child. She named her Virginia Leftwich, after her mother, but called her "GiGi," which is Chinese for "sister." Ruth became her mother's friend and apprentice; they cooked, gardened, sewed, and cleaned house together. Secure now in her parents' home with her new child, she found the separations were tolerable. For the first time since Ruth had left Tsingkiang for Korea in 1933, she felt she had really come home.

In 1946, Billy and his new song leader Cliff Barrows, an exuberant, handsome man, held rallies in twenty-six cities in the British Isles. (The Grahams had met Barrows and his attractive blonde wife, Billie, at a Bible conference in Asheville months earlier.) Later that year, Youth for Christ had a larger budget, and Billy was told that Ruth could travel with him occasionally. Her early trips abroad were educational, if not humorous, for she was even more naive than he was. Her first trip was in December. She was to travel to New York and then fly to London where she would meet her husband. By the time the taxi drivers and waiters had collected their tips, and the airline agents had penalized her for overweight baggage, she boarded the DC-4 with two cents in her billfold. She lost her first dinner somewhere over the Atlantic and then changed into her homemade red wool robe late that night in the men's restroom by mistake: She discovered the error the next morning when she retrieved her dress and realized it was hanging on the wrong door.

When the plane landed she spotted Billy behind a fence just off the runway and like a homing pigeon, she headed toward him. A stewardess in hot pursuit informed her, "You have to go through customs first." Her husband, enormously amused, added to her discomfiture by moving into the lobby while the agent was slashing her bags with yellow chalk. "They're going to throw you in jail!" Billy broadcast repeatedly. When the agent, long-faced and grim as though he had been checking bags since the Norman Conquest, asked Ruth if she had any gifts to declare, she thought a moment and whispered, "Just one. But don't let *him* see it," she nodded toward her husband. Fishing into her handbag, she discreetly slipped out a photograph of GiGi that she planned to give Billy for Christmas. It may have been the first time the man had smiled in months.

That night, when they checked into the exclusive Grosvenor House (financed by a friend who had instructed them to have a second honeymoon), Ruth marveled at some of the mysterious contraptions in the room—like the bidet. "Why on earth couldn't you put your feet in the basin or use the tub?" she asked. And the tub— why she'd never seen one so big and declared that the wire soap dish looked like a "bicycle basket."

After a month of bitter cold, foggy weather, and a bland postwar diet of powdered eggs, potatoes, and bready sausages, an incident occurred which demonstrated that being married to an evangelist had its trying, if amusing, moments. En route to Belfast, Billy and Cliff Barrows warned their wives that the Irish Christians considered cosmetics to be the paint of sinners. They urged Ruth and Billie to wipe off their modest makeup. The women dutifully obeyed. Powderless and minus eyebrows, Billie played the organ during the service while her husband led the singing (they had been mistakenly advertised at this crusade as "The Barrows Brothers"). And Ruth sat in the audience, certain that the very people they needed to reach were the ones who now would be least attracted to these pale, frumpy Christians.

With thoughts such as those in mind, she appeared at a service several nights later with a dab of Tangee Natural shining on her lips.

After the service two Irish women waylaid the Grahams.

"We received a tremendous blessing from your message," one

woman said to Billy, while she looked directly at Ruth. "But we lost it when we saw that your wife was wearing makeup."

Surprised, Billy studied his wife's face, unable to detect the virtually transparent lipstick. "I'm sorry," he said, "she has no makeup on."

Ruth smiled sweetly.

Nor was this incident forgotten, it seems. Years later when Dr. Edwin Orr, president of the Oxford Association for Research in Revival, was addressing a group of men in Belfast one gentleman raised his hand to ask a question.

"Is it true that Mrs. Billy Graham wears makeup?" the man asked.

Surprised, Orr evaded the question and again the arm shot up.

"What do you think of makeup?" the man asked.

"I don't know," Orr replied. "I've never tried it."

When the laughter subsided, the man's hand shot up again, and a neighbor jabbed an elbow into his ribs, exclaiming, "I say! Leave Billy Graham out of this, can't you? Don't you remember, John Wesley had a bad wife too?"[1]

In the fall of 1947, thrilled that his wife was again pregnant, Billy bought a two-story, partly furnished summer house across the street from her parents. The upper walls were white clapboard, the lower were fieldstone flecked with mica. The eaves curled low over the large windows like a worn felt hat pulled over an old man's ears. With the forty-five hundred dollars they borrowed from the local bank they began making the forty-five dollar a month payments. She and her mother scoured mountain junk shops for antiques and secondhand furniture. Her sister Virginia, home from nursing school at Johns Hopkins, helped them sand the drab green paint off the Victorian furniture sold with the house, refinishing the wood until it glowed like honey. Lamps evolved from adhesive tape canisters, old bottles, a small wooden bucket, and even an ironware sugar bowl.

In May, Billy began to wonder if he was losing his authority on the home front. The first of what would be many hints came when Ruth was in the hospital with their newly born second daughter, Anne, and he decided on a whim to chop down the rhododendron thicket enclosing the yard. He gave the order and the workmen hemmed and hawed, staring sheepishly at their dirt-caked brogans, before one

---

1. Years later, during the Greater London crusade, the controversy over makeup again resurfaced. With great amusement, Ruth noted aloud to her husband "that the mark of streetwalkers in a certain section of the city was that they wore no makeup."

of them finally replied in his mountain drawl: "Don't you think we'd best ask Miz Graham first?" They knew she would be horrified if she returned home and found that they would be visible to every driver and pedestrian on Assembly Drive, Montreat's main thoroughfare. Billy had given a thoughtless command and he knew it, but he was too frustrated to rescind it. Ruth and Anne came home just in time, and in his jubilation, he forgot the matter.

That summer, William Bell Riley, the president of Northwestern Schools in Minneapolis, summoned Billy to visit him in Golden Valley, Minnesota. Riley, a devout man and longtime admirer of Billy's, was eighty-six years old and dying. While a thunderstorm shook the windowpanes, he jabbed a gnarled finger at the young evangelist and, as though he were delivering a fiat, declared that he was to succeed him as the president of the interdenominational institution, comprised of a liberal arts program and a seminary. Billy's impulse was to say no, but he was intimidated by Riley's proclamation. Ruth was opposed: He was not a scholar, she told him, he was an evangelist. Against his wife's wishes and his own good sense, he replied in September that should Riley die within the next ten months, he would accept the position until a new man could be chosen. On December 6, 1947, the man died, and at the age of twenty-nine, Billy found he was the president of a school with more than seven hundred and fifty students—and empty coffers. He gave the school the motto "Knowledge on Fire" and began attempting to hammer the place into another Wheaton. His frustration mounted as his desire to preach and his new academic responsibilities tugged him in two directions.

Having no intention of going along for the ride, Ruth did not embrace the role of "first lady." One day, a Northwestern Schools' administrator telephoned her and cheerfully asked when she was moving to Minneapolis to occupy the president's mansion. Realizing that her husband would not be spending much time there because of his travels, she replied, "Never." As with his interim at Western Springs, Ruth considered this new job nothing more than a sidetrack, an interference in what he had been ordained to do—preach to the unsaved. Her feelings were justified. But in retrospect, she assessed those detours as valuable, for they gave Billy an empathy for clergyman and academician that he otherwise would not have had.

In the fall of 1949, he launched a crusade that would capture the country's attention. His fourth crusade that year, it was held in a tent virtually the size of a city block in downtown Los Angeles. Eye-catching signs and newspaper advertisements proclaimed, "Dynamic Preaching—Heavenly Music—6,000 free seats." Ruth joined him for what she thought would be the crusade's third and final week, leaving four-year-old GiGi with the Bells and fifteen-month-old Anne with her sister Rosa in Los Alamos, New Mexico.

The 1949 Los Angeles crusade is legendary in Billy Graham history. Books, magazines, and newspaper articles hail it as his starting-block. The myth, which was passed both by word of mouth and in print, said newspaper mogul William Randolph Hearst sent a memorandum to his reporters which read: "Puff Graham." The result was that hordes of photographers and journalists descended upon the meetings and Billy's name and face were circulated around the country. As with many legends, a portion of its fabric is woven with exaggeration.

It is true that William Randolph Hearst endorsed him, but this was partially because thousands of American, English, Irish, and Scottish people had noticed the young evangelist first. According to Hearst's son William Randolph Hearst, Jr., his father was interested in what attracted the attention of the greatest number of people. In the past, he had endorsed both Billy Sunday and Mary Baker Eddy. This suggests that Billy Graham was not an obscure farmboy preacher who by the grace of Hearst became a star. The memo "Puff Graham" never existed, claimed Hearst, Jr. "Pop would have never sent a memorandum to an editor of his papers with the words 'Puff Graham.' He was not given to talking or writing in such cryptic style, and I never heard him use the word 'puff.' It was not a word used in the journalism profession except by press agents." Hearst, said his son, was "committed intellectually to help spread the Christian Gospel," and he highly approved of Graham's influence on America's youth.

What Hearst did do, recalled Don Goodenow, picture editor of the old *Los Angeles Examiner* in 1949, was send teletype messages to his managing editors, urging them to "give attention to Billy Graham's meetings." Reporters and photographers from the *Examiner* and several other of Hearst's some thirteen papers were dispatched to the services. Each Friday night, Goodenow arranged a full page of photographs of him preaching; they appeared in the Saturday morning paper, and many were picked up by the wire services. Favorable letters from readers poured into the *Examiner's* editorial department and newsmen began referring to Billy Graham's "charisma." He was eloquent and powerful, they wrote, and he had a commanding baritone voice. "He did have an appeal for young people—no doubt about it," Goodenow recalled. "And even in the atmosphere of the newsroom, which can be callous at times, he was taken seriously."

People appeared at the tent en masse, their interest generating more press, and subsequent news stories generating more public interest. Billy's image was elevated to a new high: "Churchmen say he's started the greatest religious revival in the history of Southern California," read the *Indianapolis Star,* November 2; and "Old style religion is sweeping the city of angels with an evangelistic show overshadowing even Billy Sunday," said the Associated Press, on November 4.

Three hundred and fifty thousand people filled the tent at the corner of Washington Boulevard and Hill Street as the three-week crusade stretched into eight. Billy was dumfounded and exhausted. He ran out of sermons and in desperation mounted the pulpit one night and read, word-for-word, half of Jonathan Edwards's "Sinners in the Hands of an Angry God" (ending with a few words of his own).[2] It was a disaster. What may have precipitated a great awakening in the eighteenth century passed over the heads of the audience. He learned an important lesson then, Ruth said. Never again did he replace the Bible with another text.

Three thousand men, women, and children responded to the altar calls, but statistics do not tell the whole story. There were others who responded in private, like the man who wandered into the tent hours after the crowds had gone and the lights had been extinguished. Johnny, the night watchman, was sleeping under the platform when the man stumbled through chairs in the sawdust-scented darkness. "Who's there?" called Johnny, startled into consciousness. "I just came back to find Jesus," came the reply.

After the Grahams had witnessed the power that filled the tent night after night, they realized, as Ruth described it, "that this was without a doubt what God had called Bill to do."

In a poignant scene that boded what fame would do to their personal lives, Rosa returned Anne to Ruth and the child didn't recognize her mother. When she ambled over to greet her father while he was talking on the telephone, he swiveled around and stared at her blankly, thinking she was a lost little girl who had wandered into the wrong room.

Believing that his path had been clearly blazed for him, Billy began persuading the trustees of Northwestern Schools to relieve him of his

---

2. James Graham, son of Jimmy and Sophie Graham from Ruth's China past, was in Los Angeles at the time and came to Billy's rescue by supplying him with sermon material.

post. In 1950, during a crusade in Portland, Oregon, Billy was offered a contract that would put him on the radio throughout the United States. In mid-August, he telephoned George Wilson, business manager of Northwestern Schools, asking him if he would handle any mail resulting from the broadcasts. Wilson agreed and suggested that they should set up a nonprofit corporation so that all incoming funds would be tax deductible. A lawyer in Minneapolis drew up the articles and bylaws, and thus the Billy Graham Evangelistic Association (BGEA) was born. At first, Billy would run the organization, conferring daily by telephone with George Wilson and associates in Minneapolis. Later, a board was appointed to oversee the running of the organization and Wilson was appointed executive vice-president. That November Billy began a radio program that Ruth christened the "Hour of Decision." Initially transmitted by two hundred and twenty-three American Broadcasting Company stations in the country, by 1960 that number would exceed one thousand, not including countless short-wave stations throughout the world.

In the late fall of 1950, Ruth prepared for Christmas early, wrapping the presents, decorating the house, trimming the tree with colorful lights—and again trimming the bassinet with material from her wedding veil. On December 19, their third daughter was born. They named her Ruth Bell, but her mother nicknamed her "Bunny," because "she looked like a rabbit." They were home December 22, and Ruth spent what she would recall as one of her most "blissful" Christmases—"mainly on the sofa with Bunny in my arms, waited on by a loving family and feeling close to Mary, the Mother of Jesus."

With three children to manage, it was becoming increasingly difficult for her to travel with her husband. Longing to be with him, she felt even more isolated when she would hear radio reports and read news accounts of a crusade. On a rainy day in March of 1950, while Billy was holding a crusade in Columbia, South Carolina, she wrote: "The clouds were hanging low on the surrounding mountains. The whole outdoors was sodden and gray and gloomy. Then in the middle of it all I looked up from my kitchen sink and thru the window up on the side of the mountain was a bright patch of sunlight where the clouds had broken. The only patch of brightness in all that dismal scene. I thought how if I were free I'd love to climb up and sit in that patch of sunlight awhile." But then, in a touch that is vintage Ruth, her survival instinct, her buoyant optimism, resurfaced. She added: ". . . God is not limited to Columbia. The same God so marvelously working there is in the house with me. I shall have a little revival of my own."

In 1952, Billy (aided by his wife) wrote his first book, *Peace with God*. On July 14, Ruth gave birth to their fourth child—a husky first son they named William Franklin Graham III. Billy could not hide his jubilation as he proudly carried him into the house for the first time: "I'd have loved another girl," he said with a grin. "But every man needs a son."

The following year he spoke at Church House, Westminster, in London. Impressed, the English clergy and laity invited him to hold a major campaign there. The result would be the twelve-week Greater London crusade, held in Harringay Arena in the winter of 1954. Traveling with him, Ruth would endure her longest separation from her children.

9

The Greater London Crusade

I used to worry about Billy. When he started out, there was all that adulation. I was worried he might be tilted off balance by it. But then I met Ruth. Then I relaxed, knowing he had that strength on which to lean.

Paul Harvey

The SS *United States* cut a wide, frothy furrow through the North Atlantic, her red and black stacks drawing gray smudge across the light blue sky as she progressed northeast at thirty-five knots.

Midship in a handsome stateroom of soft rose, beige, and brown, sat "The Revival Widow," as Ruth had been dubbed by the press. Watching the gentle bobbing of the three portholes in front of her, she perched on the bed, writing a letter home while Billy conferred with team members. "Dearest Folks," she wrote, "here we are . . . already halfway to England. What a ship this is. . . . You should see our quarters! I'm sure John Wesley never had it so good." Her cheerfulness was a façade; behind it was the sadness she would always feel when she left her children.

It was early afternoon aboard ship, February 20, 1954. The rising sun would be smoldering behind the mountains in Montreat. When her mind drifted there, she could see it: mist wafting over the world, a filmy gray veil dropped from the heavens; shadows, like animals, shyly creeping out from under the thicket around the yard; rhododendron leaves tightly whorled in the brittle, wintry air; twigs and branches wearing thick sleeves of ice along the rich black banks of the rill twenty feet east of the patio. "I'm so glad Bill has these few days of quiet and rest and wonderful food. . . . The menus are fabulous. And they urge you to ask for anything you can think of whether on the menu or not. For hors d'oeuvres I ordered pâté de foie gras one day as I'd read of it but didn't know what it was. I still don't. . . . Also had kangaroo tail soup. It was as nasty as it sounds. All I can think of that I'd really love, now that the voyage is drawing to a close, is corn bread and turnip greens."

She was submerged, the quiet joy of writing loved ones flowing through her veins, through her fountain pen, shimmering on the paper before drying a ghosty black. Yet she kept one ear to the door, like an antenna, listening for the quick step and staccato knock of Rob, their officious English cabin boy. He was so dutiful and his arrivals so unannounced that he kept her busy darting into closets. The first evening aboard she was standing in their hallway in her "sheer nightie" when he appeared in all his crisp efficiency. Dashing into the baggage room, she just managed to snatch a robe out of her suitcase before another cabin boy opened the rear entrance in search of a passenger's luggage.

"Ah! Ah! Ah!" Rob wheeled around the corner, flailing after him like a crazed windmill. "*Madame* is in there!"

All said, Ruth concluded, before folding the ship's creamy stationery, "I've been wishing for a little less service and a little more privacy."

In three days the Grahams would arrive at Southampton for the beginning of the twelve-week Greater London crusade at Harringay Arena in the north end of the city. Owned by the Greyhound Racing Association, the arena could hold some twelve thousand people. The London crusade committee had leased it for thirty-three thousand pounds at a time when money was scarce and preachers didn't draw crowds in England.

Billy, whose ministry was not yet well established outside the United States, was tense. He had insisted that Ruth accompany him. Uneasy about leaving her four children for such a long time, she told him that she would go only if she could sail home after the first month and return for the last—a friend had offered her a round-trip ticket for that purpose. Bill agreed, and she carefully packed just enough items to get her through the next four weeks. Her plans, however, were to disintegrate. She would stay for the duration because her husband would tell her he could not do without her. Accompanying him, she would learn, did not necessarily mean she spent much time with him, either. During her three-month stay they would find time for only a few meals together each week.

She had hoped that when they reached Southampton, they would disembark relatively unnoticed. But on Monday morning, February 22, it became clear that would be impossible. Shortly before breakfast, the chief steward arrived at the Grahams' door, holding a three-page radiogram. He explained that his copy of the morning news included an item which the captain, in an attempt to spare the Grahams any embarrassment, had ordered struck from the ship's newsletter. He handed Billy the original report. At the bottom of the first page, directly above an announcement of Queen Elizabeth's travel plans, and below the news that Senator Paul Douglas was appealing to President Eisenhower to recommend more tax cuts, was this:

"London: A Labor Member of Parliament announced today he would challenge in Commons the admission of Billy Graham to England on the grounds the American evangelist was interfering in British politics under the guise of religion."

Billy discovered that the sudden uproar stemmed from a mistake in the calendars that the BGEA had mailed earlier to generate prayer and financial assistance for the crusade. The caption beneath one of the photographs read: "What Hitler's bombs could not do, Socialism with its accompanying evils shortly accomplished."[1] When Billy's public relations director, Jerry Beaven, had written the phrase, he had not realized that "Socialism," with a capital *S*, was synonymous with the Labour Party. Intentional or not, it was an unfortunate choice of words in a country still raw from the wounds of World War II. It seemed to some in Great Britain that Billy Graham was meddling in politics.

The mistake had been caught earlier, before most of the calendars had been mailed. A few, however, had slipped through. One found its way to Fleet Street and landed on the desk of Hannen Swaffer, the acid-tongued columnist for the left-wing *Daily Herald.* Thus began the furor, culminating in Labour Party member Geoffrey de Freitas's issuing the statement that Billy had read in the radiogram. "For a while there," Ruth wrote, "the wireless was kept buzzing with

---

1. John Pollock, *Billy Graham* (New York: McGraw-Hill, 1966), p. 116.

accusations, explanations, and apologies. And it kept us busy praying too, that the Lord would overrule this inadvertent mistake to his glory."

The crusade's chairman, General D. J. Wilson-Haffendon, sent Billy a telegram, graciously offering advice and his hope that the blunder might indeed prove beneficial: "It's most unfortunate that while you were at sea this flare blew up. And it has made certain that a very much greater number of people will know about your ministry. But, I think it is vitally important that you should be extremely circumspect on the whole question of politics over here because the very people whom we hope to reach through the crusade are the people who are most offended at the unfortunate use of the word 'Socialism.'"[2]

The Grahams were warned that as a result of the controversy, the press would be on them like a pack of wild dogs. Sure enough, as the ship drew near Southampton the next afternoon, Ruth stared out a porthole and watched a tug pull alongside them. Twenty-five reporters and eleven photographers shoved their way aboard the SS *United States.* The Grahams had already abandoned their room, having been warned that it would be the pressmen's first destination. Reporters and the public alike would always have a voyeuristic curiosity about how much the Grahams spent on food, shelter, transportation, overcoats, mineral water, socks, and so on. It was not uncommon for a passerby to make rude remarks, just loud enough for them to hear, beginning with "If Jesus were here today," and ending with any number of things: Would He wear a hundred-dollar suit, eat steak, fly in a jet or stay in the Holiday Inn?

Once, a reporter, watching Billy disembark from the S.S. *Queen Mary,* sarcastically remarked to Grady Wilson, "When Jesus was on earth He rode a lowly donkey. I cannot imagine Jesus arriving in England aboard the *Queen Mary.*"

"Listen," Wilson replied dryly, "if you can find me a donkey that can swim the Atlantic, I'll buy it."

The horde of pressmen had poured noisily into the SS *United States'* salon and confronted the Grahams like a band of sea rovers. "I knew they were after Bill's scalp," Ruth wrote that night, "and there was nothing we could do but pray for wisdom and be as courteous and gracious as we could."

---

2. Records of the Billy Graham Evangelistic Association, Limited, Folder 1, Box 4, Collection 9, Archives of the Billy Graham Center, Wheaton, Illinois.

"We see you still wear makeup," a reporter confronted Ruth.

"Is it true that your husband carries about his own special jug of water for baptisms?" another asked.

"What kind of hat are you wearing?"

"It's just a lid," she replied dryly.

The next day the British press reported that Mrs. Billy Graham had been wearing a round white hat that she had called "a lid." And Billy, wearing gray flannels and a black-and-gray tie, was smiling on the front page: "No Clerical Collar But My! What a Lovely Tie!" the caption read.

The reporters streamed off as the ship docked, shouting final questions and repartee as they passed. "Mrs. Graham," called one, "we're disappointed in your husband. We expected bright, handpainted ties, flashy socks, and a sort of mass hysteria. And we find he's quite an ordinary chap."

Greeted by one of the largest press receptions ever held in Southampton, the Grahams disembarked quietly, not realizing that the scores of newsmen, the cameras mounted on trucks, the gawkers were there to see them. But as soon as Billy set foot on the quay, a battery of microphones were shoved into his startled face.

"Who invited you over here anyway?"

"Do you think you can save Britain?"

"Don't you think your higher crime rate indicates you're more needed in your own country?"

"What will you do about Russia?"

One cynical question followed another, all unwittingly supplying the publicity that neither the London crusade committee nor the BGEA could afford. At the edge of the crowd, burly stevedores stared in annoyance at the hubbub, and Ruth, empathizing with them, moved in their direction, away from the mob. Towering above the crowd, the SS *United States* gently rocked in the harbor, passengers and members of the crew poking their heads out portholes, hanging over rails and gateways, "their faces," Ruth recorded, "a curious mixture of amazement and a sort of 'what-on-earth-have-we-had-on-board' look."

In Southampton, as they passed through customs, they were greeted with encouragement.

"God bless you, sir," said a customs agent. "We need you here."

"I'll be praying for you, sir," a soldier promised.

It was a warm reception after a stormy voyage. The Grahams

boarded a third-class car and rode to London's Waterloo Station, where they were again greeted by a record-breaking crowd. Above the shouting porters, above the hissing steam and clanking metal, thousands of voices rose in majestic hymns. People surged toward the Grahams to welcome them and to present Ruth with flowers, and in the happy confusion, she became separated from Billy. (She didn't relax until she finally spotted him making his way through the crowd—with All-American fullback Don Moomaw, there to help with the crusade, running interference for him.)[3]

They moved into rooms 501 and 502 of The Stratford Court, a modest brick hotel, with a small but friendly staff, just off Oxford Street. Situated on the sixth floor of a wedge-shaped building, it was directly above a Dolces shoe store. Across a side street was a pub from which people erupted in the dark early morning hours, laughing and talking boisterously. Her bedroom was adjoined by a sitting room; her husband had a duplicate arrangement next door so he could come and go without disturbing her. The rooms were dreary, colorless and bare; the wind howled around the eaves and seeped beneath window frames in an eerie, icy wail.

The evening of the first meeting, March 1, boded misfortune. The stars shone through charcoal clouds; the air was moist, portending snow. The Grahams waited, restive, in one of the sitting rooms. He was quiet, concerned. She was writing in her red leather journal. Bad weather would surely turn people away from the service, they feared. The anxiety culminated in the shrill clang of the telephone.

"It's begun to snow," Jerry Beaven's discouraged voice came over the line. "There's nothing the newspapers won't do to ruin the meeting," he added with heavy irony.

Billy fell silent as Beaven told him that thus far only two thousand people had trickled into Harringay Arena, and the more than two hundred reporters and photographers were already confident of the American evangelist's opening night bust. He thought of the prayers and hard work of the thousands of British Christians who were depending on him: He wondered what failure would do to their faith. Beaven added that Senators Stuart Symington and Styles Bridges, having just arrived in London following an official business trip on the Continent, had announced to the press that they would not be

---

3. Don Moomaw later became the pastor of Bel Air Presbyterian Church, where Ronald and Nancy Reagan often worshiped. In 1980, he gave Reagan's inaugural prayer.

attending the service because they had a dinner engagement. The news that they had backed out was unsettling. Months earlier Billy had addressed the Senate prayer group in Washington, and he had been promised that two of their members would be on hand to introduce him to the crowd at the crusade's opening service. The Grahams wondered if the dinner engagement was a trumped-up excuse, if the senators did not want to endorse him because of the scandal precipitated by the BGEA calendars.

"Bill looked sort of stunned when he told me," Ruth wrote as they waited for their ride to the arena. "And I thought I heard him praying in the other room just now. . . . The Lord has a purpose in this."

A dark green sedan and a driver (compliments of the Ford Motor Company) were waiting outside the hotel. "There are butterflies in my stomach," Ruth scribbled before sliding back her chair.

Bundled in hats and coats, they rode mutely from central London to the north end, lulled by the thrumming of the engine, hand in hand as the snow began its feathery downward spiral. In less than forty-five minutes, Harringay emerged, looming like a monstrous, windowless brick barn. Its parking lot was virtually empty; a shadowy stream of people skirted the milky aura from the few naked bulbs below the roof, not to be deterred by snow or religion from an evening at the dog races. It was a sad spectacle, at least to Ruth, who could not help juxtaposing the two: the arena offering life was virtually empty, while the race track thrived, filled with men sitting in witless wonder, watching dogs run in circles. So she thought. At a side entrance, team member Willis Haymaker waylaid the Grahams and told a different story. "The building is filled to capacity!" he whispered, his face taut with excitement. And the two American senators, he added, were there, waiting for Billy in his office. They were astounded. When Beaven had telephoned an hour earlier, there had been only two thousand people in the arena. But thousands more had been en route by Underground, and they had converged at Harringay en masse moments before the Grahams had arrived. It was true that Senators Symington and Bridges had a dinner engagement—at Ten Downing Street with Winston Churchill—but that wasn't for an hour yet. And though the American ambassador to the Court of St. James's had advised them to steer clear of the evangelist, they had never intended to renege on their promise.

Alone, Ruth ascended the large wooden platform and sat in her chair, which was next to Billy's, behind the podium. Beyond were tiers of wooden bleachers; below, twenty-five hundred additional flap-bottomed wooden chairs had been arranged on the floor, and for the next three months they would snap shut when the crowd rose, cracking in succession like a string of firecrackers. She would have preferred a seat in the audience where she could lose herself in the expanse of people and observe the service unnoticed. "You long with them to worship the Lord," she wrote. "And being stared at seems so out of place. But what can we do?"

During the next seventy-one nights, she would escape the platform whenever possible, flowing against the tide of people to the far end of the oval arena, climbing to the highest tier, just below the exposed steel girders. From this perch, Billy was just a voice, his blue eyes and keen features extinguished by distance. Yet the people were moved by the message of salvation, responding to the amplified voice, compelled and convicted by something stirring within them as they sang the familiar lyrics, "Just As I Am, Without One Plea."

The singing at Harringay would forever, in Ruth's mind, remain unrivaled. One night in March, more than a thousand Welshmen made the four-hour train ride to Harringay from Cardiff. Cliff Barrows asked them to sing. Turning off the house microphones, he led them, a capella, in their majestic rendition of "Guide Me, O Thou Great Jehovah," and, later, in "I Will Sing of My Redeemer." Moved almost to tears, Ruth recalled, "I couldn't sing—only listen." Indeed, the singing at Harringay was so beautiful, that *it,* the press began claiming, was what moved the people to answer the altar call. Subsequently, Barrows eliminated the choir's singing of "Just As I Am, Without One Plea." The people still came—and the press began claiming that "the silence" was responsible.

Occasionally, Ruth would leave behind a clue of her whereabouts. One night a kindly old Englishman, who looked like a bulldog in thick spectacles, noticed that the woman beside him did not have a hymnbook so he gave her his. Had he perused it after the service he would have found scribbled inside, "Thanks for sharing your hymnbook with me. God bless you. Ruth Graham."

Night after night people streamed into the arena until it could hold no more; the bobbies and team members firmly shut the doors, obliterating all but the faces pressed against the glass. Billy began preaching twice, sometimes three times daily to accommodate the crowds. "Not since the Dwight L. Moody revival in the late 19th Century has Great Britain been as deeply stirred," a journalist wrote, reiterating the words which were becoming increasingly familiar in the press.

The crusade made the headlines almost daily, and in an attempt to learn more about this "Hot Gospeller," as the British called him, they began to hound his wife.

"What is it like to be married to him?"

"Is he hard to live with?"

"Are you jealous of all the attention he gets?"

She was gracious, even humorous on occasion, but she disliked being followed and quizzed.

Elements of London society busied themselves inviting the Grahams to elegant teas and black tie dinners; the Grahams were taken on special tours of English museums and landmarks; they were presented both formally and privately to royalty. On March 10, they lunched at St. James's Palace with the captain and officers of the Coldstream Guards. Arriving shortly before noon, they were met by Major Richard Carr-Gomm, a tall, swarthy man with a heavy black beard and mustache and a long scar down one cheek. He had attended many of the services and would, toward the end, recommit his life to Christ.

He led them across the courtyard, up a flight of steps and into the Guards Room, a large sunny area filled with Buckingham and St. James's Palace guards, handsome in fitted navy jackets and trousers with broad red stripes. Several of them leaned against a rail, warming themselves before a crackling fire; bare-headed and smiling, they seemed painfully young. Momentarily, they were seated around a U-shaped table where they ate an elegant lunch and talked about the services at Harringay, which several of the guards had already attended.

Interesting though they were, these social engagements were also taxing. Suddenly, because Billy was a famous evangelist, he and Ruth were supposed to know how to dress and which fork to use when in the company of dukes and duchesses, earls and countesses. It was, to say the least, intimidating. One week after their visit with the guard at St. James's Palace, an aristocratic couple invited Ruth to tour the Wallace Collection at Hertford House, Manchester Square. As she studied the objets d'art she made the mistake of asking the prickly curator what Richard Wallace had done "for a living."

"What do you mean, 'what did he *do?*'" he asked her icily.

"Well," Ruth explained uneasily, "I was taken to Kenwood and they claimed it was the home of the Guinness Beer people..."

"No, Madame," he interrupted, "Mr. Wallace did not have to work. He was a landed gentleman."

There were other adjustments to make, such as feeling comfortable with the element of entertainment that was infiltrating religion. One of the highlights of the Greater London crusade was to be the guest appearance of Roy Rogers and Dale Evans. Ruth was happy to have Roy and Dale come—until she heard that they were also bringing Trigger. "I think it *wrong* to have a horse in a religious service," she wrote in early March.

Ruth was accustomed to simplicity in worship. Horses and rhinestones grated on her sensibilities. She was repelled by the presence of television cameras peering into the faces of the men and women responding to the altar calls.

Though aware of the need for publicity—much of which was generated by the crusade committee in the form of billboards and banners—she shrank from it. She was accustomed to the quiet, unglorified tactics she had seen on the mission field. It never would be her *modus operandi* to entertain people to Christ. But she would also soon learn that just because a certain method was a bit jolting to her it was not intrinsically bad. She had to apologize silently to Trigger, for example. On March 20, the cloudy Saturday that Roy, Dale, and Trigger performed, forty thousand children filled the dog track next door to Harringay Arena. After Trigger's dancing and prancing about had captured the youngsters' attention, Roy and Dale gave moving testimonies.

Roy and Dale were recognizable everywhere they went, and as Ruth observed what that did to their personal lives, it made her apprehensive. On Sunday, March 21, they invited the Grahams to dine with them at the Savoy Hotel. The Hollywood couple was so well known that they had to have a table sent to their room: Had they attempted to eat lunch in public, they would have been mobbed.

They ate on a pink, damask-covered table as a spring breeze gently swayed the curtains in the suite. Beyond the open window Cleopatra's Needle rose seventy feet above the Embankment. Roy told them he had just quit smoking, not only for his health but because he knew he was constantly being watched and emulated; he did not wish to set a bad example. For their entire week in London, they would have to hide when they weren't on stage. "Poor Roy and Dale are literally prisoners of fame," Ruth wrote. "I wouldn't trade places with them for one billion dollars. I said billion. One little bit of fame is bad enough."

SHE, THE WIFE, WAS A MIDDLE-AGED NURSE, a Christian who sang in the Salvation Army Songsters. He, her husband, was a good man, honest and industrious at his blue-collar job, kindly and faithful at home. They lived amid gardens and dunes in Southport, on the Irish Sea.

They had heard about the Greater London crusade for months and had tucked away shillings so they could attend. It was to be a welcome vacation—shops in the morning, services at night. They purchased their train tickets, made hotel reservations, and whiled away the days in quiet, blissful excitement. Then fate intervened, as it so often does, robbing the childlike soul when it fears least and enjoys living most. One week before they were to leave, he became suddenly and violently ill; he smiled as she held him the last moment of his life.

With him went her will to live. All religion and logic was devoured by a black grief that daily sucked her mind away. With bags and ticket she boarded the train, lumbering two hundred miles southeast to London, her empty stare fixed to a window. She visited the shops. She attended the services. In a mechanical ritual she lived out the last scene that she and her husband had written together. She intended, when it was over, to kill herself.

But something stirred her during the service on her last night there. When the evangelist invited the people to come forward, she rose heavily to her feet, following hundreds of unfamiliar backs, watching their drab wool shapes bob and wind in front of her as though seen through a pane of glass. She was led under the bleachers to the left of the platform, then down a cold, narrow corridor. But halfway to the tent called the Inquiry Room, where these new converts were to be counseled, she could go no farther.

That is where Ruth found her, pressed against the wall, her face blank like an empty rubber mask. Twice Ruth asked if she could help; twice she was greeted with silence.

"I should so love to help," Ruth gently coaxed.

The woman looked at her, then away. Finally, in a monotone, she told her story. When she had finished she asked bitterly, "Why are so many horrible creatures allowed to pollute the earth years without end when a virtual saint is snatched away without warning, without explanation?" The woman herself had been asked such questions in the past and had always had an answer. Now, she had nothing.

"What could I say?" Ruth wrote that night. "I with a husband, so happy and content. My words came like dust."

She prayed with the woman and copied her address. She would write to her, she thought, for in person she had failed. In fact, she feared that she had been failing ever since she had arrived in London almost a month ago. Each night she joined the six hundred counselors and the dozen interpreters in the Inquiry Room, waiting to be used, secretly hoping she would be ignored. It wasn't that she didn't want to help; it was simply that she felt inadequate.

Such a strange assortment of men and women converged upon that place each night: dancers, actors, countesses, miners, adulteresses. An undertaker moved by Billy's sermon on Lazarus came; an escaped prisoner wandered back to turn himself in to God, and to the authorities; a Russian nobleman who spoke no English came, and when he was asked by an interpreter how he could have understood the message well enough to respond to it, he replied, "When I entered this place I was overwhelmed by the presence of God. How can I find Him?" A tow-headed, blue-eyed little boy came after running to Billy and asking him breathlessly, "Mr. Graham, could you tell me where they are finding God?"[4]

A few people, however, treated the Inquiry Room like the Personnel window of a department store—it was the place to register complaints.

On March 23, a smartly dressed woman approached Ruth, not realizing that this woman wearing the white silk ribbon with "Advisor" printed on it was Billy Graham's wife.

"Can I be of any help?" Ruth asked.

"Well, not really," the woman replied coolly. "But you could answer one question for me: Why do Billy Graham and his team stay in such an expensive hotel?" She was a beauty consultant in a fashion shop and all of her clerks had been talking about it. "A room costs ten pounds a night," she added smugly.

Ruth patiently explained that the rooms actually cost two pounds ten, and she hoped that the woman would walk away without asking how she knew. She preferred not to embarrass her. But the woman asked, and the blood rushed to her face when Ruth reluctantly told her.

---

4. One night, after the service, Ruth ran into famous American photographer Carl Mydans. He was rushing out of the Inquiry Room as she was going in. Moved by what he had seen inside, he blurted, "Let me out of here! This is no place for a photographer."

As her first month in England drew to a close, two miseries nagged at the back of her mind: "I don't know where one single contact I have made over here has resulted in one single conversion to Christ. Not one; and I get so lonesome for the children I can hardly stand it." Her depression was acute at night. She didn't dare look at photographs of the children or conjure up their faces in her mind. After turning the lights out she would quickly pray, "Please take care of each one," then climb into bed and pull the covers to her ears.

On March 27, she instructed a team member to purchase her a return ticket. The first month had passed and she was going home, she thought. But when she told Billy her plans, he canceled them.

With mock severity he warned the team members, "If you get her the ticket, you're fired."

He needed her. She was his most trusted confidante; he was emotionally dependent on her. A year after Harringay when he was in Glasgow, he wrote her:

> I don't have to tell you that you are in my mind every moment and that I love you with all my heart, and miss you so much that it hurts. . . . Naturally I think of you a thousand times a day and each little experience I wish I could share with you. Last night I told Lorne Sanny and Charlie Riggs to gather all the stories for me daily. I said, "Last year every evening Ruth would bring me a number of stories of conversions of people who had come to Christ. I don't have her this year to report to me every night; therefore I am depending on you fellows." You see what an important place you had on the team. Your letters have been a balm in Gilead. They have given me inspiration, quieted my nerves. They bring me so close to you. Be assured that my love grows for you every day and I miss you more than I ever thought I could miss any person.

The thought of staying in London another two months depressed her. She felt she was more needed at home. "If I've got to stay," she wrote March 30, "I wish I could be used. I've told the Lord I want nothing to be in His way of making use of me if He can."

April 1, Billy wavered and told her that she could leave. Overjoyed, she telephoned her children and told them that she would be home in a week. She packed her bags and immersed herself in various activities, trying to push away a lingering uneasiness that irritated her like a pebble in a shoe.

The next few days were raw, the sky solid with clouds as though a gray tarpaulin had been unrolled beneath the sun. On April 4, she left her hotel alone and walked to Hyde Park where she found a small crowd assembled in the Speakers' Corner, listening to Donald Soper, a Methodist social preacher and well-known soapbox orator. He was adept at making fools of those who dared to challenge him.

"This person says he believes the Bible from cover to cover!" he roared, pointing an accusing finger at a young man. "He looks like the type that *would* believe the Bible from cover to cover!"

Ruth worked her way through the laughing mob, moving closer to Soper, just in time to hear him fire at her husband. She wasn't surprised. Billy Graham's face watched traffic from billboards and rode by on the sides of city buses; he was a target in political and religious circles and the butt of jokes in nightclubs.

"I have no patience with those who preach sudden conversion," Soper shouted. "To think an entire life can be changed in a half hour's time is a diversion of Christian truth!"

His diatribe, she found, was more depressing than annoying. "One had the feeling he was siding with the laughing unbelievers in his ridicule of simple-hearted Christians," she wrote. "It was time to close and just then I felt some drops of rain. A great black cloud had piled up overhead and it was as if Heaven wept to see a man of God (supposedly) stand and sow doubts in the hearts already full of bewilderment."

Dressed in a black-and-white check wool coat, bareheaded and without an umbrella, she hurried toward a nearby hotel for shelter. As she walked briskly along the rain-spattered pavement, she realized that a young Englishman had fallen into step with her. As she turned a corner he turned with her. Then he mumbled something.

"Pardon?" she asked.

"A pity the rain had to break it up," he said. "Where are you going?"

"Back to my hotel," she replied coolly, quickening her pace.

He followed her doggedly as she crossed a wide, busy street, darting perilously in front of cars.

"An American, huh?" he asked cheerfully, ignoring her obvious discouragements.

"That's right," she replied briefly.

"Would you have time for a cup of coffee?"

"No thank you," she said. "I'd better get back to my hotel."

"What about tomorrow night? Are you busy?"

"Yes. I'll be going to Harringay," she said. Then, suddenly filled with mischief, she asked, "Couldn't you come?"

"I suppose I could," the man said with uncertainty. "And how about Tuesday night?"

"I'll be going to Harringay again."

"Again?" he asked, incredulous. "You won't be going to Harringay every night next week, will you?"

"Every night," she assured him.

After a long, uncertain silence, he asked, "You wouldn't be connected with Billy Graham, would you?"

"His wife," she said, her laughter tumbling out as she turned on Oxford Street. "I *do* hope you'll come to Harringay," she called as he hastily retreated.

Though Billy had given Ruth permission to return home, she knew he didn't want her to go. For the next few days she packed and unpacked, unable to decide what to do. Then, on April 5, she received a letter from a retired missionary:

Dear Mrs. Graham,

Have just heard of your problem—to stay with your husband or go to the four children—and am praying.

In case God says "Stay," I feel constrained to send you a quotation from a friend's letter to me many years ago when we had to let the last of our five leave us and we had to stay in China. She wrote, "You have the right to ask the 'Mighty One' to do more for them than He could if you were with them. 'Open thy mouth wide.'"

He has been faithful to the promises and kept and used all five. I am writing this at the request of our youngest, who says she can testify to the fact that the Lord didn't let them down!

If the Lord says "Go," He will care for your husband better than you can, and as your choice   His, He surely will make that will clear."

That night the answer came to Ruth as she sat in the arena, the din of human voices undulating at the dog track next door, rising and falling in a distant roar like a music box thrumming idiocy in a weary, wounded world: Less than a decade previously England had lost one-fourth of its wealth and sixty thousand civilians in the blitz; London, suffering a coal shortage, was still in a brown-out; bombed-out buildings yawned from the cityscape like open sores; only the wealthy wore bright clothing, while most Englishmen were drab and tattered like sparrows; the House of Commons was demanding Winston Churchill's resignation and debating whether or not Britain should manufacture the hydrogen bomb. And the voices rose and fell in rhythm with the orbits.

It wasn't an epiphany exactly, but as Ruth sat high in the bleachers, thoughts and feelings sifted through her brain and finally focused. "It spoke for itself," she wrote. "The average man does not realize his peril. He fiddles gaily on while Rome burns about his ears. It's the gravity of the whole situation that gives me pause. If Bill feels he needs me—if I can in any way be of help over here—perhaps I should stay."

She canceled her reservation and unpacked her bags.

Her problem wasn't her effectiveness—it was her looking for visible results. Her husband could see the fruits of his ministry immediately in the crowds that gathered below his podium. For her, there would rarely be instant satisfaction. It wasn't the nature of her mission. But there were those rare, wondrous moments when she got her reward. Twelve years later, again in London, a creamy envelope was delivered to her hotel room. It was postmarked Southport, and a modest script flowed in lines straight and centered as though someone had taken great pains to be neat:

Dear Mrs. Graham!
I'm so happy to know you are in England. You won't remember me but in your big London Campaign I came down to hear Dr. Graham. My husband had died suddenly the week before and I came to London to end everything. *But*—in the meeting as I listened to the message—God spoke to me. You were so kind and understanding—it helped me so much to know, even in your busy life, you could think and pray for me!

My life is busy—am still singing in the Salvation Army Songsters and trying to love and serve my Lord.

On April 11, the Grahams drove one hundred miles south for a weekend at Beachy Head in East Sussex County. It was a rare escape, a moment of pause in their frenetic lives. The next morning, while the clock ticked steadily on and beyond church time, they ate breakfast and then strolled along the white chalk cliffs. The thick turf ended suddenly and the sheer rock cascaded six hundred feet into the English Channel, its placid waters heaving lethargically, twinkling like a multifaceted crystal. Behind them rolled the Sussex downs where William the Conquerer had invaded England some nine centuries before.

"We lay on our stomachs and peered over the edge, giddy from the dizzying height, and watched the sea gulls wheeling and preening themselves in the sun and nesting in the jagged rocks below. The water lapped gently on the rocky beach," Ruth wrote. The peaceful rhythms of the English Channel and the soft buffeting of the sun on their backs beckoned them to linger, but they had to leave for an evening church service to hear an Irish evangelist. The peaceful mood quickly dissolved when Billy reminded her of the Irish Christians' disapproval of make-up. Reluctantly, she removed hers. That night she ventilated her feelings in her journal, defining a philosophy that she would later pass on to her own children:

> I'll just pray God will open Bill's eyes and heart to realize what a stumbling block a Christian's appearance can be to the unconverted, and not be too concerned with offending the saints. How difficult it is for a girl to see anything attractive in Christianity when Christians look so unattractive. It has become a matter of deep conviction with me. We Christians, through frowning upon relatively harmless playthings like makeup, bleached hair, nail polish, etc., make the Christian life a bugbear to young converts instead of a joy. I think it is especially easy for [people] to mistake their prejudices for their convictions.

On April 16, Good Friday, Billy preached in Hyde Park to more than forty thousand people. Ruth, avoiding the platform that had been built for the event, wandered through the crowd, pausing every few dozen steps to listen to the orators spontaneously spawned during such services.

"Billy Graham wouldn't be over here if he weren't making money," pontificated a young man with a crew cut and thick glasses. "You know he wouldn't."

"It's all a form of mass hysteria," asserted his companion, a handsome, smooth-skinned Indian who punctuated each soft-spoken remark with delicate flutters of his poetical hands. "Six months after Mr. Graham's gone—it's the same thing with Danny Kaye and the rest—they'll get over it."

By this time, dozens had gravitated toward the two men like aimless beads of water, forming a curious puddle at their feet. Ruth craned her neck, peeking through crevices between ears, shoulders and collars.

"Did you all see Mrs. Graham leave the platform?" the Indian asked the crowd.

Heads nodded in unison. They had indeed seen someone leave the platform—former movie star Colleen Townsend Evans, who had given her Christian testimony and then left for an appointment.

"Did you notice how everyone was looking at her?" the Indian asked, his voice rising, portending drama. "People aren't looking at her husband, they aren't interested in him. Everyone was trying to get pictures of *her*. They like to look at *her* just like they would a Hollywood movie star."

Ruth almost choked on her laughter.

Suddenly, a woman standing directly in front of her launched into a defense, claiming that Mrs. Billy Graham wasn't the one who had been sitting on the platform at all. On she chattered, turning and nodding here and there to address the crowd, her eyes finally resting on the amused woman behind her. "Why here's Mrs. Graham now!" she exclaimed.

The Indian smiled vacuously as Ruth stepped forward and shook his hand.

On Monday evening, April 19, she would indeed find herself on the platform, thanks to her husband who had announced, unbeknown to her, that she would deliver a brief message that night. He clued her in that morning, and the rest of the day she was miserable with anxiety, her hands trembling like dry leaves on a blustery fall day. Billy, meanwhile, paced the room, offering what he thought were helpful suggestions in an effort to soothe her.

"Tell them about your childhood," he suggested. "Didn't you ever have any narrow escapes?"

She thought a minute and then replied that once in Tsingkiang she and the Talbot boys found a grenade and, thinking it was a metal pineapple or scale weight, hung it by its ring from a branch in the mulberry tree over the pet cemetery. The gateman recognized their new toy and alerted Dr. Bell, who wrapped the grenade in a paper sack and dropped it into a lake.

"Listen," Billy said, obviously unimpressed, "your audience went through the blitz, remember? Why don't you just practice projecting yourself like Colleen Evans?"

"Oh, joy!" she exclaimed. "That's a help. The closest I ever got to a Hollywood contract was a high school play in which I played the part of an old maid missionary."

That night, she moved to the podium, turned to her husband, her mouth strategically close to the microphone, "I could kill you," she said. Her next few words were drowned in a din of laughter.

She was not at her best when shoved onto the stage. "Somehow," she recorded later that night, "God helped me through without my throwing up on the platform or falling up the steps."

The third month of the Greater London crusade unreeled at the same frenetic pace as the previous two. Billy had lost fourteen pounds, and both he and Ruth were exhausted. The press had reversed their original cynical opinion of him; several reporters had gone forward at altar calls. In part, the media's change in attitude was due to his refusal to respond to criticism and insults. "I do not intend to get . . . into endless arguments and discussions with them," as he explained his policy in a letter to Ruth the following year. "I am going to take the position of Nehemiah when he refused to go down and have a conference with his enemies. He said, 'I'm too busy building the wall.' We are too busy winning souls to Christ and helping build the church to go down and argue."

The final two services of the Greater London crusade were on May 22, a rainy Saturday. The first was in White City Stadium and seventy thousand people jammed into the stands and playing field, umbrellas and newspapers held over their heads. The second was at Wembley, where people had camped overnight in the raw weather, hoping to get in. American and British flags tossed in the sharp winds high above Empire Stadium. At the entrances, bobbies on horse and foot directed traffic. Inside, a tremendous scoreboard blazed, "Jesus said, I am the Way, the Truth and the Life."

More than one hundred twenty thousand people packed the stadium. Ruth was seated behind the platform in the Royal Box with eleven members of the House of Commons, the mayor of London and his wife, and the wife of Archbishop of Canterbury Geoffrey Fisher. Cold, damp air seeped through her wicker chair, under the edge of the wool rug draped over her knees, permeating her with a bone-aching chill. The clouds were ponderous, the air shimmering as though the sky would split any moment and release a downpour. She surveyed the array of multicolored flecks stretching out before her. That this many people would stream into a stadium and stand shoulder to shoulder to hear a man preach the word of God overwhelmed her and filled her eyes with tears.

There was a sudden flurry of movement below her as her husband and the Archbishop of Canterbury passed through an entrance, a pack of photographers surrounding them.

"There ought to be a law stating how close a photographer can get to one's face," the mayor of London said in Ruth's ear.

Billy's sermon was simple, the message of salvation clear. Realizing that because of the crowd and the immensity of the stadium, thousands of people would not be able to come forward if they wished to, he asked those who wanted to make a decision for Christ to wave their handkerchiefs. He bowed his head before a fluttering white sea.

PART III

10

Little Piney Cove

I surrendered for the obscurity of the mission field. I thought
the height and depth of surrender was to lose myself in
heathen obscurity for God. I find my surrender was neither
high enough nor deep enough.

All summer I have rebelled at this publicity. I've climbed
into a shell. I've tacked "Private, No Admittance" over my
life, and it won't work. I belong to God and He placed me
here, and He will undertake for me and give me poise, grace,
love, wisdom—all I need to bring Him honour in the life He
has appointed.

Ruth Bell Graham, summer of 1954

After Harringay, Billy Graham's life belonged to the public. The tourists descended upon the rustic house like pigeons to a
monument.

Each Sunday afternoon in the summer of 1954, one, if not two,
commercial buses lumbered through Black Mountain from the neighboring Baptist, Episcopal, or YMCA conference centers, and approached the Montreat gate, a small set of arches built of native rock
with MONTREAT spelled in white stones across the top. One had
to pass through it to enter or leave the town, unless he was riding in a
tour bus or a truck. Then he swung into the dirt bypass girdling it to
the north. From time to time truck drivers lulled by the thrumming
of their diesel engines forgot themselves and crashed through the top
of one of those arches, and during the weeks before repairs, it always
looked as if someone had knocked the town's teeth out.

Rumbling up Assembly Drive, the buses then parked across the road from the Grahams' house. Doors flapped open, disgorging the curiosity seekers in a stream of rumpled suits, sunglasses, grins, and cameras. They flocked into the yard, shutters clicking, picking splinters off the rustic gate, snatching stones, leaves, twigs—anything that might serve as a souvenir. In a cheery squawk, they summoned the Graham children to come outside and have their pictures taken.

Ruth and Billy shielded the family from the public, refusing to place them on display for either the tourists or Billy's audiences. Though occasionally pressured to march his children to the platform to give their Christian testimonies, Billy's answer was always no. Even so, he wasn't home long enough to protect them from his fans and critics. Fortunately, Ruth was a she-bear on the subject. She requested of the journalists that they refrain from interviewing the children and taking their photographs. Usually, they complied. But if her warnings weren't enough, she simply made the children completely unavailable.

But she could not keep an eye on four rambunctious youngsters every minute. The summer of 1954 she began noticing that three-year-old Bunny, by nature more gregarious than her two sisters, had more change than her small allowance could account for. Upon questioning, GiGi tattled, "Well, Mother, just watch the next time a bus stops." The following Sunday, Ruth watched Bunny slip from the house to the front gate.

"Are you Billy Graham's little girl?" one of the tourists asked.

She nodded innocently, her red pocketbook yawning at her wrist as she waited for them to deposit a nickle or quarter for each picture they took.

Ruth put a quick halt to Bunny's entrepreneurial endeavours. Training nine-year-old GiGi was a different matter. She was a timid, enchanting child with a proclivity for mischief (often culminating in wrongdoing and a bout of repentance). "She tried harder to be good than anyone—but couldn't," her mother recalled. Once she scampered through her backyard, tied a rope across Assembly Drive, and then sent seven-year-old Anne to try to collect a dollar toll from the passing cars. Crouched behind a large rotted stump, she sometimes hurled mudballs and crabapples at the tourists. One afternoon when someone stopped her on the roadside and asked, "Could you please tell me where Billy Graham lives?" she sweetly replied, "Who's he?"

Ruth decided it was time to move when she discovered someone

Nelson Bell and Virginia Leftwich Bell, c.1916.

Ruth's family, Christmas 1958: back row (left to right): Clayton holding daughter Margaret Ann, Peggy Bell, Virginia holding son Severn, her husband John Sommerville; middle row: Rosa's husband Don Montgomery holding daughter Robyn, Rosa, Virginia and Nelson Bell, Ruth and Billy Graham; front row: Franklin Graham III, GiGi holding Ned, Bunny, Anne and cousins Johnny and Nelson Sommerville.

Christmas 1934 in front of
Tsingkiang home. Back row (left
to right): Ruth and her father;
front row: Virginia, Clayton, Mrs.
Bell and Rosa.

Back row (left to right): Ruth
and Rosa; front row: Dr. Bell,
Virginia, Mrs. Bell, 1933.

Rosa and Ruth in the kitchen of their home in Tsingkiang, China.
Missionary Cassie Lee Oliver holds Nelson Bell, Jr.

Rosa, friend Betty Yates and Ruth walking between Wheaton's Blanchard Hall and the gymnasium, 1938.

Ruth with her date Harold Lindsell during her first year at Wheaton College, 1937.

Mrs. Cliff (Billie) Barrows and Ruth on Ruth's first trip abroad with her young evangelist husband; Scotland, 1946.

Ruth graduates from Pyeng Yang
Foreign School in what is now
North Korea, 1936.

Rosa, Ruth and friend Kay
Gieser at Wheaton, 1938.

Friends Hampton Talbot, Ruth, William Talbot and Sandy Yates (and
Ruth's German Shepherd Prinz) posing by the Iron Ox placed in Kiangsu
by the Chinese to lap up the Yellow River when it swelled from its banks
and flooded the lowlands, 1936.

Vacationing in Jamaica, 1964.

An early Youth for Christ crusade at
Muskegon, Michigan, 1945.

Billy and Ruth, c.1958.

The newly engaged couple in the yard of his family's Charlotte home, 1942.

The new bride, August 13, 1943.

Just married in Montreat, North Carolina, August 13, 1943.

Aboard the S.S. *United States*, heading for the Greater London Crusade, 1954.

In the living room of their mountain-top home.

Relaxing at a ranch, 1952.

Ruth and Billy at their Montreat home, c.1981.

peeping over her bedroom windowsill while she was drying her hair one morning.

She was jittery, exhausted, and unable to sleep. Her own responsibilities had dramatically increased because of the growing demands on her husband's life. He was too busy to manage the family budget, so the job had become hers. He no longer saw his paychecks, and Ruth was all too frequently summoned to the bank to take care of their overdrawn account. The scene became an almost ludicrous rerun. William Hickey, the president of Northwestern Bank, would telephone her himself:

"Ruth, this is William Hickey . . ."

"I'll be right down," Ruth would interrupt.

Handling the finances was further complicated by the fact that she not only had to make ends meet, but she had to remember that the world was watching every penny she spent. She realized then that she would rarely be able to indulge herself in jewelry or expensive clothing, even if the items were gifts. Refusing extravagant presents was sometimes quite troublesome: She requested that a group of ladies she had addressed send her $1,000 honorarium to an orphanage in Mexico. They complied—and then sent her a Neiman-Marcus gift certificate for the amount. Ruth bought a gold bracelet with it and gave it to a relief organization with the stipulation that they sell it for twice its value and use the money for mission work in Third World countries. One Christmas, her good friend June Carter Cash sent her a hooded, full-length autumn haze mink coat because she had noticed Ruth shivering on crusade platforms.

"Look," June said when Ruth explained that she couldn't exactly appear in public, much less on Billy's platforms, wearing the fur, "wear it to the barn. Wear it in the car. Wear it out walking with Billy in the snow on the mountain. But stay warm!"

So Ruth, using it for warmth instead of show, wore it on the mountain or in the car, once appearing at a friend's house on a bitterly cold day wearing the coat and a pair of asbestos gloves. Finally, with June's permission, she auctioned it off as she had the bracelet, only to have a friend buy it for twice its value and give it back to her for her birthday: "My wife and I are giving it back to you," the man explained cheerfully, "with the understanding you never get rid of it again."

Prosperity also knocked on her husband's door, enticing him with the spoils of mammon. In the late fifties he rejected NBC's offer of a million dollars a year to host a two-hour Sunday morning talk show;

he said no to Paramount Pictures Corporation executives who wanted to make him a movie star; later, he rejected ABC's offer of a starting salary of $150,000 if he would serve as a consultant. He would donate personal gifts, such as prime real estate in Florida and California, to the BGEA and Wheaton College. He refused other favors, such as a year's lease of a jet and pilot. By the eighties he would have given about half of his approximately $500,000 family inheritance to various Christian organizations.

Ruth wondered how she would overcome the tensions imposed by fame; and she wondered how she could provide their children with a normal environment. In typical fashion, she kept her anxieties to herself, talking about them in her prayers and journals; she fought back the resentment that rose to her throat when the tourists invaded their property. She knew that these people meant no harm, that most of them simply were expressing admiration and gratitude for her husband. Any unkindness on her part would be unfortunate. "It's an odd kind of cross to bear," she wrote at the time. "Yet those who have not been through it would consider it some kind of glory."

In early 1954, the Grahams had been offered a good deal on a 150-acre cove, located two miles from their house between two ridges— or hogbacks—on one of the Seven Sisters that climb to Mount Mitchell, twelve miles away. The land was occupied by two mountain families who grew corn on one slope and culled timber on another. The people decided to sell out and the cove was offered to the Grahams for a mere forty-three hundred dollars.

Shortly after the turn of the century, a six-foot-six mountain man named Solomon Morris built the narrow dirt road that wound from the hogback's base to a level area, several hundred yards below the summit, where the mountain families later built their pole cabins. He hacked a clearing in the brush halfway to the top. Then, following with a mule-pulled plow and drag pan, he cut and smoothed a road wide enough for a wagon. Morris planted more than a hundred apple, pear, cherry, and black walnut trees and carried dozens of white pine seedlings from Mt. Mitchell. These, along with a thousand white pines the Grahams received from a Forestry Incentive Program, reseeded many times over until their full, pungent branches eventually umbrellaed the mountain.

Before the Grahams agreed to buy the property they drove there to inspect it. They were greeted by suspicious eyes peeking through cabin windows on a slope thick with rhododendrons, mountain laurel, and wild flowers. Just yards away, the red clay-chinked stone foundation of Solomon Morris's original house reclined in the moist, fragrant shade of the white pines he had planted almost half a century earlier.

Billy surveyed the property with skepticism, but Ruth felt her blood race at the potential.

"I leave it up to you to decide," he said just before he left for the West Coast.

Ruth borrowed the money from the bank and bought the cove while he was gone. When he returned he was incredulous.

"You *what?*" he asked.

After he recovered from his initial shock, they began making plans. They decided they would build near the end of the dirt road, beyond the cabins and just behind the tall bank of white pines Morris had planted. Bill wanted to cut the evergreens to afford them a view of the valley. Ruth believed that no tree should be cut unless it was absolutely necessary. They compromised by deciding to build farther up the ridge. The mountain people evacuated the property, leaving a tarpaper shack, two pole cabins, three lean-tos, a hog pen, and a potato cellar, along with the foundations of other cabins that had burned to the ground over the years. Bulldozers began gouging a shelf in the hogback.

Ruth's first project—to be a surprise for Billy—was to remodel one of the pole cabins so the family could escape the tourists on the weekends. While he was out of town, the workmen tore out partitions, opening the cabin into one spacious, L-shaped room; they built a fireplace from fieldstone found on the property, replaced the asbestos roof, and scoured the rooms from beams to floorboards; Ruth furnished the cabin with a double bed and covered the loft with mattresses for the children. The "kitchen" consisted of the fireplace and a grill outside; spring water was piped into a wooden tub at the back door; and the bathroom was an outhouse some hundred paces beyond the secondhand wraparound porch Ruth had bought from a carpenter.

Shortly after she finished her secret project, her husband returned home. She drove him up the mountain at dusk, not telling him where she was taking him or why. Hugging the rutted, unpaved road around sharp bends, the Jeep finally crunched to a halt in front of the remodeled cabin. Oil lamps glowed in the windows and a wisp of gray wood smoke rose from the chimney. They sat at the hearth drinking the cocoa she had heated over the open flames, their romantic mood dissolving into laughter when he drained his cup and discovered the chewing gum she thought she had tossed into the fire moments earlier. While the house was being built, the cabin was a welcome refuge where Ruth's family, parents, and friends would convene for picnics of fried chicken, biscuits, potato salad, and apple pie before the open fire.

In the weeks that followed, Ruth, aided by an architect, designed the new home. It would be a U-shaped, story-and-a-half structure facing a small semicircle of lawn and a vista of Black Mountain, the Swannanoa Valley, and row after row of hazy ranges. Though she built the house for her husband—it was to be his refuge from the frenetic world around him—it would be a manifestation of her spirit. She built and furnished it with materials from her past and cemented them with her imagination. It would be her artistic masterpiece, and she would spend a lifetime enjoying it.

She studied books on architecture and discovered that she felt the strongest sense of peace and certitude when she looked at the chapter about log cabins. Like the red Jeep she roared up and down the mountain in and the face of the man she loved, ruggedness attracted her, as in the natural beauty of old wood and stone. Cracks, nail scars and weather-beaten materials "had character," she explained, "as if they'd existed for a long time and seen a lot of living." Smooth, synthetic beauty did not appeal to her.

Billy, in contrast, was not at home in rusticity. His idea of comfort was a hotel. "When Bill gets to Heaven and finds it's not like a Holiday Inn or a Marriott," Ruth often joked, "he'll be back." His only request regarding the new house was that it have comfortable chairs and adequate lighting.

It's not surprising that she hired the same team of rugged mountain men that had remodeled her parents' home to build hers. Her fondness for the neighboring clans had begun when she hired "Old Dad" Roberts to come work for her at her first house. He was a short, wiry man with black hair and a bushy mustache, and he had dark eyes like volcanic glass. He raised his voice almost to a chant when he talked about religion, and he had a talent for smelling rattlesnakes—they smelled like cucumbers, he claimed. When he detected the enemy, he would freeze and sniff, then he would slowly lay down his hoe or rake and say, "I smell me a rattlesnake." While the workmen gathered around him to watch, he would begin stalking. Finding what he was looking for, he would snatch the diamondback behind its head and snap its neck like a raw green bean. He would slit its neck with a penknife, tie a string to its tail, and hang it over a tin can to drain the carcass for "snake oil."

"It's good for the rheumatiz," he would explain.

Roberts was as honest as a tuning fork, and when Ruth began building her home, he went to the mountain with her. Ambling through the property, he disassembled old still furnaces (moonshiners were not strangers to this part of the world), rolling boulders along a stream bed to the construction site where they eventually became part of the native rock walls around the house.

Her contractor was Gregg Sawyer, a mellow, good-natured man. Unlike several of the temperamental artisans who worked for him, he submitted to Ruth's preferences. A taut leather belt encircled his ample middle, holding up a pair of perpetually wrinkled khaki trousers; usually, he wore a plaid flannel shirt, sleeves rolled up to the elbows. He had a habit of cleaning his wire-framed spectacles between his thumb and forefinger, smudging the lenses until it was a wonder that he could see a blueprint or drive a wooden peg into a floorboard. His chin was sandy with stubble and he wore a battered felt porkpie hat. Zeb Sawyer, his brother and partner, was the best fireplace builder in the valley. Both were craftsmen of the first order and in later years would be commissioned to restore former Governor Zebulon B. Vance's birthplace in nearby Weaverville.

Zeb Sawyer's skill in building fireplaces and clean-drawing chimneys reached its zenith with the construction of Ruth's house. While a bootlegger mixed the mortar, Sawyer built fireplaces in the guest room, Ruth's bedroom, the living room, and the family room. The latter two were as cavernous as they would have been in the seventeenth and eighteenth centuries, when the family baking and cooking were done over the fire.

Except for the frame, the house was built of old wood, most of which came from log cabins Ruth discovered in the mountains. Dressed in blue jeans and an Army jacket, she would drive her Jeep through western North Carolina, stopping at gas stations to leave her telephone number with attendants in the event they heard of cabins for sale. Six months after her first inquiry, she began receiving calls. She bought a two-story cabin for four hundred dollars and a dog-trot (two cabins connected by a breezeway) for a hundred and twenty. Most cabins sold for about fifty dollars, and when she didn't buy the entire building, she would pay several dollars per wormy chestnut, oak or yellow poplar log. Often the owners of the cabins would throw in a few bonuses with the sales—like an old lazy Susan table with a broken leg, a smokehouse, or a broadaxe that had been used to hew cabin logs in the past century.

She discovered a large, century-old Victorian house that was being torn down near Asheville and for forty-five dollars per thousand feet bought all of its usable heart-of-pine lumber. "Couldn't buy it new for a hundred and twenty dollars a thousand," Gregg Sawyer chuckled as he eyed her find. She became an expert at hand staining new lumber, rubbing such curiosities as leftover lipsticks and shoe polishes into the wood until it was highlighted with subtle shades of red, gray, and brown, like the old wood she preferred. From a school that had been torn down in Asheville, she salvaged tons of old brick, and with it she floored the living room, a porch, and the glassed-in hallway that connected two wings of the house. She bought miscellaneous items from a salvage yard.

Her building philosophy baffled and annoyed many of her workmen: "Use the new lumber for framing and the old lumber for finishing," she reminded them daily.

It didn't make a bit of sense to them. They had all been born in log cabins, spending every night of their childhoods sleeping on feather beds, with the stars shining through the gaps in the shingles. They had worked hard to leave all that behind. Prosperity meant linoleum floors and department store furniture. They couldn't understand why Ruth wanted the hundred-year-old lumber on the outside where everyone could see it, nor could they figure out why she wanted the massive exposed beams in the living room ceiling roughed up with a broadaxe. Two rock masons quit on the spot when she asked them to build walls without the mortar showing—to look like dry rock walls.

"If I can't lay rock the way it's s'posed to be laid," one mason told his boss, "then I'm not a-going to lay it."

A carpenter quit when she gave him weather-beaten log cabin doors and asked him to install them in the front hall closets. He picked up his satchel and sauntered outside to the Sawyers: "I weren't mad at none of you men," he explained after announcing he was leaving. "But ever'thing I done up there, I had to do wrong. A man can't take no pride in this kind of work."

Troy Fortner, a tall, broad-shouldered plasterer, came close to leaving. He was respected as a master craftsman, his ceilings smooth as beaverboard. Ruth told him that she wanted her ceilings imperfect, with the wide sweeps of the trowel visible as they would have been two hundred years ago.

"Go on back to the boiler room and practice," she told him cheerfully.

"O.K., Mrs. Graham," he said, his strong face breaking into a smile, "I'll do it for you on one condition—you won't tell anybody who did it."[1]

The other men stayed on the job, after Ruth volunteered to replace all broken drill bits and pay for the extra time it took to sharpen saw teeth dulled by nails embedded in the old wood. They continued muttering behind her back, saying they hoped nobody ever found out who had built her house, for they feared it just might ruin their reputations.

As the house began to rise from the earth, Billy once more became suspicious that he had been relieved of all home responsibility. It was obvious, especially when the workmen would walk right past him to discuss business with his wife. His frustration began to surface.

"Why is it," he demanded one afternoon, "that my authority seems to end at home?"

"Listen," she said, "do you want me to call you every time a door needs painting, the furnace needs repairing, the septic tank needs emptying, the drains need cleaning . . . ?"

"No," he had to admit.

"I'm assuming the home responsibilities," she explained, "to free you for your more important ones."

He relaxed, seeing the wisdom in her words.

By late 1955, the logs were in place and chinked with rust-colored brixment resembling, yet more durable than, the red-clay chinking of the mountain cabins. The men built a split-rail fence around the yard and from the leftover lumber constructed Ruth's and the guestroom's beds. Damming the stream below the house, they built a small swimming hole so cold it took your breath away when you first jumped in. It, like the small pool Dr. Bell had built in Tsingkiang, became the center of attention in the warm months, and it was enjoyed not only by the children (and their mother) but by tadpoles, water bugs and an occasional water snake.

Ruth furnished her home with castoffs, hunting in such unlikely places as the town dump, where the workmen found a heavy slab of wood that had once been Lake Susan's diving board. It soon became the fireplace mantle in the Grahams' living room, carved with "Eine

---

1. Though Ruth realizes that in telling this anecdote she has done just what Troy Fortner asked her not to do, she at least waited until after his death. "Troy is in heaven now," she explained. "So I feel free to say he did it—and did a superb job at that."

Feste Burg Ist Unser Gott" (or "A Mighty Fortress Is Our God"). She also rummaged through furniture stores, antique shops, and junk shops. One day, she and a local antique dealer named Tom Rezutto followed a seldom-traveled dirt road to look at an old bench on a cabin porch. Hewn from a solid board and complete with legs with Chippendale turnings, the bench was covered with dirt and chicken droppings, its only occupants obviously of the feathered variety. The owner, an old mountain man with a face like a dried apple, was sitting on the porch when Ruth braked her Jeep beside his yard.

"Would you like to sell your bench?" the antique dealer asked.

"Nope, don't think I care to sell it," he said, staring just past them, his eyes faded like an old cotton dress. "I like to sit on it of an evenin' and watch the cars go by."

"How about thirty dollars?" Ruth suggested.

"Give me the money and take the bench," he said.

She made a deal with the workmen that for every old 'possum lantern they brought her she would buy them a new one. She had them wired and hung beside the outer doors, in hallways and on the front porch. The kitchen and its adjoining keeping room are early American in decor: Hand-forged tools and copper pots adorn the fireplace with an old black-iron Betty lamp tapering above the musket over the mantle. Colorful braided rugs cover the floors; Indian corn and a wrought iron smokehouse hook hang from the exposed beams; the furniture is overstuffed and inviting.

The living room is full of light, its ceiling high, its floors made of old brick oiled to a soft shine. Two of its walls are assembled of cabin logs and the others from leftover chestnut paneling. An expansive, deep-set window overlooks the lawn; two smaller ones overlook the ridge. Treasures from Ruth's rummages in English junk shops are scattered about. On the handcarved mantle is a medieval helmet with bittersweet flowing from its mask like a misplaced plume; a pair of coach horns is propped in a corner; a heavy jousting helmet turned upside down on a wooden base serves as a wastepaper basket. Hanging on the walls are two original letters by John Wesley, the Graham coat of arms, an etching of the Madonna and Child, an oil painting of a Chinese peasant, and a brass plaque that reads: "Pray for China." Old leatherbound volumes (acquired through years of visiting English and Scottish antiquarian bookstores) fill bookcases on either side of the fireplace. It is a warm, comfortable room, one that invites people to sit and stay awhile.

Over the years her creation would come as a surprise to people who had heard tales of Billy Graham's mythical mansion (even the IRS once listed them as owning a hundred acres of arable land and an Olympic-sized swimming pool—there's not a level area big enough for a tennis court). The first time singer Stuart Hamblen visited them he unfolded himself from the car and surveyed the place for a moment. "I thought you lived in a fine mansion," he drawled. "Thank God for all them logs." When the retired three-time world champion heavyweight boxer Muhammad Ali visited in the fall of 1979, his reaction wasn't quite as approving. "I thought he lived on a thousand-acre farm," he marveled to the press. "And we drove up to this house made of logs; [it was] the kind of house a man of God would live in." (He graciously refused Billy's invitation to spend the night there.)[2]

In early 1956, the Grahams moved to the mountain. They named their homestead Little Piney Cove. By this time the workmen had reconsidered their early negative attitudes about her ideas. They were so proud of what they had wrought that some of them asked if their wives could see it. The women arrived with housewarming presents, such as a Dutch oven or a handmade quilt. "This place sort of grows on you," said workman James Sawyer, "and before you know it you catch yourself a-liking it."

Most significantly, Ruth and the mountain people had developed a mutual affection and respect. She admired their honesty and craftsmanship; not only were their skills virtually lost arts but so was their native gentility. Likewise, the mountain folk found Ruth to be trustworthy, appreciative, and deferential; her loyalty, they sensed, was nondiscriminating.

One workman was Joe Tolliver, a tall, husky man who had been an alcoholic before he "got saved," as the natives put it. No sooner had Ruth moved up the mountain than Tolliver slid back to the bottom, drinking like a wild man and staggering home covered with blood after barroom brawls he didn't remember. Darlene, his slender, pretty wife, would wait for him and then clean his wounds, hoping with every breath that he would change. Finally, she began visiting Ruth and pouring out her despair. One day, just before she left Tolliver, she asked Ruth if, as a last resort, she would talk to him.

---

2. "The 'Greatest' Meet: Graham, Ali Discuss Problems," *The Asheville Citizen Times*, September 17, 1979.

Ruth found him stretched out on his bed, pale and weak.

"Why?" she asked him.

A veil of shame dropped over his eyes, "I'm guilty of ever' sin in the book, Miz Graham," he admitted. "I'm too weak to resist."

"I'm scared for you," she told him softly.

Soon after, Ruth received a plain white dimestore envelope containing a short note written by Darlene.

"In case anything happens to me, will you keep my baby?"

"Yes," Ruth replied.

Then there was Bud Lominac, whom Tolliver had introduced to Ruth in early 1956. Lominac, Tolliver told her, was a drunk, but if she would just take him on as a caretaker he would surely mend his ways. Ruth needed a man to cut the firewood, mow the lawn and do other odd jobs around the house. She let Lominac move into one of the cabins.

Early one morning, as he and Ruth headed to a distant valley where they were dismantling an old cabin, she offered him a cup of coffee.

"Don't mind if I do."

"Do you like it strong or weak?" she asked.

"Strong!" exclaimed Lominac. "You know, Miz Graham, it don't take near as much water to make coffee as some folks think."

Over the months his cabin became so filthy that the other workmen mentioned it to Ruth.

"Mr. Lominac," Ruth told him one day, "you have two choices. Either clean that cabin or get you a wife."

"Iffen you don't mind," he replied with a grin, "I'll clean up the cabin."

He did so and spent many hours there, propped up in bed with his bottle. Days would pass without his showing up at work, and when he did put in a token effort, he cheated on his time. One week he didn't appear for some five days and Ruth sent a workman to check on him. When the man returned from the cabin, he reported sheepishly that he had found Lominac in bed, "a-readin' the Bible."

"You should have looked *under* the Bible," she said.

Lominac would never admit that he drank. He might reek of a hundred proof and he would still look Ruth squarely in the eye and say thickly, "Before Gawd, Miz Graham, I don't drink." With reluctance, she fired him, replacing him with Floyd Roberts, Dad Roberts' son, who with his wife and five children lived in a small cabin just outside the Montreat gate on Rainbow Mountain. Their brick-colored, unpaved road snaked up from Assembly Drive and disappeared into the woods.

Ruth had become acquainted with him when she lived in the house across the street from her parents. She often joked that she kept him around just to hear him talk and to engage him in lively bantering sessions. Pontificating about politics, he would launch into a diatribe about the evil deeds of "*Adof Hilter* and *Joe Stallion*." Ruth, meanwhile, periodically chided him because he refused to take his family to church.

"Church's full of hypocrites," he usually replied.

"Well, Floyd," she would say, "there's always room for one more."

Roberts became so fond of the Grahams that he named his sixth and seventh children after them. Thus, the real Billy and Ruth Graham lived up a steep road to the left after one entered the Montreat gate, and their namesakes lived up a steep road to the left after one exited. Unsurprisingly, some of Montreat's younger and more mischievous residents occasionally directed unsuspecting Billy Graham fans to the wrong Billy and Ruth.

Needless to say, the mountain folk didn't always appreciate the thousands of cheery Presbyterians and Baptists who stampeded below their mountain into Montreat each summer for conferences and perhaps a peek at where "the Baptist pope of the Presbyterian Heaven" lived, as one minister referred to Billy. So if a misguided tourist strayed from the herd and lumbered up Rainbow Mountain instead of Little Piney Cove, he couldn't count on, much less deserve, any sympathy. The lost soul was bound to pass by one certain unpainted cabin where lived a woman who didn't exactly qualify as the hostess of a Welcome Station. Embattled and wizened from too much work and too little comfort, she had little regard for the tourists. On a typical summer day, she could be found sitting on her front porch, unperturbed, her shotgun propped on a nearby chair.

Legend has it that one sweltering summer day, two men in a Cadillac made that wrong turn. When they reached the cabin the car rocked to a quick halt, stirring up pinging gravel and billowing red dust. A window was rapidly rolled down and a smiling face greeted the woman's inscrutable one.

"'Scuse me, ma'am, but could you please tell me where Billy Graham's . . . ," the man's voice trailed off as the oddity of the situation struck him. "We must have made a wrong turn, 'cause this doesn't look like . . . ," he added lamely.

Within seconds the Cadillac was careening down the mountain, a double-barreled shotgun load of rock salt whizzing past the rear bumper.

With so many tourists violating the local residents' territory in search of Billy Graham, it was a wonder that the mountain folk and their neighbors didn't resent the Graham family. But they were fiercely loyal to them. Ruth was known to carry casseroles or pots of soup to them when there was illness in a family, and she was always there to offer comfort in bereavement. She did the same for her Montreat neighbors. On one occasion a widow returned home from church to find that Ruth had not only left her a potroast for dinner but had cleaned her oven. And if a big city journalist made the mistake of telephoning one of the mountain folk to ask about the Grahams, he was answered by a resounding CLICK. If he asked a neighbor, he was likely answered with an inscrutable smile and a platitude.

Floyd Roberts eventually quit his job with the Grahams when Ruth repeatedly told him that she needed him to work inside the house as well as in the yard. But indoor chores, he often reminded her, were "woman's work." It was an amiable parting.

He was succeeded by John Rickman, a gentle, kindly man who also lived on Rainbow Mountain. A former alcoholic, Rickman had been converted to Christ after Nelson Bell found him unconscious in the woods. Dr. Bell carried him to his own home, sobered him up and then hired him to do odd jobs around the house. Later he sent Rickman up the mountain to work for the Grahams. They took him on, providing that he wouldn't drink. After a few slips (which they pretended not to notice), he kept his promise and would work for the Grahams for twenty-odd years before dying of cancer. An uncle, of sorts, to Franklin and Ned, he taught them how to handle guns safely, and he taught all of the children how to drive.

In the late seventies, Ruth began noticing that Rickman was pale and listless; she caught him leaning on his rake, panting and wiping his brow when he thought no one was looking. Finally, she persuaded him to see a doctor, and it was discovered that his years of chain-smoking had finally exacted their toll. He had cancer of the throat. She visited him in the hospital the day before he died.

" 'Let not your heart be troubled,' " she read to him, " 'Ye believe in God, believe also in me. In my Father's house are many mansions. . . .' "

A gnarled hand covered hers and she looked up to see Rickman, whose larynx had been removed, carefully mouthing, "many, *many* mansions." Then they prayed, his face crinkled into a smile, a finger pointing heavenward.

The next day, his daughter Shirley watched him struggle in his hospital bed as he tried to hold on.

"Papa," she said gently, "don't fight it. Go on to Heaven."

His craggy face smoothed like peaceful water as he obeyed.

In the early sixties Ruth noticed that Gregg Sawyer's skin was yellowish and it was found that he had a fatal pancreatic disorder. One afternoon as they worked on a gate, he began thinking out loud.

"I figure I'm not good enough for Heaven," he said.

She smiled, her hands never stopping as she worked on the rocks, and she told him a true story:

"Well you know, Mr. Sawyer, when Mr. [Dwight L.] Moody was in Scotland holding meetings, a little boy wanted to get into the building. He was a little urchin. Now when I say a little urchin, I mean his face was dirty, his clothes were ragged. And every door he went to was closed because the place was jammed. He was turned away. Maybe if he'd come in top hat and tails they would have been a little more respectful to him.

"But anyway, the little guy got turned away and turned away until finally he wound up at the back door with tears running down his little face. And just about that time a carriage pulled up. People went to help the gentleman out of the carriage and a big, tall man stepped down. And he noticed this little guy with the dirty face and tears running down and he put his hand on his shoulder and said, 'Sonny, what's wrong?'

"The boy said, 'I want to hear Mr. Moody and it's full up and nobody will let me in.'

"And the big man took his hand and said, 'Come with me.'

"When they got to the door it was thrown wide and people bowed him in. The big man found the little boy a seat on the front row. Then he mounted the platform. It was Mr. Moody.

"When we get to Heaven, Mr. Sawyer," she concluded, her eyes filled with light like a sunny day, "that's the only way any of us are going to get in—if Jesus takes us by the hand. None of us are good enough. We're too dirty."

Cocking his head to one side, he studied her over his glasses for a moment. Then he grinned, shaking his head appreciatively. "Well, now," he said, "that makes sense. A man can understand that."

11

Her Jungle

Having always longed to do pioneer missionary work, I must keep reminding myself as I look out over the New York skyline—this is our jungle.

Ruth Bell Graham, 1957

On Saturday, May 11, 1957, Ruth leaned against the pillows in her Pullman car as soft lamplight soaked into the blanket tousled over her legs and illuminated the India paper of her battered King James Bible. Two and a half hours had passed in hypnotic beats since she had awakened at 2:00 A.M.

The train lurched to a halt in Washington, where the day before, Billy had met with President Eisenhower and Vice-President Nixon. Boarding, he greeted Ruth with a hug in their two-bunk stateroom. As the train lumbered to New York, they talked and then slept until the porter brought them coffee and toast at 9:00 A.M.

Two years earlier, John Sutherland Bonnell, pastor of New York's Fifth Avenue Presbyterian Church, had approached Billy with an interesting question.

"Billy," Bonnell asked, "when will you begin a crusade in New York?"

"I am not ready for that," he replied. "I want more time for study and prayer before tackling that project."[1]

Nonetheless, that same year, the Protestant Council of the City of New York, representing seventeen hundred churches of thirty-one

---

1. "Dedicated Deciders in Billy Graham Crusade," *Life,* vol. 43, no. 1 (1 July 1957), p. 92.

denominations, invited him to hold a crusade in Madison Square Garden. He accepted and his organization began setting it up. By now, the city was plastered with 650 billboards, 40,000 telephone dials reading "Pray for Billy Graham," 35,000 window posters and 40,000 bumper stickers. In addition, the BGEA's arsenal included a million letterheads, 2.5 million envelope stuffers, 250,000 crusade songbooks and 100,000 Gospels of John.[2]

Vice-President Nixon would attend the crusade on behalf of the President and speak to 100,000 in Yankee Stadium for ten minutes on July 21. Many of the country's top entertainers and jet-setters would come. It would be the longest, most expensive and most exhausting crusade Billy had yet held, as the scheduled six weeks of services stretched into sixteen. By the time it was over 2.3 million people would have attended, with 160,000 jamming Times Square for the final meeting September 1. But the phenomenon that would change the course of history for him—and for his family—was that on June 1, his ministry would be televised, launching him as the nation's pioneer "televangelist."

Journalists from virtually every major magazine and newspaper in the United States and Europe were trickling into Manhattan even as the Grahams sat in their Pullman car. He was restless, unnerved by the task ahead of him. To him, his mission was not necessarily one of choice. It was one of obedience. He knew it was God propelling him along a ribbon of steel to the central nervous system of the nation, the hub of sophistication, art, and fashion.

Politically, it was a volatile time in the United States. On May 17, 1954, the U.S. Supreme Court had declared that racial segregation in public schools was unconstitutional. Violence and controversy erupted in the already stormy South. In September of 1957 President Eisenhower would send a thousand Federal troops to Little Rock, Arkansas, to quell Governor Orval E. Faubus's attempt to block the integration of a local school. Reporters wanted to know why Billy Graham didn't stay home and help his people solve the racial problem instead of traveling north to "save" New York City.

Over the past four years he had gained increasing respect in the country for his stance on racial segregation. During the 1953 Chattanooga, Tennessee, crusade he had instructed his ushers that blacks were to sit wherever they pleased. There was no segregation at the

---

2. Curtis Mitchell, *God in the Garden* (New York: Doubleday, 1957), p. 32.

foot of the cross, he maintained repeatedly. Many people fancied that he was moving in rhythm with a twenty-eight-year-old black Baptist minister named Martin Luther King, Jr., who had mounted his own platform in 1955 when Rosa Parks, a black woman, had been arrested in Montgomery, Alabama, for refusing to surrender her bus seat to a white man. While Billy Graham rebelled against the ungodliness of racial discrimination, King set in motion the first mass civil rights movement in American history.

At the 1957 New York crusade King would sit on Billy's platform. Three years later the two men would fly together to Brazil to attend a banquet for Baptist leaders. There King said: "If it had not been for the ministry of Billy Graham, my civil rights work in the States would have been much harder."

Shortly before Billy left Montreat for Washington, he and Ruth hiked to the small mountainside field near their house, a quiet spot where he often wandered alone to pray. They stretched out on the grass, sleepily watching their four sheep graze. As they talked and prayed about New York, he confessed to her that though he was challenged, he was also frightened. She shared his feelings, she told him. "But at the same time," she added, "self-confidence would be worse."

Now, as they ate breakfast on the train, they were talking and praying again. She gently peeled back the fragile pages of her Bible, smoothing it open when she found each verse: "'If Thy Presence go not with me carry us not up hence. . . . My Presence shall go with Thee. . . . Lo, I am with you always . . .'" The opportunity came from God, she told him. And He would be with them.

In a steady, dreary rain, the train stopped briefly in Newark, an hour late. The press, much to Ruth's relief, had tired of waiting and had left. But in Manhattan they were greeted by a mob of reporters, friends, and for the first time, police. A burly sergeant and a detective stood sentry on the station platform while the Grahams left the train. Ruth was surprised, for it had not occurred to her that there was any possibility of violence. The presence of guards was the beginning of what was soon to become commonplace.

Moments after they arrived at the New Yorker Hotel, one of Billy's associates began ushering Ruth to her quarters, away from the hundreds of journalists who had been waiting more than an hour for her husband.

"Oh, no," Billy said, grinning as he scotched Ruth's getaway. "She goes to the press conference with me."

She sat beside him, feeling "like a fool," as she recalled, while he answered the reporters' ten pages of questions:

"How sinful do you think New York is?"

"Is it a criticism of the church today that people respond to you as an evangelist and not to the churches themselves?"

"Why is a revival needed when the membership in churches is zooming?"

Drained, he remarked to a reporter as he walked toward the elevator, "My wife and I have lost our privacy. And I don't think anyone who has lost their privacy doesn't long to have it back. You don't realize what a priceless possession it is to be a private individual. To be looked at, to be stared at everywhere one goes, never to go into a restaurant without being looked at. . . ."[3]

During this crusade many of the wealthy and famous showed interest in Billy as never before. Jackie Gleason invited him to lunch. Tallulah Bankhead invited the Grahams to tea. He was a frequent guest on talk shows. On Sunday, May 12, Ruth sat in a balcony and watched him on the set of "The Steve Allen Show," along with Dean Jones, Milton Berle, Tallulah Bankhead and Pearl Bailey. Amid the dancing, fanfares and one-liners, he emerged in a simple gabardine suit.

"And the presence of God was there," Ruth observed. "Right in the midst of all that fun & foolishness, . . . Bill sat and God was with him. . . . Oh, the consuming . . . ambition of the stage—and even when you reach the top, what do you have? Full lives and empty hearts."

She couldn't wait to escape the crowds, the flashbulbs. Whenever possible she would sequester herself in her hotel suite to read and meditate. Along with her Bible, she read Frank W. Boreham's essays and the recently published *Through Gates of Splendor,* written by Elisabeth Elliot, whose husband Jim was one of five missionaries murdered by the Auca Indians in Ecuador. "I have never been more deeply moved or challenged," she wrote at the time.

Her life had radically changed over the past fourteen years, changed in a way she could never have imagined in those early days

---

3. Ibid., pp. 36–37.

in Illinois. And yet her priorities had not wavered. They burned like a quiet inner flame; they coalesced into an untouchable energy, her quintessence. She had redefined her notion of her mission field. It was not Tibet—it was everywhere.

The moment they emerged from their room, they were hounded by journalists and television crews. Everywhere they turned, it seemed, someone was snapping their picture.

"After so much publicity you begin to feel exposed," she wrote May 13. "Every paper you pick up has a picture or a story—or both. And you feel a bit like a beetle under a stone when the stone's just been removed. Well, I was feeling very uncovered when I picked up my Bible and read, 'He shall cover thee with His feathers, and under His wings shalt thou trust.' I can't say what a comfortable thought that was. All I needed."

Journalists crowded into the BGEA team prayer meetings. They wandered through the crowds at night, hunting for celebrities to photograph. Ruth's annoyance with the press mounted when the "czar of the Los Angeles underworld," as Mickey Cohen was called, appeared in Manhattan. She had recently seen the tough-talking ex-convict on television, where he referred to gangsters and racketeers as "fine men," and law enforcement officers as "degenerates." She feared that he was attempting to re-establish himself in the underworld. She also suspected that his interest in the crusade was only a publicity stunt. Nonetheless, she hoped he would come to know Christ during the services, but she didn't see how that was possible when the press was between him and the pulpit.

She watched the assault the night of May 21 and her indignation peaked. Julie Nixon Eisenhower, at the service with her father, recalled it was the "angriest" she ever saw her. Sitting in the lower tier, just in front of Cohen, Ruth noticed an Associated Press photographer stalking the front row like a cat. Oblivious of the woman inches away from him, he squatted and focused his camera on Cohen. Smiling, Ruth blocked the lens with her songbook just as the shutter clicked. She shook her head at him like a mother reprimanding a naughty child.

"It's my job," the photographer explained when Ruth bumped into him after the service. "And I will do all I can to get the pictures."

"And it's our job to do all we can to stop you from getting them," she replied, again with a smile.

"So, at least we understand one another," he said as he walked away.

Moments later she met Cohen in Billy's stadium office. She had been praying for him since the 1949 Los Angeles crusade when his wiretapper Jim Vaus had accepted Christ and Billy had unsuccessfully urged Cohen to do likewise.

"We're praying for you," she said.

He smiled nervously, kissed her on the cheek and left.

"He has not given in to God—he would not that night," she recorded. "As he said goodbye, I felt like that verse in the Scriptures, 'He went out. And it was night.'"

While Billy Graham, "the fair-haired evangelist with that clean collar–ad look [was] fighting the toughest battle in his phenomenal career,"[4] as columnist Dorothy Kilgallen wrote, he was chosen Father of the Year in Religion. On May 23, he took time off from his usual fourteen-hour work day to escort Ruth to the awards dinner at the Waldorf Astoria. Guests included Ronald Reagan (who with his wife Nancy would one day invite them to the White House), the John Kellys (parents of Grace Kelly), Ed Sullivan, Charles and Mark Van Doren, and Mickey Mantle (who was wearily signing autographs without so much as glancing at his fans). When Billy rose to accept his award, he told the guests that it was his wife who deserved it, not he, because she had been both mother and father to their children.

After the dinner, Ruth returned to the hotel and discovered that the A.P. photographer she had confronted days earlier had left her a message. He wanted her to sit in the front row that night so he could take her picture. She sent him a message back.

"Yes I will, if you promise not to photograph any celebrities."

He never showed up.

Saturday, June 1, marked the beginning of Billy's television career. The month before, American Broadcasting Company executives had approached him with their idea of televising the services. Soon, seventeen broadcasts had been scheduled for the crusade—a modern miracle made possible by a $100,000 donation. Having ridden the

---

4. Dorothy Kilgallen, "D. Kilgallen Goes Behind the Scenes to Tell Life Story," *Los Angeles Herald Examiner*, 20 May 1957.

train back home for the week, Ruth and the Bells gathered before the television set, switching the channels past Jackie Gleason and Perry Como until Billy floated onto the grayish screen before them. He preached on John 3:16, his face pale, his gestures too energetic for the small box.

And yet, his words carried power, and as Ruth watched the hundreds of people stream forward, she was overwhelmed. "Thank God for the incomparable opportunities of preaching Christ these days," she wrote. "For men's willingness to listen. It may not be but for a time. But thank God for it! And may we all take advantage of every opportunity while the time lasts."

Six million people tuned in for the first broadcast, three times as many as had attended the sum of the crusades the year before. Ruth knew then that if television were to become his new pulpit, their lives would be laid bare before the world as never before. It was, however, but a small exchange for transformed lives. A Presbyterian minister, a Roman Catholic priest, a bartender, a Calypso dancer, a prostitute and one of her customers—all had made that walk through the Garden as a gesture of their desire to make peace with God. "One watches, lost in wonder, love and praise," Ruth wrote.

Joy and pain, blessings and bitterness; they are usually yoked together. The New York crusade was not exempt. By 1957 Billy had reached a point in his career where he was rapidly polarizing his fellow Americans. He was evolving into the most powerful religious figure of the century. That alone made him controversial, a target for criticism.

In a *Life* magazine article published during the crusade, Reinhold Niebuhr, prominent theologian and vice-president of Union Theological Seminary in New York, took the evangelist to task.

The success of mass evangelism, Niebuhr said, "depends upon oversimplifying every issue of life." Billy Graham's preaching, he added, "promised new life, not through painful religious experience but merely by signing a decision card. Thus, a miracle of regeneration is promised at a painless price by an obviously sincere evangelist. It is a bargain."

Niebuhr's first point was perhaps relevant—his next one is questionable. Though Billy Graham said his "present crusade is aimed at New York City," Niebuhr wrote, "relatively few New Yorkers attend the Graham meetings. The bulk of his nightly audience comes from out of town."[5] Had his assertion been correct—and it was not—one wonders if it really mattered whether the people trickling into Madison Square Garden were from New York City, Yonkers, or New Jersey. During the services following the July 1 article, members of the audience were asked to raise their hands if they lived in New York City. At least 80 percent of the people did.

Attacks also came from extreme liberals of various denominations who claimed that Billy's crusade was a sort of religious circus where the evangelist instead of the Holy Spirit was the ringmaster. Criticism also came from the extreme Fundamentalists who condemned Billy for cooperating with "Christ deniers, radicals and liberals," referring to the high-powered businessmen and clergy who made up the crusade's executive committee. The attacks upset Ruth. She ventilated her anger in a journal, then tore out the pages and burned them because "God would give me no peace of heart. We must leave them to Him. These men are, after all, God's anointed. May we like David refuse to lift our hand (or tongue) against them."

One of the most noted developments in Billy himself—one that was largely responsible for his losing some supporters and winning others—was his growing ecumenism. Nelson Bell was partly responsible for this change. Billy later claimed that he "never took a major step without asking [Nelson Bell's] counsel and advice." His influence, along with Billy's own experience as a minister, had given him a respect and understanding for different denominations. "Even though I was a Southern Baptist," he recalled, "I still had an 'independent' streak in me that came from my days at the Florida Bible Institute. Dr. Bell showed me that the strength of my future ministry would be in the church. He actually taught me to be a churchman."

Ironically, Billy's toleration for other denominations stopped just outside his front door. If someone else chose to be a Presbyterian or a Methodist, that was fine with him—as long as that someone wasn't his wife. For fourteen years he had listened to the badgering of his Baptist friends who thought it was mighty sorry if a man's wife wouldn't join his church. He tended to agree and had tried to tug Ruth away from the Presbyterian church more than once. But pulling her away from that tradition was like uprooting kudzu; no matter how much or how hard he yanked, it was always there, hearty and happy come rain or sun. The attacks were tenacious and clever, and

---

5. "Dedicated Deciders in Billy Graham Crusade," *Life*, vol. 43, no. 1 (1 July 1957), p. 92.

not all of them made by Billy. Once a Baptist friend appeared "for breakfast" and spent the morning proselytizing. After each battle, she remained steadfast and smiling with the maddening immutability of Mona Lisa. Finally realizing what he was up against, Billy jokingly announced that he would give a hundred dollars to whoever could make a Baptist out of her. (Though the reward would forever go uncollected, more than a few Baptists offered to split the money with her if she would allow them to immerse her.)

Not everyone appreciated the role Nelson Bell and his daughter Ruth were playing in Billy's life. In 1954, Dr. Bell and Billy had worked together to found the evangelical magazine *Christianity Today*. The magazine had a rather unusual beginning. One morning in 1954, after a sleepless night spent at his desk, Billy came downstairs and made an abrupt announcement to Ruth: "God has given me a vision," he said, "the plans for a new magazine which I am to call *Christianity Today*." The magazine, he continued, was necessary, for there was not an "intellectually respected magazine for evangelicals" in existence at the time. He immediately shared his idea with Dr. Bell and found to his amazement that Dr. Bell had been thinking about the same thing. Working side by side, the two men turned their dream into a reality. As Ruth recalled, "I watched and listened as my husband and my father talked and planned, marveling at the vision and wisdom God had given them, each one respecting the other, each one so beautifully balancing the other." With Dr. Bell as its executive editor, the magazine's first issues had begun circulating less than a year before the New York crusade.

To some observers, the organization was a dynasty, not a business; it was built of old and trusted friends who had banded together over the years. "The BGEA wasn't formed," Ruth often asserted, "it simply evolved"—much as a family evolves. Over the years, she would develop warm friendships with the wives of Billy's associates, including Mary Helen (Mrs. T. W.) Wilson, Wilma (Mrs. Grady) Wilson, Betty (Mrs. Lee) Fisher, Ethel (Mrs. Walter) Smyth, Helen (Mrs. George) Wilson, and Wanda (Mrs. Howard) Jones. "Though scattered around the world," Ruth noted, "we share a sense of family love and fellowship. There is mutual support, and any of us facing some difficulty is backed by the others' prayers. If one of our children strays, the prayers of not one but dozens of mothers will follow that child."

Jerry Beaven (who helped plan the early crusades, and who would resign from the BGEA in 1963) recalled that he resented Billy's treating Ruth and her father as his chief advisors. To him, it was rather like Jimmy Carter's asking Amy for advice. "It's no secret," Beaven said, "that I, in all my years, didn't agree always with their advice and didn't always feel they were the best people to advise him—advise him on anything." Ruth, he said, had grown up in China, then retreated to the sheltered world of Wheaton College, and had finally "retired" to the mountaintop in Montreat. Dr. Bell, meanwhile, had spent most of his life in China, "which is not exactly in the mainstream of the world's affairs. So I felt that those two were not the best ones to advise Billy on how to conduct his life, his ministry, his gradually growing world influence. I felt [theirs] was a very narrow view. There were times my advice didn't concur with theirs and Billy almost always took theirs. And, if you're very pragmatic and look at success, it must have worked. He's done pretty well."

On Saturday, June 15, Ruth returned to Montreat for several days and was greeted with the chilling news that her four children and a friend had plunged over the mountain in the Jeep. There were no serious injuries, just cuts, scratches, bruises, and one fractured arm. The Jeep was virtually demolished. The same day, however, there was a photograph in the local newspaper of a Thunderbird and a twenty-ton tractor-trailer that had collided in nearby Oteen. The car's three occupants had been killed. She couldn't help feeling as though her own family had been spared. "I had cold chills to think what might have happened," she wrote. "My heart was speechless with gratitude."

That same day, she found a note on her pillow telling her to telephone Darlene Tolliver: Joe Tolliver was dead. He had died alone, a hand groping toward the telephone as though he were trying to cry for help.

On Sunday, she drove to the Tolliver home to pay her respects to his family. The living room was small but well-kept; the casket was heavy and lustrous. She stood there, thinking about that day so many years ago when her husband had knelt on the floor beside Tolliver's bed, praying for him, leading him to Christ. Tolliver had won the war then, and lost every skirmish leading up to what he knew was to be his reward. It was a glory without honor.

At the small hillside cemetery, Bud Lominac lurched up the hill toward the church, his body twitching uncomfortably in his Sunday suit. Ruth moved up the grassy slope toward him and took his big, rough hand. Like the Thunderbird and her Jeep, she was again confronted with a fatality and a close call. Lominac had not changed his hard-drinking ways, and yet he had been spared Tolliver's fate. His turn might be next.

"God loves you wherever you are, Mr. Lominac," she told him with feeling. "Whatever happens to you, remember God *loves* you."

"Yes, ma'am, Miz Graham," he muttered, staring blankly past her. "How's Franklin?"

12

Home on the Mountain

"When God asks someone to do something for Him entailing sacrifice, He makes up for it in surprising ways. God has not let me down. Though He has led Bill all over the world to preach the gospel, He has not forgotten the little family in the mountains of North Carolina. I have watched with gratitude as God has guided each child."

Ruth Bell Graham

Beside the bedroom fireplace bordered in old blue and white Dutch tiles, the empty antique Windsor cradle waited. The wedding veil had disappeared long ago. On January 12, 1958, Ruth's fifth and last child was born. She named him Nelson Edman (or "Ned") after her father and Dr. V. Raymond Edman, former president of Wheaton College. In an eerie fulfillment of her dream of being a "pioneer missionary alone," she found she was virtually alone in the large responsibility of raising five children. She would have to be both mother and father.

As a wife, Ruth was no longer the young bride whose feelings were easily hurt. She had learned to laugh at almost everything, as illustrated by this example of how she dealt with Billy's chronic preoccupation:

One day the Grahams were expecting guests for dinner and Ruth asked Billy, "What would you like to have on the menu?"

"Uh-huh," came the reply.

Deciding to have some fun, Ruth began rattling off a rather unusual bill of fare.

"I thought we'd start off with tadpole soup," she began.

"Uh-huh," he replied.

"And there is some lovely poison ivy growing in the next cove which would make a delightful salad."

"Uh-huh."

"For the main dish, I could try roasting some of those wharf rats we've been seeing around the smokehouse lately, and serve them with boiled crabgrass and baked birdseed."

"Uh-huh."

"And for dessert we could have a mud souffle and . . ." her voice trailed off as his eyes finally focused.

"What were you saying about wharf rats?" he asked.[1]

No longer was Ruth the young bride who was quick to give an opinion she knew would irritate her husband. She had learned long ago: When she indeed knew what was best for him, there were better, more diplomatic ways, to make her point. She became adept at making him think her ideas were his own; she would make a suggestion, which was, unsurprisingly, generally greeted with "Uh-huh." Then, after a sufficient time lapse she would say, "I think your idea about such and such is a grand one." And he would look at her with a bemused expression, not sure he recalled being the author of the plan.

As a mother, she was less subtle. And perhaps it was poetic justice that the children, too, found ways around her.

She began modeling her home after the familiar—the nest she had known in her childhood China. She attempted to train the children as she had been trained, playing many of the same games with them, emphasizing the same values. Her childhood home and the one she was establishing for her family in Montreat had interesting similarities. First, the Bells were less than two miles away, and Ruth saw them daily when she wasn't traveling. To the children Nelson Bell was an attentive, caring grandfather who advised and sometimes disciplined them while their father was away. Second, Montreat was a Presbyterian oasis consisting substantially of retired and furloughed missionaries, retired and itinerant ministers, and people who simply wished to live in a secure, peaceful environment. With the exception of some of the students at Montreat-Anderson, the small junior col-

---

1. Ruth Bell Graham, *It's My Turn* (Old Tappan, New Jersey: Fleming Revell, 1982), p. 67.

lege clustered around Lake Susan, most Montreaters were genteel Southern Presbyterians. Montreat had a zero crime rate, according to North Carolina annual crime statistics. And there was only one town drunk that anybody knew of.

Montreat was a comfortable, happy pocket in this kingdom of mountain folk and vacationing flatlanders. It was untainted, like the icy creek water sluicing through the foothills, beaten clean by mica-flecked stream beds. It was as simple and pure in its Christian faith as the mayor's starched white shirt; and yet it was as casual and warm as the old suede shoes worn by the minister.

In the beginning Ruth would rely on the child-rearing principles her missionary parents had relied on, and she assumed the results would be the same. But the considerable differences between the two environments were to render Ruth's tactics somewhat ineffective. In China, much that wasn't Christian was blatantly evil, if not repulsive. But in the world now surrounding her home, sin was rather more difficult to recognize—indeed, it was often attractive. Neither the Montreat gate nor Ruth could completely shield her children from its enticements.

There were times when she felt the bite of frustration. With the exception of the usual childish spats, her childhood home in Tsing-kiang had been a happy, peaceful one, as she recalled. Her new home, in contrast, was unsettled. The children bickered and pecked at each other like roosters. "We can lick this evil," she wrote in 1959. "With His help we *will*. A happy, well-disciplined, well-ordered, loving home is our spiritual right." The problem was that she was too new in the battle to realize the differences between her childhood home in China and her home in Montreat. Perhaps the only way she could have ensured that her children would be as sweet and fearfully well behaved as she had been would have been to release rats and scorpions in their bedrooms, let a horde of knife-wielding bandits loose in the woods and have Japanese bombers drone over the roof day and night. As it was, the flying squirrels and hoot owls offered little diversion for their mischievous minds.

During Ruth's early childhood, she rarely went a day without seeing her parents. The dangers and hardships indigenous to the China mission field served to draw the family closer together. In Montreat, Billy's long and frequent absences, combined with the violation of privacy, might have fragmented the family. A more implicit danger was that Billy's absences and preoccupations could have made Ruth insecure and unhappy. Had that been the case, she would have inevitably passed her misery on to her children, particularly her daughters. She could easily have become resentful and demanding, evolving into a selfish, brittle woman whose love for her children was conditional.

Had her mother become demanding, Anne surmised, "It would have been very difficult to be her daughter because you can't live up to her." As it was, Ruth was not competitive, nor did she attempt to live vicariously through them or to use them as weapons. She made each one feel special; she respected each one's individual rights; she seemed to consider herself their guardian, not their owner. "Each child has to be dealt with differently," she recalled telling herself. "When in a quandary as to how to deal with one of the children, the thought always came to mind, 'How has God dealt with me?'"

As a mother her *modus operandi* was not much different from a missionary's. Her top priority was to mold her children into Christian soldiers. She was not content with just reading them Bible stories and including them in bedtime prayers. She actively and persistently evangelized them just as she might have evangelized the Tibetans. This method would certainly not work for everybody; a tyrannical, hypocritical, or unjust mother might have turned the children against God as well as herself. But there would be a happy ending in this story because God, she believed, was working on her just as hard as she was working on them. In her journals she often reminded herself of George MacDonald's warning that the quickest way to make someone bad is to try to make that person good. She could, she later discovered, only change herself and become an example instead of a judge. Thus, the focus of her personal life became the old roll-top desk in her bedroom. On it were numerous translations of the Bible, concordances, devotional books, notepads, and mugs of felt-tip pens. It was here that she came from time to time throughout each day, cup of coffee in hand, to sit down and "indulge herself in the Lord"; it was here she came to remind herself, as she would so often say, of her "reference point."

Prior to the mid-fifties she had been able to help her husband by traveling with him whenever possible. From time to time, she brought the children along, but she usually left them with the Bells. After the 1954 Harringay crusade she realized she could not afford to stay away from the children for long stretches. Leaving them occasionally was inevitable. Leaving them for substantial periods of time was unwise. When she returned from London in the late spring of 1954 she found a resentful Franklin and an even more insecure, and thus unmanageable, GiGi.

Sunday, June 14, was typical:

That afternoon she gathered GiGi, Anne, and Bunny into the Jeep and drove them up to the cabin below the then unfinished house. They sunned, read, picked cherries, hunted turtles. Then GiGi and Anne performed skits based on nursery rhymes. Ruth hung a blue and white bedspread from the loft for the curtain. She and Bunny were the audience.

When Anne began acting out "Little Miss Muffet" GiGi climbed a ladder, ostensibly to drop the "spider" beside her. The spider turned out to be a lump of manure. GiGi hurled it with the cheek of a mockingbird dive-bombing a squirrel.

"It's the only thing I could find that was brown and we could pretend was a spider," GiGi explained as her mother scrubbed a teary Anne.

One unfortunate scene led to another, and Ruth ended GiGi's tantrum with a spanking.

After a supper of hot dogs roasted over the fire she read the children a Bible story and GiGi began asking questions.

"Mommy," she asked, "if I die, will I go to Heaven?"

"You tell me," she replied.

"I don't know."

"Want me to tell you how you can know?" Ruth asked.

"I don't think you can know for sure."

"I do," Ruth said.

"O.K., how?"

"First," she explained, "you know you are a sinner, don't you?"

"Oh, I *know* that," GiGi assured her enthusiastically.

"Then you confess your sins to Him," Ruth said.

"I do that. You know when I got so mad at you this afternoon I told Him I was sorry three times just to make sure, in case He didn't hear me the first time."

"He heard you the first time," Ruth said. "Listen, 'If we confess our sins, He is faithful and just to forgive us our sins and cleanse us from all unrighteousness' (1 John 1:9)."

"Are you sure He heard me?"

"I know He did," Ruth said.

"But it doesn't say 'GiGi.'"

"It says '*whosoever*,'" Ruth said.

GiGi said nothing and her mother continued. "Now you have done the first two. You have become a child of God. You are born into God's family, just as eight years ago you were born into our family. Your body was born then, your soul is born again now."

"But I still am not sure," GiGi said.

"GiGi, would you call God a liar?"

"Of course not!"

"But you are. He said if you confess He will forgive; if you believe, you have eternal life. You have done both, but you don't think He will keep His promise. That is the same as calling Him a liar."

Ruth held up a piece of paper and said, "Whoever wants it can have it."

GiGi snatched it from her fingers.

"What makes you think I said you?" Ruth demanded.

"You said 'whoever,'" she replied.

"Exactly."

They knelt beside the cabin's bed and prayed.

"Mommy," GiGi said breathlessly as they drove away, "I feel like a new person."

The next day, this "new person" scampered down Assembly Drive to the Montreat gate and uprooted a dozen water lilies that had just been planted in time for the arrival of the season's first tourists and conferees. Ruth escorted her to the town manager's office with the evidence wilting in her tight little fist, her face pale as she worried aloud that she was going to be thrown into jail (her mother saying nothing to dispel the fear). She confessed and apologized.

That night as Ruth tucked her into bed she asked plaintively, "Mommy, have I been good enough today to go to Heaven?"

"Now how much," Ruth wrote that night, "should I impress on her Salvation by Grace when really for a child of her disposition one could be tempted to think salvation by works would be more effective on her behavior?"

The training of the Graham children began early in more ways than one. First, whenever possible, each day was begun with a Bible lesson at the breakfast table. Second, it was Ruth's hope that her children would accept Christ at a very young age. Third, schooling at private Christian institutions began before the children had reached their teens. GiGi was sent to a boarding school in Florida when she was twelve. Though she had been eager to taste independence, the results were mixed. Leaving home so young added to her insecurity, she would later claim. "I was scared," she recalled. And she missed her family far more than she ever had imagined. But in retrospect, just as Ruth's leaving home at age thirteen had prepared her for "a lifetime of goodbyes," as she put it, so GiGi's leaving home at age twelve would prepare her for marrying and moving to Europe at the tender age of seventeen.

The foundation for Ruth's method of child-rearing was, not surprisingly, the Bible. During childhood she had been taught to love it and respect its authority. She read it to be corrected, informed, and inspired. She studied it, drawing from it ideas like this one: "Because sentence against an evil work is not executed speedily, therefore the heart of the sons of men is fully set in them to do evil" (Ecclesiastes 8:11). From that verse Ruth determined that "punishment, when needed, should be prompt."

Of necessity, she was, in the main, the sole disciplinarian in the family. Had she made a habit of threatening, "Wait until your father gets home," her children would have dreaded his return. And Billy would not have looked forward to coming home and meting out punishment for crimes he had not witnessed. She had a catalogue of punishments for different offenses: first fight—ten minutes in room; second fight—fifteen minutes in room; sassing and rudeness—switching with a shoe tree or flyswatter; procrastinating going to bed— earlier to bed the following night. Often, her chastisements were more humorous than severe. Occasionally, GiGi recalls, when two of the children had had a spat, Ruth would sit them together nose-to- nose until they kissed and made up. Franklin recalls the time when he was being insufferable while his mother was driving the children to a fast-food restaurant in Asheville. She finally stopped the car and locked him in the well-ventilated trunk.[2]

"Don't worry," she cheerfully assured the startled carhop who appeared just as the trunk yawned open. "He enjoyed it."

"I'll have a cheeseburger without the meat," Franklin ordered with a grin as he dusted his jeans.

Another Bible verse she implemented in her child rearing was: "Feed the flock of God which is among you, taking the oversight thereof. . . . Neither as being lords over God's heritage, but being

---

2. Though Ruth thoroughly enjoys retelling this story, she does not recommend that other mothers begin sending their children *to the trunks* instead of *to their rooms.*

examples to the flock" (I Peter 5:2–3). From this verse she determined that being a disciplinarian wasn't enough: She also had to be an example. The more she corrected and shaped her children the more convinced she was of what she viewed as her own flaws: "The children misbehave," she wrote, "I reprimand them sharply—more probably peevishly. The very tone of voice irritates them (I know because if it were used on me it would irritate me). They answer back—probably in the same tone. I turn on them savagely (I hate to think how often! And how savage a loving mother can be at times). And I snap 'Don't you speak to your mother like that. It isn't respectful.' Nothing about me—actions, tone of voice, etc.—commanded respect. It doesn't mean I am to tolerate sass or back-talk. But then I must be very careful not to inspire it either."

While Ruth was criticizing herself in her journals, she was, perhaps without realizing it, changing and maturing as much as her children were. She was beginning to rely more on her own instincts and imagination; she was becoming more flexible, more confident. She never discarded the principles once implemented in her childhood home; she simply began modifying the methods to fit the needs.

The changes began in small ways. When Ruth was a child, the Sabbath had been a fun, but reverent, day of making candy, singing around the coal fire, and playing Bible games. One sunny Sunday afternoon in the early sixties, Virginia Bell drove to her daughter's house unannounced and was horrified to find Ruth and the children frolicking in the swimming pool. Shortly after GiGi had left for boarding school she wrote that she had fallen in love. Ruth kept her concern to herself and did not resort to lectures or clandestine meddling. Later, when Anne entered her teens, she bleached her hair and began wearing makeup. She began modeling for several of Asheville's finer clothing stores. Ruth granted her freedom. "These weren't moral issues," Anne recalled. "Mother totally trusted me and encouraged me and loved me. Therefore I was always the person she thought I was. She used to say, 'If you trust a person they'll live up to your trust.'"

Ruth even implemented rules from a dog-training magazine she subscribed to:

1. Keep commandments simple and at a minimum. One word to a command and always the same word. Come. Sit. Stay. Heel. Down. No. Etc. Etc. (I talk my children dizzy.)
2. Never give a command without seeing it is obeyed.
3. Be consistent.

4. When the dog responds correctly—praise him. Not with food. (And also don't reward the children materially. Your praise should be enough.)

A true mother, she recorded, "is not merely a provider, housekeeper, comforter, or companion. A true mother is primarily and essentially a trainer."

And yet the fighting, the disobedience, and the rebelliousness—typical of most families—continued. At least, they were not the saints some of the neighbors thought "Billy Graham's kids" ought to be—an expectation which alone was enough to turn any normal child into a rascal. Then, in the middle of this day-to-day turbulence, a quietus would be ushered in by the preacher himself. Billy would come home and peacefulness, like the calm before a thunderstorm, would settle over the mountaintop.

The scene in the early years was always the same: Ruth and the children forming a happy knot on the vibrating wooden depot platform, watching the glassy ribbon of train windows flow by while they waited, hearts racing, in the damp mountain air. Then Billy, his rumpled suit hanging more loosely than it had when he was last home, would emerge, his face beaming but weary. In his suitcases there were certain to be stuffed animals or dolls and toy cars.

Suddenly the world on the mountaintop would change. The children would temporarily lose interest in their neighborhood playmates, and they were better behaved because they were excited. They also knew that their father wouldn't tolerate impertinence or disobedience. Even so, his spankings were rare. GiGi can recall but two, the last one being most memorable: She sassed him, stomped her foot, slammed her bedroom door, and locked it. After she finally let him in and he had commenced swatting her, she blurted, "Some father you are! You go away and leave us alone all the time ..." Suddenly he stopped, his eyes filling with tears. "It just broke my heart," GiGi recalled. "I'll never forget that because I realized that this was a sacrifice he was making."

In the main, discipline was rather much forgotten when Billy was home. "Daddy would come home from a trip and break all the rules," GiGi said.

"Oh, let them stay up a little later," he'd say to Ruth when it was time to turn the television off and tuck the children in bed. "I hardly get to see them." He'd give them candy, gum, and soda pop during the week when he knew the rule was that they were only to be indulged on Sundays. And when the five young faces looked up to Ruth after their father had just granted them permission to break her rules, she would say with a smile, "Whatever your Daddy says is fine with me."

When he was home he conducted family devotions and told the children stories and played games with them, especially at bedtime, when he'd imitate a spider and creep through the house while the children scattered and screamed in delight. He was affectionate, frequently stopping them in the hallway to hug or kiss them, or perhaps sneak them away for a hike on the mountain. It delighted them when he and Ruth would "smooch," as the children called it. He was boyishly demonstrative, sometimes whisking Ruth away from the stove to waltz her around the kitchen; throughout the day he held her hand or sat her in his lap, the two of them laughing and teasing like highschool sweethearts. "His love and tenderness toward her were something we daughters looked for in our husbands," Bunny remarked.

His presence, however, did not ensure his undivided attention. Sometimes he would sleep through his first two days at home. "It's like being in a hurricane," he once explained, "and all of a sudden it stops and there is nothing but quietness." He would confide in Ruth, telling her details of his life that she had not been on hand to witness, voicing his joys, plans, and discouragements. Though she had worries of her own, she kept them to herself; sensitive to his needs, she listened, encouraged, and soothed, for even evangelists have their moments of anxiety and doubt. One evening as they sat on the porch watching the setting sun light the thunderclouds piling over Rainbow Mountain, he began fretting aloud.

"God has never failed you yet has He?" Ruth asked.

"No," he replied thoughtfully, "but He's come pretty close to it sometimes!"

Nor did business stop just because he was home. He had scores of daily telephone calls and letters to attend to. Television crews and journalists would arrive for their "thirty-minute" sessions, which characteristically stretched into half-day marathons with Ruth hanging nearby, smiling, appearing calm, as she listened in. But despite her cool, gracious façade, her hands trembled as she carried in the coffee or brought her husband a Coca-Cola. Like a she-bear she was poised to attack, ready to protect what was hers from what she viewed as the occasional irresponsibility of the press.

The children also had to share their father with the inevitable tourists. In the late fifties and early sixties, anyone could and often did amble up the mountain. One Sunday morning Ruth took the children to church while Billy stayed home and rested. He decided to surprise the family with a picnic lunch. Never much of a gourmet (when he fended for himself it meant canned tomatoes, Vienna sausages, or a can of cold baked beans), he met them on the driveway with seven peanut butter and jelly sandwiches and an unopened can of pork and beans. Just as they were settling down to eat, a jalopy full of admirers chugged up the mountain, past the Private Property signs, steam pouring out from underneath the hood as it overheated in front of the swimming pool.

Billy sauntered over and inquired if he could help them with their car troubles. Then, magnanimously, he added, "Come on up and share our picnic lunch. There's plenty of food for everyone."

The children looked anxiously at Ruth, who assured them with an uncertain whisper, "Sharing always makes a picnic more fun."

Staring at this legendary evangelist with unabashed awe, the tourists sheepishly refused and rolled their steaming heap back down the mountain.[3]

There were the unwelcome visitors who bore special messages from God, or worse yet, thought they themselves were God. When Ruth was pregnant with Ned, her housekeeper Beatrice Long entered the living room one day, characteristically planting one foot slowly in front of the other, as though there was not one thing on God's earth worth hurrying for: "Miz Graham, there's a man at the door who says he's Jesus Christ and Mr. Graham is 'specting him."

Ruth went to the door and found a heavy, perspiring man who immediately repeated his claim.

"You are not Jesus Christ," she told him firmly, "and my husband is not expecting you."

An argument ensued and the man announced he *was* coming in.

"You are *not*. And besides," she unwisely added, "you must remember, after the resurrection, Jesus didn't knock on doors, he walked through them."

With that remark the man paused, lifting his eyes heavenward for instruction. Ruth grabbed the opportunity, quickly shut the door, and

---

3. Chris Jarrett Kyle, letter to Ruth Bell Graham, 1982, Ruth Bell Graham Papers, Montreat, North Carolina.

latched it. He drove his green Chrysler New Yorker to Assembly Inn on Lake Susan and told the desk clerk his story. "My only mistake," he concluded, "was I knocked on the door instead of walking through it."

"Don't you realize," the clerk responded, "Jesus made no mistakes?"

The man then announced the end of the world was at hand, tossed his wallet and wristwatch into the lake and rolled his car in after them.

Ruth had other such encounters, and each time she handled them deftly, doing so whether her husband was away or in his study, oblivious to what was happening. "Before they put that gate up," recalled Beatrice Long, "cars would come up there every day and pretend they were lost. Some of them would wander around the yard hoping someone would come out and speak. Sometimes she'd go out. Sometimes she wouldn't. She was never rude. She was nice and kind to them but they never did see him. He wouldn't know what was going on." It was best he didn't know what was going on—he might invite them in for lunch.

In the sixties, a man toting a large Bible appeared at the Billy Graham office in Montreat. The man bore a message from God, he claimed. He wasn't leaving until he'd delivered it. After he had camped in front of the office for three days, a secretary telephoned Billy, informed him of the situation, and asked him what should be done. In a blink, he was down the mountain, shirtless, sitting on a tree stump in the sun. All afternoon he patiently listened as the man prophesied. When he was finished with his message, Billy shook his hand and thanked him. That scene would have been common had Ruth, who possessed the slyness and discretion of an Oriental majordomo, not intervened.

All too quickly the peaceful interlude would end as Billy piled his hastily packed baggage into the car trunk and left for either the train station or the airport. Often one of his aides would pick him up and whisk him away, the throaty roar of the automobile fading as it descended the perilous drive. As his fame grew it became futile for the family to say good-bye to him in public because he was usually inundated with dozens of admirers who wanted his autograph or just wished to shake his hand. Once Anne accompanied him to the airport and was immediately washed to the background when a sea of well-wishers flooded her father. After rapidly shaking one hand after another, he finally turned to his daughter, shyly standing behind him. Pumping her hand, he blurted, "Nice to meet you!" before bolting toward his gate.

When it was time to say good-bye neither Ruth nor Billy displayed emotion. There was the tight hug and kiss. But in private, their individual reactions were quite different. "Many a time," Billy said, "I've driven down that driveway with tears coming down my cheeks, not wanting to leave." No matter what part of the world he was in, whenever possible he would telephone Ruth every night. His feelings were best expressed in a letter he wrote her from Los Angeles on August 11, 1963, two days before their twentieth wedding anniversary:

> How can I find words to express my appreciation for all you have meant to me. Your love and patience with me in my ups and downs . . . have meant more to me than you will ever know. Your counsel, advice, encouragement and prayer have been my mainstay—and at times I have almost clung to you in my weakness, in hours of obsession, problems and difficulties. "Whoso findeth a wife findeth a good thing, and obtaineth favor of the Lord." One reason that in spite of my own lack of spirituality, discipline and consecration I have found favor of the Lord is *because of you.* I found a good wife and as a result have found favor with God. . . . It seems that in the recent months my capacity to love you has been increased—I did not think that age would bring greater and deeper love—but it has and is. I *love* the wife of my youth *more* every day! When we are apart, I miss you so much more than I used to. A week seems like a month. Yes, I am thankful to God for you. What a wonderful helpmeet He provided—certainly our marriage was planned in heaven. I am thankful for the five precious children you bore me—each one a bundle of joy. And what a wonderful mother you have been to them! No child ever had a greater mother than our children. You may compare yourself to Susanna Wesley and think you are a failure—but she did not rear her family in a modern, secular society. For our generation you are near perfection.

Ruth's emotions were revealed in her poetry:

> We live a time
>   secure;
>   sure
>   It cannot last
>   for long
>   then—
>   the goodbyes come

again—again—
like a small death,
the closing of a door.
One learns to live
with pain.
One looks ahead,
not back,
. . . never back,
only before.
And joy will come again
warm and secure,
if only for the now,
laughing,
we endure.[4]

On rare occasions her feelings spilled out in front of close friends, such as actress Joan Winmill Brown, who was visiting her while Billy was out of the country on a long campaign: One morning, Ruth received a letter from a missionary acquaintance whom she had not seen in years. Joan later recalled what it said: "Oh, I guess you don't remember me, Ruth, now that you're married to such a famous evangelist. It must be a very glamorous life. Here I am stuck in the mission field with my husband." "Well, at least she's with him," Ruth said, her eyes filling with tears as she quickly left the room.

"Maybe she cried in her room," GiGi speculated, "but we did not know it at all. When Daddy would leave she would get busy doing something. We'd have projects—like hunting for antiques—and we'd right then begin looking forward to his coming home." After he was gone and his physical presence was little more than a memory, Billy would once again become the figure they saw more of on television than in person. He was the authority figure who was no longer there to punish. Once while Billy was gone, his secretary entered the kitchen and discovered Franklin playing with matches.

"Franklin," she said sternly, "you *know* your Daddy told you not to play with matches!"

"No he didn't," Franklin countered. "He told me not to let him catch me playing with matches. And I'm not going to let him catch me."[5]

---

4. Ruth Bell Graham, *sitting by my laughing fire* . . . (Waco, Texas: Word Books, 1977), p. 153.
5. Chris Jarrett Kyle, letter to Ruth Bell Graham, 1982, Ruth Bell Graham Papers, Montreat, North Carolina.

He was the husband who was gone an average of six months of each year. By all rights, Ruth should have evolved into that resentful, brittle woman. But she didn't. Anne, who stayed home during high school and thus saw her mother the most, discovered why that sad transformation never occurred. A sensitive, pensive girl, Anne would climb into her mother's bed to talk each night. After a kiss and a hug she would then retreat upstairs to her own room. And no matter how late it was when she finally began drifting off to sleep, she could see her mother's light shining on the trees at the rim of the yard. In the early mornings, the story was the same. "She'd be studying her Bible. And if I entered her room at these times and found her on her knees, there was no use saying anything to her then because she wouldn't hear me. That's how Mother coped with Daddy's being gone so much."

13

The Beginning
of a Mission

I am grateful not even one little sparrow falls to the ground
but what He knows—and understands. This is our
opportunity to explain to the world.

Ruth Bell Graham, 1966

On a ridge between the Red and Sulphur rivers, a hundred miles northeast of Dallas and just south of Oklahoma, stood a two-room log cabin on a small patch of weather-beaten dirt. It was Lamar County, near Paris, Texas, August 15, 1930, and the heat slammed down like a hammer as Mae Thielman gave birth to her second set of twins. She named the youngest of her seven children Calvin Coolidge and Malvin Joe.

For the next thirty-two years Calvin Thielman and Ruth Graham would move in their separate orbits and then connect in an obscure indentation in the Blue Ridge called Montreat. They would become partners in their personal warfare against the poverty, pain, and loneliness they had witnessed in their childhoods and seemed from then on to discover in every pocket of the world.

The cabin rested on a small cotton farm run by Calvin's father, Charlie, an alcoholic who became abusive during his debauches. He died when young Calvin was fourteen months old, leaving Mae to chop cotton and later work in a factory, eking out a bare survival for herself and her children. She was a devout Presbyterian who wanted more than anything else to instill a love of God and learning in her children. With Calvin, she succeeded in doing both. By the time he graduated from West Texas University, he was a respected student and athlete, headed for a career in law until he felt the unmistakable call to the ministry.

In 1952, he and his wife, a petite blonde named Dorothy Barnette, moved to Columbia Seminary in Decatur, Georgia. There Calvin became friends with Billy Graham's brother-in-law Leighton Ford and Ruth's brother Clayton. Through them he became well acquainted with the Grahams and the Bells. In 1961, he was hired to fill the double post of Montreat-Anderson College chaplain and minister of the Presbyterian church, which sat on the top of a hill at the hub of the school's raw fieldstone plant. The grounds, which in the summer bustled with conferees and flatlanders escaping the heat, had changed little since that waning afternoon almost twenty years earlier when Ruth Bell and Billy Graham had been married there. She had attended it regularly since. Shortly after he was hired, Calvin gave her charge of the college Sunday school class, consisting almost exclusively of Montreat-Anderson students.

From the beginning her class was popular. A gifted teacher, she was adept at sensing the mood of the group and responding impulsively with her blend of homespun logic, candor, and humor. Like an athletic coach she stirred the students until they rallied to her causes, which included holding street meetings, helping the poor, and distributing hundreds of large, bright yellow DON'T MISS CALVIN buttons throughout the campus when church attendance had dropped.

Hers was no mean task. The small college was not immune to the rebellion and hostility that had infected the people of the so-called generation gap. In fact, since Montreat-Anderson College was known as the place "where you go if you can't go anywhere else," a sizeable band of society's rebels, along with those afflicted by academic indolence, landed there. Ruth, Calvin said, "never paid any attention to the generation gap. For her, it didn't exist. She was not shocked by anyone's hair to his knees or clothes. I can remember some people that were very physically unattractive or terrible misfits that other people would not like, would not want to be around and would not work with. And yet, she would take time with these people and show them kindness."

One day Calvin said to her, "Don't you think you could more profitably put your time on some other people where you could get more mileage?"

"Well, God loves these people too," she replied. "Just because they're unattractive or warped in their thinking doesn't mean the Lord doesn't love them. And if we don't take them, who is going to take them?"

It was as though the Tsingkiang mission station had been relocated in Montreat. The new minister rooted out the needs and then telephoned Ruth.

"I sometimes feel guilty for calling her so much," he later admitted as he sat in his small, paneled church office. Autographed portraits of astronauts, baseball players, and LBJ were propped on the crowded bookshelves around his cluttered desk. He was typically dressed in a shapeless sweater, baggy Levis, and Wallabees. An unruly shock of graying hair fell over his brow. "But I've always got kids who have medical payments to be made, who are about to flunk out or don't get their grades because they can't make their final payment. And she has always assisted. . . . She's very generous with other people, but not with herself." He would later speculate that she had helped "hundreds" of people through college.

When Calvin wasn't telephoning Ruth, he was calling on her father. Dr. Bell had retired from a successful surgical practice in 1955, respected not only for his professionalism but for his humanity. He was said to have charged the poor only what they could pay, or nothing at all, just as he had done in Tsingkiang. Observers speculated that he gave away at least a third of his gross income. His load had not lightened upon leaving the mission field. As a doctor, he had been on call at night; as a prominent Presbyterian layman, he was often out of town. Sometimes he worked around the clock while his wife sat up anxiously, crocheting or reading, until fatigue or one of her headaches drove her to bed.

Though Virginia Bell began her daily diary entries with "head," "no head," or "terrible head," she rarely mentioned her pain to anyone.

Likewise, Ruth was stoical—so much so that she rarely even admitted in her journals that she was ill.

"You never really see her down or depressed," Calvin said, "or if she is, she covers it in such a way that you don't know it. I've seen her when she's had migraine headaches that were so severe that she was almost unable to see how to walk and yet she wouldn't complain. I'd say, 'Do you have a headache?' because she was glassy-eyed and it was evident the light hurt her eyes and she was really in pain. She would brush it aside with the comment that it didn't amount to anything. The only time I've known her to hide out is when she gets one of those severe headaches. She's been plagued with them and she never made a to-do over them at all. And she always works very hard at beating the schedule of getting well."

In fact, Ruth was a medical frustration: though she was a cheerful, cooperative stoic while in the hospital or clinic, she was quite another sort of patient at home. She treated her ailments whimsically, indulging in unsavory health foods ranging from buttermilk with a twist of lemon to blackstrap molasses over toast—the latter had all the appeal of bread dipped into a bucket of tar. She derived infinite delight from offering these odious creations to houseguests.

She experimented with different types of analgesics; she swallowed a variety of obscure vitamins, lecithin and alfalfa, conveniently storing the tablets in empty lipstick tubes which she carried in her pocket or purse.

If a doctor ordered her to stay in bed for two weeks and do "absolutely nothing," her notion of compliance was to putter about the house in a flowing robe and do all the chores she normally did. "What the doctors don't know won't hurt them," she often chirped. That attitude prevailed in most of her dealings with people. She avoided confrontations, gently if not humorously contradicting only once, her words wafting on the current of her mellow Virginia accent. If her antagonist of the moment remained obstinate, Ruth would simply smile and say no more. What she would do next, no one could predict, for she was as quietly stubborn as the sphinx and just about as inscrutable.

In the main, her stubbornness was not born of self-interest. Rather, it was part of her determination to keep on course, to carry on with her duties no matter how she felt or who or what was interfering. She had observed the missionaries' self-sacrifice and tenacity in China and she expected no less from herself. Like the missionaries, she enjoyed an extraterritoriality of sorts, for she was not always guided by the standards of the society she lived in. Her sense of justice was bigger than the law, which in her mind wasn't always moral. And she didn't necessarily do the practical or the expected. She followed her own impulses—signals transmitted by her faith in God, her tenderheartedness and her eccentricities.

The result was an unpredictable, disorganized, baffling human being, far more loving than legalistic. She had an unusual live-and-let-live attitude toward nature, allowing such harmless intruders as bats, cobwebs, flying squirrels, goats, nonpoisonous snakes, or perhaps a runaway turkey, to inhabit her homestead with impunity. Indeed, creatures, like children, seemed strangely drawn to her: A guest marveled one morning when a tiger swallowtail alighted on Ruth's shoulder and rested there a good minute before floating away; hummingbirds sometimes watched her eye to eye as she planted geraniums; flying squirrels carried Christmas yarns from the attic and built nests in old Jeep tires; field mice hid birdseed in her shoes. Once a train of ducklings followed her from a lakeshore, across a lawn, and through the front door of a nearby house.

She was spontaneous, impulsive, and delightfully uninhibited: Once she entered a shop in the Atlantic airport and requested one of the psychedelic packages of rolling papers behind the counter.

"These are great to write notes on and stick in your Bible," she cheerfully explained to the clerk.

"Oh yeah," the young woman sarcastically drawled.

A practical joker, she was not above squirting Grady Wilson's new pastel suit with disappearing ink or sneaking a slice of rubber swiss cheese into his sandwich. Once, when she cooked beef bouillon with tiny meatballs for lunch, she placed a bowl of tinted water and live tadpoles in front of associate Lee Fisher. He didn't notice anything odd until he dipped for a meatball and it swam away from his spoon. Once she served a guest a slice of pie covered with shaving cream. On another memorable day, she left a dead black snake inside a bag outside a friend's kitchen door and then hid behind a tree to watch her open it.

Her life, like her dresser drawers and closets, was dominated by clutter. It was common for her to have twenty or thirty books scattered around the house, each in the process of being read. She might devour a volume from beginning to end or she might abandon it after the first twenty pages if it bored her. Finishing a book just because she had started it, she once said, "was like going into the pantry and thinking you had to eat all the peas before you could open anything else."

Though she eventually had a bona fide office upstairs, complete with a desk, library, and disarray of knickknacks, her "office" was wherever she was. Often, particularly when she was weary, she worked on her bed, propped up amid her jumbled projects. When she traveled, the clutter traveled with her like iron filings after a magnet and relocated wherever her next bed was. The dining room table also made a fine desk, and on it one might find a heap of maps, scrapbooks, and photographs. And wherever she had been there was a trail of notes, written in her unique calligraphy on snippets of white or yellow paper. These included grocery lists, reminders, telephone numbers, spiritual insights, sermon ideas and illustrations, quotations that she found particularly amusing or profound (perhaps from the caretaker or children), and ideas for improving the house. They might be on a cupboard door, next to a telephone, inside a book, under bed covers, in her Bible, on a table, taped to a car visor or wall, or perched on a log in a cold fireplace. (One can well imagine her delight in later years at the invention of self-stick notepaper.)

Her proclivity for disorganization wasn't helped by her reluctance to throw anything away. Most of her memorabilia—including ticket stubs, dried wedding bouquets, her wedding dress and letters—eventually migrated to the attic. Billy was just the opposite. Often after he left home Ruth would rummage through the trash to retrieve items (like his college diploma and a hundred-dollar check) that had been buried in the things he had haphazardly dumped into his wastepaper basket.

Like the whimsical notes to herself and the partially read books scattered throughout her house, her life was full of projects and "unfinished" people—not only her children, but her neighbors and the young men and women in her Sunday school class. She opened her door to all of them, often inviting into her living room the sorts of people her neighbors would have feared to let into their yards. Had she ever kept a guest book, it would have held the names of drug addicts, thieves, the mentally unsound, and juvenile delinquents from the local detention center who had committed crimes ranging from vandalism to murder. Occasionally, she would invite people like former street fighter Nicky Cruz or South American evangelist Luis Palau to talk with them. And she would buy pizzas, barrels of fried chicken, or bags of hamburgers for her scarred, skeptical acquaintances, feed them and challenge them with the Christian faith.

Because of her own ministry, she was able to keep her husband in touch with students. Not only would she occasionally coax him to speak at the college and small community gatherings, but once when she was ill, he taught her Sunday school class.

Important people, ranging from celebrities to politicians, visited the Graham house. But it was the lonely, the misfits, Ruth welcomed with special warmth. They were the people she virtually adopted.

Her first "orphan" was an elderly man named Arthur Radcliffe, a midwesterner who had taught horticulture in North Carolina and later managed a flower shop. An eccentric bachelor, "Old Man Art," as he was called, was as short and sinewy as a licorice stick. Ruth had become acquainted with him through the Montreat Presbyterian Church, where he was an usher. When he reached his seventies, about the time Ruth started teaching her Sunday school class, he was placed in a Greensboro, North Carolina, nursing home. Miserable when separated from the soil and plants he loved, he ran away and hitchhiked back to western North Carolina. One day he appeared on Ruth's doorstep.

"I'm not going to let the highway patrol take me back!" he declared, his voice rising. "I'll die before I'll go back to that nursing home." Then he begged, his eyes gleaming, "Why don't you just let me die right here in this old cabin you got at the end of the road?"

She renovated it and Radcliffe moved in. He papered his walls with magazine photographs of flowers and he plugged the cove with plants and shrubbery. Whenever a friend would drive up to visit him, Radcliffe would be found stretched out in the loamy soil, gouging and planting, because he was too feeble to stand or squat. When he died, after living in the cabin two years, the wishes of his handwritten will were carried out: His body was given to science and a white pine was planted on the ridge in remembrance of him.

Just before Christmas, not long after Radcliffe had become part of that earth once so much a part of him, a rumor circulated about a family virtually starving in an abandoned toolshed on a brambly patch of dirt in Black Mountain. On a raw December day, Calvin Thielman and two deacons investigated. They found the unheated shanty and a mother and five small children living inside. There was no plumbing. The only convenience was an electric light bulb glaring over the crazed mosaic of a broken concrete floor. The father, a carpenter named Luther Dover, was dying of cancer in Asheville's Memorial Mission Hospital. When Calvin visited his ward several days later, he found him lying on his back, the skin covering his gaunt face as thin as cigarette paper.

"I went up to your house and went out to your family," Calvin finally drawled after moments of small talk. "It looks like it's going to be a pretty rough Christmas for the children. And some people at our church have more than they know what to do with. They would be glad to help give the children some things for Christmas and to help you have a place to live if that would be all right with you. We don't want to do anything without your permission and I guarantee you it won't take anything away from anybody else, it won't take anything away from them."

Dover's eyes filled with tears. "I reckon they would appreciate that," he whispered.

When Billy Graham heard the story of the Dovers he sent for Calvin. "I'm always hearing that the government is giving away money right and left," he said. "Find out if they're receiving the aid they should be receiving." He handed Calvin a generous check. "There's more where that came from," he said.

Ruth discovered the ages of the Dover children and bought clothing and toys for them. By mid-December, the Dover family had been moved into an abandoned house. Plumbers had replaced its rusty water pipes. Rooms were furnished and Dover's doctor allowed him to come home for the holiday. Shortly after the family moved in, Ruth's Sunday school class arrived with sacks of groceries. Christmas Eve she sent her husband and the children down the mountain to deliver the gifts she had chosen and wrapped.

Several days later, Dover, gasping for breath, was carried back to the hospital in the bed of a pickup truck. Calvin went to see him, finding him wracked with pain and receiving little attention.

"Can't you give him oxygen or do something to make him more comfortable?" Calvin asked an orderly.

"Well," the man stalled, "I have to get clearance from the head doctor and I don't know where to get him. . . ."

Outraged, the preacher stormed through the hall, telephoned Ruth and told her the situation.

"You let me handle it," she said firmly.

She knew when to throw her weight around and did so happily when necessary. She was calmly settling the matter over the telephone before Calvin had walked twenty paces. "And *boy!*" he recalled, "when I went back down the hall the nurses were moving and everybody else was moving. A private nurse was by Dover's side and a doctor had arrived. . . ."

The last moments of Dover's life he held his wife's hand, his breathing shallow, laborious. "I'm gonna die," he whispered. "I want you to see that all my debts is paid. And I want my children raised as Christians."

Cloaked in wool, her breath turning to smoke against the wintry air, Ruth stood at the rim of the small crowd when he was buried in the mountainside cemetery. Unbeknown to all who clustered around the new gash in the frozen earth, she had paid for the funeral.

14

The Terror by Night

Whether it was a loud car or motorcycles I loved these things when I was growing up. I never pretended to be the stereotype of a fellow with a Bible under my arm. But my parents pretty much let me be me.

William Franklin Graham III

The six of them—children and mother—perched around the kitchen table, beginning the day with readings from a box of multicolored Bible verses. Momentarily they heard the heavy booted feet of Zeb Sawyer in the foyer, arriving to begin his chores.

"Morning," he said.

Ruth invited him to read the Scripture lesson, something she always did if one of the workmen appeared during breakfast. He sheepishly withdrew one of the cards from the box she handed him, seated himself, and commenced cleaning his glasses between his thumb and forefinger.

He read Hebrews 12:6: "Whom the Lord loveth, He *chaseth*. . . ."

His misreading was a harbinger of what would happen with Franklin throughout his teens. It would indeed seem that the Lord would chase him as he veered from the straight and narrow, his problems and temptations nipping at his heels.

He would require his mother's full attention, something she could not always give; he needed the strong hand of a father, but the pressure of Billy's ministry was staggering. By the time Franklin reached his teens, more than thirty million people had attended his father's crusades, while countless others had heard him over the radio or on television. He was so recognizable that he could no longer eat in restaurants without people lining up ten and twelve deep to ask for his autograph; he couldn't appear in an American hotel lobby or airport without being mobbed.

Frequently he resorted to disguises, rarely leaving the house without a pair of large sunglasses and a cap pulled low over his eyes. Perpetually preoccupied, sometimes he didn't pay as much attention to his camouflages as he ought to have, and some of them were rather curious. Once he wore a wide-brimmed hat in Mexico and an autograph hound thought he was James Arness. Once in a European airport he discovered with alarm that he had lost his sunglasses, so he quickly bought a pair off a rack. Ruth later noticed, to her horror, the Playboy bunny insignia on the frames. Another time he walked along a crowded beach in Europe, clad in fire-engine-red shorts, a blue windbreaker, yellow socks, Hushpuppies, a denim cap, and sunglasses. "That's the dumbest looking human being I've ever seen," Ruth thought to herself as she watched him amble in her direction. "Oh, no!" it dawned on her. "He's mine!"

But without disguises, he was painfully vulnerable. In the mid-seventies the Grahams were on a boat in Acapulco Bay, Mexico, with future Vice-President George Bush and his wife, Barbara. After a picnic of raw oysters on a deserted beach, it was time to swim back to the boat. It would take an hour to follow the shoreline to their hotel.

"Since the trip back will take so long," said Billy, who was in the midst of writing a sermon, "I think I'll just walk back along the beach."

Without wallet or sunglasses, wearing nothing but a pair of white swim trunks he had borrowed from Bush, he set out, not knowing that the beach he was walking along was the property of a Mexican Naval station, off-limits to civilians. He rounded a corner and was greeted by two submachine guns backed by unsmiling Mexican soldiers. As Billy, who spoke no Spanish, tried to explain, and the guards, who spoke no English, tried to understand, he was directed to sit on a nearby bench and wait for one of their English-speaking superiors. The officer arrived, heard Billy's explanation, and released him, with the order that he could not walk along the restricted beach. Standing, Billy realized he had been sitting on wet green paint. He had two choices: trot barefooted along the piping hot sidewalk to the first hotel and get back to the nonrestricted beaches by darting through the lobby (where he would be immediately recognized); or stay on the sidewalk the entire distance and be miserable but anonymous. He opted for the latter.

As early as 1961, there were signs of what Franklin was in for. On November 27 of that year the *Indianapolis Times* printed this: "Columnist Charlie McHarry writes that the handsome lad nightclubbing in New York with Gayle Horne, Lena's daughter, was Billy Graham, Jr., son of the evangelist." Franklin was nine years old at the time.

"But the sobering fact," Ruth observed, "is that it shows none of our children can ever live privately—conquer privately, or sin privately." She and Billy prayed, she recorded, that God would "mercifully spare [the children] any sowing of wild oats. . . . Unless committed to Thee, they will react violently against this enforced publicity and turn against Bill in bitterness as tho' he were to blame. . . . As Christians they will take all this as an opportunity for witnessing. As pagans they would seek to camouflage themselves with worldliness to escape notice."

A rakish-looking boy with strong features and a mop of black hair, Franklin had inherited his Grandfather Bell's sturdy build and love of adventure. He was happiest when scaling "Suicide Trail" on Montreat's Lookout Mountain or hunting with Calvin Thielman, who taught him much about guns and preached that he mustn't kill songbirds. One day, after hearing complaints that Franklin was indeed doing the latter, Calvin firmly reprimanded him.

"Aw, Calvin!" Franklin assured him, "don't worry! I draw a bead on a bird and I say, 'Sing.' If he sings, I let him go. And if he doesn't I let him have it."

The shooting lessons came to an end one day when Calvin was demonstrating how to handle a high-caliber pistol and accidentally shot himself in the leg.

Out of sorts in a Sunday suit, Franklin preferred faded jeans and flannel shirts; his hands were usually covered with black grease from his tinkerings with automobile or motorcycle engines. He was energetic and witty, more attracted to vice than virtue. He began his flirtation with cigarettes at age three, supplying himself with the butts dropped by the workmen while they were building the house. One day, after he had gathered a tidy little pile, he heard his father coming.

"Pretend they're yours," Franklin whispered loudly to Wallace Walker, the electrician.

"Franklin," the man laughed, "your Daddy knows I don't smoke."

Several years later, Ruth asked caretaker Floyd Roberts to let Franklin try one of his cigarettes, thinking it would make him so sick that he would never again want to smoke. Franklin smoked the first one down to a nub and proceeded to help Roberts finish the pack. So the next day Ruth asked John Rickman to give him a cigar. Again, the plan backfired.

"Why are you doing this?" Franklin asked her at bedtime.

"The things are bad for you," Ruth said. "I don't want you to get the habit."

It was a little late.

When Franklin was ten, Ruth recorded that he "had asked Christ to come into his heart" while hiking with Chuck Gieser, the son of a former missionary Ruth's family had known in China. Instead of ensuring peace, it seemed to give him something else to fight against. His mother's anxieties became acute: "I cannot sleep," she wrote at the time. "For a while I sat here in bed with the lights off, and thought and prayed. I have a headache. It would be so easy to take a sleeping pill but He knows I need sleep—and how much. And sometimes there are things more important—like seeing the world outside flooded with moonlight and watching the last log in my fireplace flicker and die; watching the shadows of the ceiling beams leaping in the firelight. And knowing He is here. I've taken time out to remember all this because of one special thing He said. He has told it to me before, many times in one way or another. It's about Franklin. Every time I pray especially for him God says: 'Love him.'. . . Which seems odd because I love every bone of him. But God means 'show it.' Let him in on the fact. Enjoy him. You think he's the greatest—let him know you think so."

Ruth agonized over him; and she felt frustrated as her other responsibilities wrestled for her attention.

By 1965, the year John Pollock was finishing his first authorized biography of Billy, life was becoming as complex and tedious as a circuit board. Frequently, Ruth lay awake at night, her mind streaking down her list of chores.

A typical day was frenetic. Take, for example, November 10, 1965: Ruth drove Anne twenty miles to the dentist, then to the oral surgeon; she carried clothing to the dry cleaner, shopped, and returned home in time to serve tea to radio commentator Paul Harvey and five other guests; at spare moments she packed her bags for London, read snatches of Pollock's galley proofs, answered mail, paid bills, and bought traveler's checks. Still ahead of her were two talks and a Sunday school lesson to prepare and Sunday dinner to plan. "And ringing thru my mind," she wrote, "are there not twenty-four hours in the day?"

It seemed that the only time she had to herself was the sleepless early morning hours when everyone else on the mountain was unconscious. Like a solitary buzzing machine in a darkened factory, her brain was active, alert. She hungrily studied her Bible and meditated, her thoughts turning to God, Whose presence was silently and invisibly there. "It may be," she wrote, "that the night seasons are the only times He can get in a word edgewise."

From time to time, her experiences were almost mystical. On February 17, 1965, she awoke at 2:30 in the morning, disturbed and dejected. Feeling the impulse to pray, she knelt beside her bed. Inexplicably, tears flowed as she found herself petitioning God for two men: Kenneth Strachan, a Latin American missionary whose wife Elizabeth had gone to college with Ruth, and Tom Allan, a pastor in Glasgow, Scotland, whom the Grahams had come to know during crusades in the British Isles. She prayed, unaware of the men's circumstances, for "a reprieve for both. An extension of their lives and services on earth." After a few minutes the impulse was gone. She returned to bed. "But why?" she wondered.

One week later forty-nine-year-old Strachan was dead from cancer. Allan, also forty-nine, died soon after from a heart attack.

And there were periods when the rhythm continued, day and night, night and day; light giving way to darkness, darkness giving way to dawn, with her seeing it all, watching from the vantage of her sleeplessness. "INSOMNIA," scrawled in black ink and underlined, scarred pages of her journals. In the cool darkness her senses became refined, a radar detecting the pulsations of the universe. Through the parted curtains she watched the moon, hanging over Rainbow Mountain, pallid, a ghostly face upturned in a black pool; she heard the whispering stream west of her window; anxieties, failures, unfinished tasks rose to the surface of her brain like old wood in the water.

She began climbing out of bed at two, three, and four o'clock in the morning to write letters, pay bills, or finish the work that worried her; she prayed and read her Bible; she began to dread the extinguishing of her light, the hour for bed. Then, one night, she felt the tugging as she read Psalm 91:5. The words were lifted from the page:

"Thou shalt not be afraid for the terror by night." She emerged from her worries strengthened, closer to her Creator.

In 1969, Franklin hit the white water of his rebellion. "In looking back," Ruth wrote, "I think I would say this is the summer Franklin began to walk his own road." He had just turned sixteen that July. He seemed unwilling, his parents saw, to take a stand for Christ. Despite their concern, their talks with him were amiable.

"I remember when long hair became a big issue—I wanted my hair to touch my ears," Franklin recalled. "When I smoked I knew they disagreed for health reasons. But they never preached at me— they said they wished I'd do it at home and not behind their backs. They didn't want to make alcohol, tobacco or long hair an issue. They knew the Lord would deal with me on these things."

Though Franklin didn't smoke in front of his family, he couldn't fool his mother. Puffing furtively out his upstairs window, he didn't realize that an updraft from the valley simply carried the smoke around to her bedroom.

Academically, Franklin continued his nosedive. Believing he needed masculine discipline, his parents sent him to the Stony Brook School, an all-male private school in New York. There he kept a brotherly eye on Bunny, nearby in The Stony Brook Girls School. Both of them were miserably homesick, and in an effort to cheer themselves up, he visited her on a regular basis, bringing her candy he purchased with money he earned from selling popcorn on campus. When his parents realized how much he loved his home and the mountains, they did not insist that he return to Stony Brook his senior year. Instead, he enrolled in the local public high school where he struggled with his studies but conquered the gang of students who thought it great sport to goad the shaggy, denim-clad fellow widely known as "Billy Graham's son." One classmate, determined to harass him into violence, would sit behind him in class and jiggle Franklin's desk every time he attempted to write. After repeated warnings, Franklin finally jumped to his feet and with the swing of a wrecking ball knocked the young man over the teacher's desk. Moments later he was in the principal's office. He was expeditiously sent home. "He walked in, grinning like a 'possum—totally unrepentant," Ruth recalled.

He wasn't exactly a calming influence in the house either, and it would have been convenient, from time to time, had his mother been able to summon him to *her* office and then exile him to school. He teased Ned unmercifully, fired his shotgun out his bedroom window, set a stereo speaker in front of the intercom, and rocked the house with Janis Joplin. In the summers he stayed out late. Again his mother did not confront him. "I'd come in at one or two o'clock," Franklin recalled. "And her light would still be on. But she never would get on me for being up late." It was often at these times, when she was calmly waiting for him, that they would have their most meaningful talks. But sometimes her presence annoyed him.

"You only wait up so you can smell my breath," he accused her one night.

"If that's how you feel," she replied, "I'll hit the sack. I'm tired."

At least in Franklin's mind, it was sometimes his mother, not God, who was doing the "chasing." One Sunday afternoon at lunch the family was discussing spirits and wondering if it were possible that some Christians returned to earth after death and, no longer restrained by bodily limitations, continued serving God. "Too many people who have lost loved ones," Ruth remarked, "have said that at times they have had such a sense of their loved ones' presence—as if they were breathing down their necks."

"I sure hope *you* don't die," Franklin said dryly.

But in the main, Ruth allowed him to do as he pleased, making it clear that she expected much from him regardless of how little he expected from himself. Her attitude about sin in general was that people who break the law or one of God's commandments should confess and accept the punishment; then they should accept forgiveness. If her son chose to be irresponsible, then he'd have to live with the consequences—such as feeling cranky and exhausted when his mother awakened him at 7:30 each morning by banging a broom against the copper stove hood below his second-story bedroom. One morning she dumped the contents of his ashtray on his head.

He began locking his door. Ruth, not one to give up easily, climbed onto the roof one morning. She crept across the shingles, holding a tin cup of water in her teeth which she planned to dash in his face when she reached his open window. Hearing her coming, he played 'possum until she was just outside his room. Then, bolting up, he slammed down the sash and grinned back at her through the glass. She was laughing too hard to be angry.

15

"Other Children"

Ruth picks some peculiar ones to come to bat for. Of course, if she helps just one person, she's done more than I have.

Pete Post, Chief of Police, Montreat

There were her "other children," waifs who seemed to drift over the face of the earth like dandelion seeds. She had an eye for them, snatching them in midflight for a moment, in the cup of her hand. She was more a mother than a missionary, more a tenderhearted friend than a judge, not so different from the heartbroken little girl who had buried Tar Baby beside the compound wall and then dug him up three weeks later to see how he was doing. Her empathy was her weakness, for often she involved herself with people who were beyond her help. No matter how often they fell, her optimism was unflagging. No matter how often they took advantage of her kindness, she did not see it. This weakness was also her strength, a fortitude sustained by faith, not success.

On Wednesday, May 18, 1966, the Grahams boarded the *Queen Mary* in New York and set sail for the month-long crusade at Earl's Court, London. The afternoon was cool, the clouds ponderous, obscuring the top of the Verrazano-Narrows Bridge as the ship passed under it toward the open sea. The night before the ship docked Ruth tossed anxiously in their cabin, sleep eluding her until 4:30 A.M. when she finally drifted off and dreamed they were in the Earl's Court stadium and only thirty people had appeared for the first service.

As they prepared to dock in Southampton on Tuesday, May 24, seventy-five reporters boarded. Unlike the mob fourteen years before them, they were courteous and friendly. From Southampton they traveled by train to Waterloo Station in London, where they were greeted by a large, cheering crowd. Many had first heard Billy at Harringay. The people sang spirited hymns as a convertible whisked the Grahams away. "It's hard just to smile and wave when there's a lump in your throat," she wrote at the time. "It would be all right if only they wouldn't sing. Then memories of Harringay come crowding back and that overwhelming sense of the presence of God. And you know you should be down there among them, lost in the crowd, singing with them . . . not riding in a convertible."

On May 28, a warm, cloudless Saturday, the Grahams arrived in Oxford at midafternoon. Like a stone tossed into a millpond, commotion rippled from them in rings of dogged newsmen and well-wishers. Oxonians glanced up quizzically as the party passed down narrow, winding streets; past flower vendors peddling paper-wrapped roses; past the stares of pale, bespectacled dons pedaling bicycles; past dark towering churches flanked by jagged rows of headstones, leaning and stained from centuries of rain and wind, jutting mutely from the earth like bloodless tongues. Europeans, Africans with crisp English accents, ragged beggars, wove around them beneath the spires that seemed to reach toward the great Intelligence, as though God could be reached through reasoning, through ritual, through tradition. They, these two Americans, were there, moving through it all like a tiny bead, aiming for the heart.

The next day Billy was to speak at Saint Aldate's, an evangelical Anglican church. A long line of Oxford students wrapped around the imposing stone building, some still in their evening clothes from the revels of the night before, others passing out humanist tracts. As he went through the crowd to the church door he was escorted by hecklers. "I'm glad to have you here," he told them affably as he passed into the cool silence of the sanctuary. Afterward they drove to Cambridge, stopping midway for a picnic lunch, for once eluding the press. And, wrote Ruth, they "missed two good shots of Bill. One of him going into the Ladies' restroom by mistake and the other of him, hat brim turned down all around, rain coat on . . . leaning on the fence like an old farmer."

That night he spoke at Great Saint Mary's. It was an evening filled with misfortune. Again, hundreds of students were queued outside, a number of them there to make sport of this guest who dared to violate their refined minds with his simple message.

"I bless you in the name of Billy Graham," a young man wearing his shirt backward chanted as he sprinkled water on his friends. In the hall next to the church residents played their radios full volume until the police intervened; a row of students sitting behind Ruth whispered insults about her husband throughout the service; the vicar forgot to turn on the pulpit light and Billy could not see to read one word of his notes.[1]

Abroad, Ruth was no different from the Sunday school teacher at home: Ironically, it was the young cynics, the confused, often troublesome teenagers, that she reached out to.

On Sunday, June 12, her husband was to speak at a church in Brixton. She sat in the family pew of the elegant woman beside her, a patrician and an acknowledged force in the congregation. Two young men, bearded, wearing blue jeans, their arms tattooed, moved down the aisle and stood with uncertainty just yards from Ruth. She glanced at them empathetically and later recorded: "I wished so that someone would welcome them warmly—offer them seats." The woman next to her stared at the men, however, her face constricted by suspicion and disapproval. "That kind sometimes disturbs meetings," she whispered to Ruth. Heads turned as Billy appeared at an entrance. He walked down the aisle, stopping long enough to shake hands with the two young men and welcome them. The moment he moved on, the woman instructed an usher to show the men out.

Later, when Billy preached to ten thousand at Victoria Park in London's East End, Ruth wandered through the crowd and noticed a group of irreverent teenagers who, when Cliff Barrows suggested a song, yelled, "No!" They wadded their song sheets and pelted the people nearest them; behind them was a stockpile of eggs. Billy preached on John 3:16 while his wife, dressed in a trench coat and dark glasses, slipped toward the offenders, her strategy planned. When she reached them she would say, "I'm much more interested in what you have to say than in what he has to say. Let's get off where he won't disturb us and explain what you've got on your mind." Before she could open her mouth she felt a hand on her arm; three BGEA team members flanked her, thwarting her plan. The teenagers scattered.

She was irrepressible, spontaneous, even reckless; she was the woman who in later years would confide to a friend that she was

---

1. Having assumed that the service was a failure, the Grahams were surprised in years to come at the number of people who told them that they had been converted that night.

never free to be socially and politically uninhibited—she felt she had to constrain herself for the sake of her husband's ministry. But in spiritual matters she was open, even aggressive, for the sake of her faith. She carried her beliefs wherever she went, sharing them with whoever seemed receptive, whether it was teenagers, hotel maids, or taxicab drivers. Here's a typical scene:

One morning in London she hired a taxi to carry her to Foyles Bookstore and soon discovered the driver was Jewish. As he whizzed Ruth past cars, careening through side streets and around pedestrians, she invited him to Earl's Court.

"You must be kidding or something!" he turned around and said. "In my faith, we have our own beliefs. And I know what you people would do. You'd try to convert me. And me—I don't want to get involved."

"Are you Orthodox, Conservative, or Reformed?" she asked, clinging to the back of the seat as he darted down another street to avoid a traffic jam at Trafalgar Square.

"The synagogue I go to is Orthodox," he replied. "It's the only one around. I wish it was Reformed. Me—I don't go to synagogue any more than I have to. I say, why should I go to church and confess my sins to God when I know I'll go right back the next week and sin all over again?"

"I wonder why you bother to eat a meal since you will have to turn around and eat another," she replied.

"Hey!" he said, laughing, lurching back into the line of traffic. "That's a good answer!"

He began attacking religious formalism, legalism, and hypocrisy, punctuating each remark with dramatic gestures, looking at her over his shoulder for what seemed alarmingly long moments. He buzzed past her address, braked to a screeching halt and backed up.

"Your comments on religion sound very much like Christ's," she smiled as she paid him.

"How's that?" he asked, startled.

"Christ said many similar things in the New Testament," she said.

"Never read the New Testament," he said thoughtfully. "But I'll get one."

On Wednesday, June 29, the radio brought the news that the United States had bombed Hanoi, and war protesters retaliated by announcing they would set off firecrackers in the counseling room at Earl's Court after that night's service. As Ruth sat in the stadium (and Scotland Yard officers stood sentry outside the counseling room), an usher slipped her a note from Meg Spalding, a young woman Ruth had recently become acquainted with:

"Dear Mrs. Graham. Please could you come and see me as I need your help. I will wait for you outside the exit where you sit. Thank you very much. Meg. P.S. It is about dope."

Meg, a pallid wisp of a girl with frizzy red hair, had seen Ruth walk in with Billy before a service the week before and had rushed up to meet her. Since then, she had sought her out in the stands, her cheery small talk masking her misery and interminable loneliness. One of five children, she had been born to a prostitute. Eventually, her home became the streets, her trade the same as her mother's. After years of being nothing more than a commodity to men, she had turned to lesbianism.

Ruth immediately left the service and found Meg huddled at the bottom of the steps. Wearing jeans, sandals, and the same brown jacket she had worn every day, she looked blankly at Ruth. Her eyes were dark and dull, her face blanched. Fishing inside her voluminous brown satchel, she pulled out a square of cloth and spread it open next to her for Ruth to sit on.

"I'm doped," she said.

"What happened?" Ruth asked.

"It's me girlfriend Pat," she said. "She died in hospital today. Drugs."

"You can't go on escaping from problems and hurts by taking dope," Ruth told her gently. "You'll have to choose between 'escaping' to Christ or 'escaping' to dope. Jesus *loves* you, Meg."

She hung her head, staring at her frail hands. "I wish I had a mother like you," she whispered.

"Listen," Ruth said tenderly, "you have Jesus. He's always with you. He *loves* you. He understands. He's more powerful than dope. I'll be gone next week. Earl's Court will be over. You'll have disappointments but He's there with you."

"I have more dope," she confessed.

"Give it to me," Ruth said.

"You want it?"

"No, I don't, but I don't want you to have it," she replied firmly.

She again rummaged inside her satchel and handed Ruth a small knot of something wrapped inside a handkerchief. In the distance Billy's words echoed off the stadium walls as though there were two voices preaching instead of one. The service seemed unreal and far away as she sat in the damp air watching Meg drift deeper into a stupor.

It was the beginning of a sad, seemingly futile friendship. She attended to Meg, and would continue doing so for years, though she was the sort of person very few in Ruth's position would have associated with. Ruth was not threatened by her; she also was wise enough to visit with her only in public places such as tearooms and the stadium. The press needed little fuel for scandal: That had become obvious two nights earlier when her husband, despite her objections, decided to visit the Soho district, notorious for nightclubs, gambling, and prostitution.

"Since you are going to preach Christ, we can expect God's protection. But," she warned, "with the omnipresent press it will seem little more than a publicity stunt."

After the evening service he, several associates and a Soho priest drove into the district; without his knowledge she followed in the backseat of a friend's car and parked behind them in an intersection. Immediately he was inundated; people flooded around the car, pouring out of buildings and automobiles; cameramen and photographers mysteriously appeared. Spontaneously, he climbed onto the hood to preach while his wife, frozen in the traffic jam, rolled down her window, deciding to have some fun.

"What's going on?" she innocently asked a stranger.

"It's Billy Graham," the man replied, "but don't ask me what he's doing down here."

"I think he's a singer," another offered.

"It's Billy Graham working off some of his inhibitions," someone else said with a laugh.

"I'm not here to condemn you and God is willing to forgive you no matter what you do," Billy Graham proclaimed, when suddenly, out of the crowd burst a small blonde who bulldozed through the aides as though they were paper dolls and lunged for him.

"God bless you all!" he shouted to the masses before jumping off the hood and diving into the backseat. He was whisked away. The blonde, it turned out, was naked beneath her coat, obviously there to scandalize him in front of the cameras.

Saturday, July 2, was the last day of the crusade. That morning Ruth met Richard Carr-Gomm, the major of the Coldstream Guards she had met twelve years earlier during the Greater London crusade. In 1965, the Grahams had learned that he planned to resign his commission to establish homes for the elderly and outcast in London's East End. The Grahams and Carr-Gomm's family had attempted to talk him out of it, distressed to see him abandon a military career that was part of his family tradition. One day, Carr-Gomm forever silenced their objections.

"When God has done so much for one," he politely informed them, "one would like to express one's appreciation."

Since then he had indeed resigned and founded what he called the Abbeyfield Society. On July 2, Ruth visited two of the houses, small, spotless structures with a tiny patch of grass scattered with flowers in front. Carr-Gomm had discarded his dignity for humility and his bearskin helmet for an apron. He now scrubbed floors, cooked, shopped, and cared for those who could no longer care for themselves, providing a roof for those who did not have one, providing companionship for those who were alone, loving those who felt unloved.

The closing service that evening was at Wembley. By late that afternoon the roads to the stadium were jammed for three miles in every direction. Ruth sat above the choir in a glassed-in terrace. She was joined by a young actress.

"I don't know about you," the young woman said at the altar call, "but I've got to go." Flanked by two men to prevent the press from exploiting her decision, she moved through the crowd, slim in her simple yellow dress, her blonde hair draping below her shoulder blades. Afterwards she said breathlessly to Billy, "I can't explain it. It was as if suddenly a great light burst upon one. It is as if one is not alone any more."

That was what Ruth had wanted Meg to experience—the end of her aloneness, the end of her feeling of abandonment. That was what she wanted for all her "other children," for all those she attended to both at home and abroad. She was attempting to share the message of God's forgiveness and love with those who could not forgive, much less love, themselves; she was attempting to help people who were just as crippled by their backgrounds as a quadriplegic is by polio.

Two years after she sailed away from Meg she met Tony Mendez, a Puerto Rican from the Bronx, where he was known as "The Kid." Compactly built and bearded, he was appended to a pool cue and a switchblade. Like his platform shoes and multicolored Indian cottons, he was uninhibited, mercurial.

His parents had divorced shortly after immigrating to the United States. In a shabby tenement on Prospect Avenue, a drug-infested strip between the Harlem and East Rivers, his mother raised him and two sisters. Early on he mastered the art of survival, picking up a dollar any way he could, rarely buying anything if he could steal it. He hustled in smoky, beer-soaked pool halls, earning sometimes a hundred dollars a day, enough to satisfy his appetite for cocaine and heroin.

On a whim—for temerity was his muse—he enrolled in a few courses at nearby Fordham University shortly after graduating from high school. There he fell under the watchful eye of his guidance counselor, a man who had grown up in the ghetto and escaped. In early 1968 he urged Mendez to leave New York. He told him about a tiny two-year school in western North Carolina called Montreat-Anderson College, and he asked him to give it a try.

"Those people are out in the sticks," Mendez retorted, laughing ruefully as Southern stereotypes floated to mind. "Man, they're backward!"

To please his friend, he filled out the application, though he had no intention of ever going South. But when he received word that he had been accepted, the thought of going there "for some reason warmed my heart," he recalled. That fall he stuffed his few garish belongings into a suitcase and flew to Asheville.

It was a shock from the moment the prop plane began circling for landing; the runway seemed no bigger than a race track, a solitary wind sock swayed languidly from a pole. Inside the terminal, which was no more than a two-minute walk from one end to the other, he looked about in disbelief: The lobby was a small square of shag carpeting scattered with plastic chairs, a mounted television set blinked in one corner; the adjacent gift shop sold, not duty-free cameras, liquors, and perfumes, but saltwater taffy, jars of dark sourwood honey, and Cherokee Indian souvenirs.

But it was the mountains that left him speechless. Fall had peaked, the hills were dashed with gold, orange, yellow, and red. The few pitiful trees he had seen along Prospect Avenue had already lost their leaves—he had never before seen the magic of autumn.

"Did someone paint the leaves?" he asked the college employee who picked him up at the airport.

"No, Tony," the man replied. "They change that way."

As a student Tony was a loner, working as a janitor in the post office and student center, hustling at pool, and spending his profits on drugs. Gambling in Asheville as well as in Montreat, he earned a reputation, and soon outsiders were roaring through the rustic stone gate to challenge him. The college's Presbyterian administrators began to wonder at the wisdom of importing this inner-city student.

On a Sunday morning that fall Mendez crawled out of bed, headachy and dizzy after drinking the night away. He pulled on a white Nehru jacket and slacks, tied a red sash around his waist and a scarf around his head. He ambled along the cracked cement walkway, passing beneath gnarled apple trees and pines on the rim of Lake Susan, Montreat's stream-fed swimming hole. The docks were warped and green (that same Victorian dark green that seemed to coat every resort porch and rocking chair in western North Carolina). On a diving platform in the center of the lake was the graffiti, "Please Don't Walk On The Water." Overlooking the water, on the western shore was the student center, a modern building filled with brightly colored plastic chairs and round formica-covered tables. The oily smell of last night's hamburgers clung to the stale air. Mendez considered it his turf, and this morning he found it was being violated by a gang of students who were seated around the pool tables—*his* pool tables. A handsome woman with a large black Bible was the ring leader; they called her "Ruth."

She glanced with friendly curiosity at the glassy-eyed, pale apparition stumbling through the line of chairs in front of her, and she thought, "That's got to be the most pitiful individual I ever saw." Hopelessly confused, he dropped into an empty chair and watched her through bloodshot eyes. "I'll never forget," he recalled, "she must have had Billy Graham's Bible because it was *so* big." She abandoned her Sunday school lesson and directed her comments toward him. Afterward, she introduced herself and invited him to come again.

"Well, I've got to go continue my game," he said, backing away.

As the days unrolled Mendez's reputation worsened—an unsurprising phenomenon in a town the size of Montreat, where news spreads like an echo in a telephone booth. Calvin Thielman, determined to reach the college's "hippies" for Christ, invited Mendez and several others to his house on December 9. Billy Graham's Indian associate Akbar Abdul-Haqq talked with them and answered questions. Afterwards, Mendez talked with him for more than an hour and then asked to receive Christ. The next day, Ruth, or "Roof" as Mendez called her, sent him a copy of the J. B. Phillips translation of the New Testament. Reading the simple prose in the student cafeteria, he understood the words for the first time and became so excited that several students reported him drunk to the dean.

Two days later, he and his best friend broke into a heated argument in the dormitory.

"I could cut your face! I could cut your face!" the friend menaced, waving a scalpel (a recent gift from Mendez, who had stolen it from the laboratory) perilously close to Mendez's nose. With the reflexes of a street fighter, Mendez whipped his bone-handled knife from his belt and plunged it into the man's stomach. When the police arrived moments later, they found the two men clinging to each other.

"Buddy, I didn't mean to do it," Mendez sobbed.

"It's okay, buddy. It's okay," moaned his friend.

Though the friend dropped all charges, the college wouldn't be so generous. Montreat-Anderson's Disciplinary Committee advocated kicking Mendez out of school. They summoned him and interrogated him about the fight, about his past, their opinion of him darkening by increments. Ruth was a member of the college's Board of Trustees at the time and was instrumental in saving Mendez from being shipped back to the ghetto.

"Do anything," she told the committee, "but don't send him back to the Bronx. He'll slide down the drain."

Reluctantly, the committee agreed to place him on probation and let him stay.

After hearing his wife talk about Mendez, Billy invited him to the house and they spent an afternoon talking in the living room. As he left, Billy wrapped an arm around him and said, "Tony, I want you to know that your friends are my friends, and my home is always open to you."

Mendez took him at his word, and the next day he loaded a bus and a van with "drug addicts and the worst on the street," as he called them, and led the way to Little Piney Cove. The caravan halted at the lower locked gate, an obstacle Mendez had not anticipated. He reassured his disappointed friends, climbed on top of the bus, and began yelling as loudly as he could until they were granted entrance. They spilled out of their vehicles, the Grahams watching from the porch, not knowing how they would fit all of them inside the house.

"Let's go out to the yard," Billy suggested.

He patiently answered their questions, and then told them, "Jesus Christ is what you fellows need. You can have your highs, but they're temporary highs. When you have Jesus Christ that's an everlasting high."

In the late spring of 1969 Billy held a crusade in Madison Square Garden, and Mendez, home for the summer, decided to attend.

The night of the first service he brought a group of hoodlums to the stadium, materializing at an entrance in gang jackets, shaggy hair, tattoos, obscene patches, and frayed blue jeans. The stadium was full, said the security guard as he looked them up and down. Though the man was telling the truth, Mendez assumed he was being discriminated against.

"Listen," he said, his voice rising, "Billy Graham and Ruth, they're just like my parents. I've eaten at their home, I've slept there. . . ."

"Yeah, yeah, yeah," the officer drawled sarcastically. "Listen, he's my brother." Then, his voice hard, he barked, "Listen buddy, keep walking."

"Come on!" Mendez motioned to his friends. They pushed past the guard and bolted through the entrance. What Mendez didn't know was that the Black Panthers had threatened Billy's life that day and security was unusually tight. By the time he and his buddies had made it to the fourth tier they were surrounded by a dozen plainclothesmen, and in moments they found themselves back on the street.

"Yeah, yeah, you know him, sure," his friends taunted him irritably.

Two nights later Mendez brought his sisters to the service, and when the invitation was given, Ruth saw the three of them go forward. She headed toward the counseling room to welcome them.

"Hey Ruth," Mendez said nervously, "I've got to see you—I've got to talk to you."

They met the next night outside the loge entrance.

"What's the trouble, Tony?" she asked, studying his troubled face.

"Well, Ruth," he said, "I've done something bad. *Really* bad."

"Not again!" Ruth exclaimed. "What this time?"

"Well, Ruth," he said, "I have a buddy. He needed some money and, Ruth, he had never robbed a filling station before and needed some help. So I thought it was my Christian responsibility to teach him how to rob a gas station."

"How much did you get, Tony?" she demanded.

"A hundred and twenty-five dollars."

"Okay," she said, "You have to pay back your share."

He blanched.

"Was your buddy a Christian?" she asked, referring to his accomplice.

"No," he said.

"Okay," she said, "then you have to pay back his share as well."

His face constricted into a mask of pained disbelief.

"Tony, do you have anything else in your possession that you've stolen?"

"Everything I got," he replied; he confessed that he didn't own a thread of clothing that wasn't "hot."

"It's a good thing it's summer," she said, "because you're going to have to give everything back."

When he returned to Montreat that fall Ruth asked him, "Did you pay back the service station owner?"

"I couldn't," he replied, shrugging his shoulders innocently. "I went to the filling station and it was closed down."

"Well, I guess so if he had many customers like you," she retorted dryly.

In the spring of 1970 Mendez again became involved in drugs. In order to locate a pusher for a narcotics agent, he mainlined heroin twice in one day, thus destroying his credibility as a state witness and, in the eyes of his classmates, as a Christian. They decided he was the same con artist he had always been, that he had used the undercover work as an excuse to take drugs. They excluded him from their circle. Ruth was indignant. "Instead of loving him extra hard and praying for him," she recalled, "they gave him the cold shoulder." Two weeks before commencement Mendez appeared at Sunday school.

"I know you think I blown it as a Christian," he explained, "but I felt I had to do it. If I was wrong, I want you to forgive me. But I want you to know me and Jesus are just like this," he concluded, holding up two welded fingers.

He left school before the end of the term, flying back to New York without telling Ruth or anyone else of his plans. In class the following Sunday she explained to her students the mistake of ostracizing a "backslidden" Christian. "When a person seems at his worst," she said, "we should demonstrate Jesus' love the most. When a child falls, you don't avoid or scold him, you help him up and comfort and encourage him."

When Montreat-Anderson refused to readmit Mendez the next fall, Ruth telephoned the president of a nearby Bible school.

"Would you like to gamble?" she asked.

"What do you mean, Ruth?" the man replied after a long, curious silence.

"How would you like to have a student who is the most irresponsible, unpredictable, undependable Christian you've ever met? And furthermore, he has a beard and he drinks and he smokes."

"Ruth," he said, again after a long pause, "it sounds to me as if he's not ready for Bible college."

"Where does a baby Christian go to get ready for Bible college?"

"That," the man conceded, "is a very good question."

After some reluctance on the president's part, Ruth persuaded him that if he would take the chance, she would ensure that Mendez's education was paid for one semester at a time. He agreed, and in February of 1971, Mendez shaved his beard, swore off alcohol and cigarettes, and headed off to Bible college.

Over the years, Ruth had corresponded with Meg Spalding, praying for her while Meg moved from one tragedy to another. In September of 1972 when Ruth was in England she learned that Meg was pregnant and planning an abortion. She had moved in with friends in London and wanted to see Ruth. Dressed in black, sickly, Meg met her in a hotel restaurant.

"I can't have it, Ruth," she said. "I can't. It would be half black, born of prostitution. I hate the father and hated meself when it was happening. I wouldn't make a good mother. I know me own limitations, I do."

Opposed to what she called "the modern-day holocaust," Ruth argued against Meg's notion of having an abortion and suggested she put the child up for adoption.

"If I can't have it, nobody will," she replied.

The next day they met in a corner booth in a coffee shop and talked for two hours. She told Ruth that her real problem was that she enjoyed being a lesbian and did not want to give it up.

"I need these relationships," she insisted, munching on the ham sandwich Ruth had ordered for her.

"There's a story of a little pig trotting happily to market," Ruth replied. "Other owners were having a rough time of it, either dragging the squealing animal by a rope around its neck or hurting it with a stick. Watching one little pig happily following its owner to market, the others asked the man his secret.

"'It's beans,'" he replied. 'I've a pocket full of them. And I drop one at a time.' So the little pig trotted happily to market, eating one bean at a time, unaware that he was on his way to becoming someone's ham sandwich.

"The Devil is smart enough to provide you with just enough pleasurable scenes to keep you following him to Hell," Ruth concluded. "I'd like you to get alone sometime and write down on a piece of paper all the reasons why you should remain as you are and in another column why you should surrender to the Lord Jesus."

She explained to Meg that being a Christian was not an escape—in fact it was a challenge, the road to a harder, yet better, life. "What," she asked, "if someone turned a cathedral into a public privy? Yet God created you a dwelling for Himself and you are doing just that."

Later that day she wrote in her journal: "We are not punished for our sins, but by them. . . . I watched the too-old face, the chain-smoking, the sunken lips, saw her wince with pain from time to time, listened to her—and I know that we are indeed punished by our sins. The Devil has won this round."

Several days later Meg telephoned her and told her that she had decided to keep the baby.

"I really want it, Ruth," she said. "All me sisters have had babies out of wedlock. But Ruth, I really want it, I do. I'll get me a job so I can get it really nice clothes and I'll teach it manners—to say 'please' and 'thank you.' I'll bring him up real proper, I will."

Ruth laughed and reminded her, "The most important thing is to teach him to know the Lord Jesus."

"Yeah," she said.

"It won't be easy," she warned. "And to be a good mother you'll have to give up your lesbian relationships."

"I'll do anything for the baby, Ruth. I've had only one cigarette all day, I have. When it comes I want you to be its grandmother or its godmother or something."

"O.K.," she agreed.

But that day would never come, for less than twenty-four hours later, she would suffer a miscarriage. Soon after, Ruth boarded a Pan Am flight for home, her heart heavy. "I am asking God boldly, presumptuously and confidently," she wrote aboard the plane, "that Meg's life might yet demonstrate the transforming and keeping power of the Lord Jesus Christ. Heredity, environment, circumstances, are all against her. Is anything too hard for the Lord? Isn't it true the greater the problem, the greater His glory through conquering it? Her heredity, her environment, her friends, her nature—all state flatly that it is quite impossible. Not unlikely. Just impossible. Anyway, it's up to Him. I feel sick at my stomach. It's the most hopeless case I've ever come across."

She wrote a poem for her:

> Perhaps
> she will land
> upon That Shore,
> not in full sail,
> but rather
> a bit of broken wreckage
> for Him
> to gather.
>
> Perhaps
> He walks those Shores
> seeking such
> who have believed
> a little
> suffered much
> and so
> have been washed Ashore.
>
> Perhaps
> of all the souls redeemed
> them He most adores.[2]

---

2. *sitting by my laughing fire* ... (Waco, Texas: Word Books, 1977), p. 65.

PART IV

16

Power and Influence

I don't think Ruth cares a hoot about whether or not she meets a celebrity.

Julie Nixon Eisenhower

On a clear, balmy March evening in 1950, Strom Thurmond and his wife, Jean, invited the Grahams to the Governor's Mansion at Columbia, South Carolina. It was one of the first occasions when a prominent politician showed interest in the evangelist who had become so well known during the pivotal Los Angeles crusade the year before. Ironically, after an evening of mingling with a number of the state's prominent citizens, the names Ruth recorded in her diary were those of the servants.

That was typical. The Grahams' association with the famous and influential has been a source of both curiosity and controversy. In 1950 President Harry Truman invited Billy to the White House for the first time; in 1955, the Grahams were invited to Clarence House to be presented to the Queen Mother; later that spring they were invited to Windsor Castle to have lunch with the Queen and the Duke of Edinburgh. Never has an evangelist been of such interest to contemporary world leaders. Ruth occasionally accompanied her husband on his visits to places of importance. In general, she was observant and unassertive; she rarely discussed the details of such events with friends or even family.

On their first visit to Clarence House, a butler reached for the evangelist's hat and Billy shook his hand with a "Pleased to meet you." Then, when the Queen Mother appeared, Ruth didn't know which to do first, curtsy or bow. Her indecision, her husband remarked afterwards, made it look as if she "had tripped over the rug." Though the Grahams were discreet about these visits, the British press was not. Reporters usually found out about them and printed detailed, often fictitious reports in the newspapers. After the 1955 lunch in Windsor Castle, reporters demanded a statement from Billy. When he refused, they printed that as the Grahams left the castle, the evangelist patted Prince Charles on the head and remarked, "God bless you, sonny. I have a little boy just like you at home." They had in fact not even seen Prince Charles.

Billy's associations with world leaders began generating criticism from other ministers and theologians, many of whom had never agreed with the evangelist or his message to begin with. One critic was the theologian Karl Barth, whom the Grahams became acquainted with in the summer of 1960 while Billy was preaching in Switzerland and Germany and his family was staying near Montreux on Lake Geneva. One afternoon the Grahams met Barth and his son Markus for a chat at a provincial inn. On August 26, Ruth wrote her parents:

"Dr. Karl Barth came down from the little inn porch—a big, kindly, rumpled man. Like most great men, he doesn't look the part. . . . We had a very interesting two-hour visit. . . . Really, his graciousness, his geniality, his kindliness, make one feel he is a near and dear relative—like an uncle or a grandfather. There is nothing of the austere or unapproachable scholar one might expect.

"They are all deeply disturbed by and concerned over Bill's giving an invitation. As far as I could see Dr. Karl Barth felt the 'convert' would confuse the act of coming forward with conversion itself. Dr. Markus Barth felt it was 'separating' the believer from the unbeliever and he feels there is great danger in Christians 'separating.' I felt the language barrier accounted for some misunderstandings and the fact that none of them had ever attended a meeting."

As they chatted around the table, Billy asked Karl Barth what he would say to a "sinner" if one came to him for help.

"I would say to him," Barth replied, raising his shoulders and upturned palms in an eloquent shrug, "'Friend, you are in great danger . . . but then, so am I.'"

Ruth observed:

"One could not help but feel that was a rather dreary outlook—

nothing of hope and certainty in it. I could hardly believe he meant it as he said it, and perhaps he didn't. His English is very broken. But none of the others offered to contradict or supplement what he said. Trying to follow their profound reasoning I felt myself getting thoroughly confused. . . ."

Toward the end of the conversation Karl Barth suggested to Billy, "You should come to Basel and teach theology for six months. And I will go out and hold your meetings for six months." A smile tugging at the corner of his lips, he concluded, "And anyway, I should love to have lunch with the Queen and meet President Eisenhower and people like that."

Ruth was not awed by glamour and fame. In truth, she was most comfortable sitting before the fire in her rustic house, chatting with a friend from her past or, perhaps, a neighbor. To her, greatness was measured by service, not office.

Shortly after a tea with the royal family in 1961, she was in Belfast for a crusade at Saint Andrew's Hall. There, on June 27, she visited a former missionary to China whom she remembered from her childhood. The woman lived in a nearby rest home.

Her apartment was small, washed with sunlight, bright with symbols from her past. The quilt covering her bed was made of Chinese silk scraps; her favorite volumes, worn and mottled, filled the bookshelves; yellowed photographs of her family were neatly pasted on the walls. The packing crates used to carry her belongings home from China were now furniture; her desk was a card table. On it were neatly stacked boxes she was packing with empty plastic bottles, note pads made from greeting cards and paper, a crib sheet made from bits of damask, cans, and trinkets she would soon ship to missionaries in Africa to distribute to needy children.

"You certainly manage to keep busy and get a lot done!" Ruth marveled.

She straightened proudly, looking her squarely in the eye. "I don't belong to meself," she said.

"I couldn't help remembering another room just five days before," Ruth wrote in her diary that night, referring to her earlier visit to Buckingham Palace. "It also had family pictures all around the wall, books, and a desk. And boxes piled on boxes. Red dispatch boxes. They were a world apart. But for all the royal elegance of one and simple poverty of the other, there was a similarity. And I couldn't help but feel I had had tea with royalty twice in one week."

To Ruth, happiness had nothing to do with self-importance, not even with survival. From the perspective of an infinite universe, wealth and fame were baubles. Far better to be on her mountain, snow piled on the rail fence, bare trees clawing at the pearly gray sky, flames licking over the logs; far better to be there, unnoticed and unimportant yet rich in heart and soul.

On June 23, 1966, during one of the crusades at Earl's Court, Winston Churchill's daughter Sarah invited Ruth to a cocktail party. At fifty-one, the former actress, who had just published her first book, was a brilliant woman filled with poetry and profundity but empty of the things that mattered. By now, she had been married three times. Ruth met her through Joan Winmill Brown, a former English actress who had answered the altar call at the 1954 Greater London crusade. Joan had been led to the Inquiry Room, conspicuous in a red coat, uneasy and suddenly repelled by the thought of having to talk to a stranger, much less pray with one. Edging toward the door, she was on the verge of slipping away when a striking woman wearing a camel's hair coat greeted her. Warm and sensitive, the woman read from her Bible and listened. "Joan, you don't walk out of here alone," she said. "Christ goes with you." She wanted Joan to meet her husband, so she led her down a hallway, into a tiny office; momentarily, Joan, speechless with surprise, was shaking hands with Billy Graham.

Joan and Bill Brown later became employed by the BGEA and in 1966 they found themselves in London, helping set up the Earl's Court crusade. They moved into a nineteenth-century row house in Chelsea, soon to find they were next door to Sarah Churchill, there temporarily while her posh townhouse off Eaton Square was being renovated. She lived in an apartment filled with English antiques, the walls covered with her father's paintings and many of her own.

The Browns came to know her when she knocked on their door one night because she had locked herself out of her apartment. Joan impulsively volunteered her husband to climb over the balcony and let her in. "Oh, Lord," Joan mumbled, watching him perilously suspended two stories above the parking lot, "I just hope that balcony holds with Bill's weight on it." Afterwards, Sarah became a frequent late-night visitor, sitting at their kitchen table, her bottle of wine before her, listening, asking questions about their Christian faith.

"I don't want to join," she often reminded them.

"But Sarah," Joan would laugh, "you don't have to *join* anything."

"It's fine for you because you have Bill," Sarah would say. "And I'm sure the Lord is everything you've said He is. But I'm so lonely; I don't have anyone."

"But Sarah," Joan would reply, "the Lord wants to be everything to you. If I didn't have Bill I would still have this joy in my heart because of our Lord. He is with me no matter what happens."

A year later, Sarah moved back into her townhouse and asked Joan to bring Ruth Graham to the cocktail party and introduce them. Ruth arrived, signed the guestbook, and moved upstairs, where Sarah appeared in a pale blue dress with spaghetti straps. Her skin was flawless, her bone structure beautifully sculpted; her long strawberry blonde hair was pinned up; heavy makeup masked the eyes that looked so hauntingly like her father's. After greeting several couples, she asked wistfully, "Where is Mrs. Billy Graham?" Ruth introduced herself, and as Joan later recalled, Sarah immediately ushered Ruth out of the crowd and began asking her questions.

"Do you think there's any help for a person like me?" Sarah asked.

"The Lord can help any person," Ruth said warmly.

"Do you have any help for me?"

"I might not, but I know One who can help you, and that's the Lord Jesus."

"Do you think one is ever really happy with religion?"

"I am," Ruth said. "That is, I am truly happy with Jesus Christ. I couldn't live without Him. When my life gets beyond the ability to cope, He takes over."

"Well," responded a man in tweed who had sidled up to eavesdrop, "I've given God a couple of cracks at my life, but He certainly hasn't made much of it!"

"God helps those who help themselves," Ruth replied, smiling. "But there are times when we are quite incapable of helping ourselves. That's when God stoops down and gathers us in His arms like a mother lifts a sick child, and does for us what we cannot do for ourselves."

The apartment walls were covered with dozens of rather bizarre paintings.

"Here, let me show you," Sarah volunteered, motioning toward the gallery, tripping and sloshing her cocktail over Ruth's leg and foot. "I'm so sorry," she added, wearily lowering herself into a gilt chair. Asking to borrow her mirror, Sarah commenced powdering under one eye while Ruth waited mutely, wondering with amusement what people would think when she arrived at Earl's Court smelling like a martini.

"Please excuse me," Ruth said. "But I have to leave to get to the crusade on time. Will you come one night as my guest?"

"I would love to," she replied with feeling.

Sarah walked her down three flights of stairs to the front door, stopping on the last step, one hand on the banister to steady herself, the other holding her glass. Her eyes, vacant, infinitely sad, followed Ruth.

"Bill and Joan Brown were very kind to me," Sarah said suddenly.

"They love you very much," Ruth said gently.

"They thought I was too drunk to understand. I saw everything. I heard everything. I understood everything."

She was seen in the crowd the last afternoon of the crusade, perched high in the stands at Wembley. After the sermon, Ruth searched for her, straining to see her face somewhere among the sea of people. She was gone, having left just moments before the altar call, threading through the masses toward an exit, head bent.

By the late fifties Billy was receiving invitations to White House prayer breakfasts, beginning a tradition that would continue through the Reagan presidency. It was here he and Ruth became acquainted with Senator Lyndon B. Johnson and his wife, Lady Bird. When John F. Kennedy was assassinated in 1963, Johnson became president, and soon Billy Graham became known as the "White House Chaplain," a tongue-in-cheek appellation that followed the evangelist through the Nixon administration.

Forthcoming were occasional telephone calls from the President and invitations to the White House and to the ranch house on the north bank of the Pedernales River, fifty miles west of Austin. Ruth was adamantly opposed to her husband's becoming involved in politics. She reminded him of this occasionally. In 1964 they dined with the Johnsons the weekend of the Democratic convention.

"Who should I take as my running mate?" Johnson asked Billy.

Before Billy could reply he received a swift kick under the table. "Why did you kick me?" he asked Ruth.

Johnson looked at her quizzically, his eyes twinkling as he waited for her response.

"Because," she said firmly, "you are supposed to limit your advice to moral and spiritual issues and stay out of politics."

"I agree with you," Johnson said.

As they left the dining room, preceded by the women, Johnson whispered to Billy, "Now, what do you really think?"

Johnson had no hesitation in letting the world know that he and Billy were friends. On May 20, 1965, the Associated Press reported that when he was tired or worried he often called Billy "to get a new injection." When he "was being called a crook and a thug and all," he said, he spent a weekend with Billy and "we bragged on each other. I told him he was the greatest religious leader in the world and he said I was the greatest political leader."

Ideally, it was not the Grahams' place to judge the President, they believed. Nor were they to endorse him. Unfortunately, the fact that they were frequently seen with a president seemed endorsement enough.

But the friendships between Johnson and clergymen were more than political, claimed Calvin Thielman, who, by a strange twist of fate, had been Johnson's campaign manager in his race against Coke Stevenson for a seat in the Senate in 1948.

Calvin was seventeen, a respected orator in his high school, when the Lamar County attorney, Royce Whitten, summoned him to his spacious courthouse office and asked him to be Johnson's campaign manager. Calvin accepted the offer and for the next few months, he and this gangly, jug-eared Texan, forever known as "LBJ," buzzed the Lone Star State in a newfangled contraption called a helicopter. It was just the two of them and a pilot, their helicopter agitating the skies above provincial towns like an eggbeater, a Texas drawl booming such messages from its P.A. system as: "THIS IS LYNDON JOHNSON YOUR NEXT U.S. SENATOR. MEET ME AT THE MARKET SQUARE AT THREE O'CLOCK."

One afternoon they landed in Calvin's hometown of Paris. Knowing that Calvin dreamed of one day being a politician, Johnson, amid a square thick with people, wrapped an arm around him and announced, "If Wright Patman ever dies, this boy will be the next congressman from this district." (Ironically, thirty-five years later, Calvin and Patman would stand side by side at Johnson's funeral.) After stumping for five in months in thirty-six precincts, Johnson won the runoff by 87 votes out of 900,000 cast. Thus he became "Landslide Lyndon," and was accused of stuffing the ballot boxes.

Many years later, when Johnson was in the White House, he called upon Calvin as many as half a dozen times to sit by his bed and pray or read the Bible to him. The President had a vulnerability that caused him to crave approval, that caused him to have "a soft spot for preachers," Calvin observed. Billy's affection seemed especially important to Johnson: In 1971 Johnson told Walter Cronkite, "Not many people in this country love me, but," he said, referring to Billy, "that preacher there loves me."

CBS anchorman Dan Rather, a native Texan who covered the Johnson presidency, believed Johnson's interest in Billy was not entirely opportunistic. "Johnson had a strong strain of religion in him," he mused, staring over black reading glasses in his modest New York office. "I think Johnson, in a way, was a believer in what Graham was doing and what Graham was trying to do. . . . In street language, he put a move on Graham. But it would be a mistake to see it as entirely cynical."

To Lady Bird Johnson, it was all very simple. "I know, at least my feeling is, that Lyndon sought counsel of an awful lot of folks from our cook on up to Dean Rusk, and the wealthy or most academic to the lowest. Lyndon had a very strong sense of need, certainly he did in the presidency, a need for being sure he was on the right path, a need for comfort, a need for an anchor. Billy was a comfort. And Lyndon believed in him and respected him. . . . And if there ever is a position in the world where you feel you need all the help you can get it's the presidency."

It was during the Johnson friendship that Ruth became familiar with the White House. Those who observed her—like Lady Bird Johnson, the press, and later Barbara Bush—commented that it was not her wont to elbow her way to the forefront and introduce herself to the important people. Instead, she would drift to the edge of the crowd, melding into the background like one of the dark oil portraits, unobtrusive amid the heavy draperies and chandeliers. The Ruth who lost herself in the masses at crusades, the Ruth who disliked sitting on the platform, remained in character in the White House.

She was "quiet, gentle, observant," recalled Rather, who occasionally saw her at the White House and later at events involving Nixon. "As a professional observer myself, maybe I recognize that. She was watching people, watching events. Listening very carefully. She was not one of these people whose mind is elsewhere. And if she's talking to you, she's talking to you—she's not looking past you. You may only have her for a few seconds, but you've got her attention and she's listening to what you're saying."

In 1968 Johnson announced he would not run for re-election. He asked the Grahams to stay with him on his last night in the White House. But the friendship did not end with his term of office.

On Sunday, October 18, 1970, the Grahams flew to Austin, and Secret Service agents drove them within two miles of the ranch. Johnson, driven by a foreman, escorted them the rest of the way. He was thinner since leaving the White House, his silver hair untrimmed and curling down the back of his neck; he was more relaxed and playful, howling cheek-to-cheek—singing duets, as he called it— with his white mongrel, Yuki, reducing guests to weepy laughter. He told long stories, ambling through the colorful turns of his imagination, savoring every detail like the raconteur he was, and read aloud long sections from his new book, *The Vantage Point*. When he tired of talking, he would ride around the ranch, checking on the guinea hens, hawks, deer, tractor blades, and his airport runway.

During the October 18 visit Ruth met Madame Shoumatoff, the Russian artist who was painting President Franklin D. Roosevelt's portrait when he died at Warm Springs on April 12, 1945. She was now in the midst of painting Mrs. Johnson's portrait, and on this Sunday, she rode with the Secret Service man who picked up the Grahams in Austin. En route to the ranch, Ruth and Madame Shoumatoff discussed subjects ranging from her leaving Russia just before the Bolshevik Revolution in 1917 to Grigori Efimovich Rasputin.

"It is quite an experience to find oneself in a new country with nothing," she told Ruth. "Suddenly one realizes one has absolutely nothing. It is a strange sensation—a sort of lightness. It's a great privilege to be deprived of all one's possessions—when one is twenty and in good health."

Madame Shoumatoff's father, she said, had once ridden on a train with Rasputin and conversed with him for two hours. "He was a compelling personality—repulsively dirty but with strange, piercing eyes. Very light with small, dark pupils," she said. Rasputin told her father that as a young man he had committed every sin, that he was consummately evil. Then one day in a field, Rasputin claimed, he had seen the glory of God and had repented. When her father asked him bluntly about the stories of his immorality, his debauchery, Rasputin replied, "I repented once. I can sin and repent again."

Ruth wondered if Rasputin could have been possessed by demons.

"But of course," Madame Shoumatoff replied. "One knows, but

one cannot speak of certain things in polite society."

In contrast with some of the more prominent people Ruth had met, she found Madame Shoumatoff "interested in others, therefore interesting." For that same reason Ruth held Mrs. Johnson in high esteem. She was a kind, gracious woman, lacking the veneer of self-importance one might expect of a first lady; she was humble, almost self-effacing, aggressive in her interest in others and quick to steer the interest away from herself; and yet, beneath her soft exterior, there was a fortitude and intelligence, a keen perception, that was all the more powerful because it usually went unnoticed. "Sometimes beautiful women develop from adjusting to difficult men," Ruth often said.

The two women became friends. Both knew the pressure of having the world view them with expectation and curiosity: "I don't want to be anybody's role model—I don't think I'm that good," explained Mrs. Johnson. "And . . . Ruth wouldn't want to be a role model, but you are forced into it willy-nilly." It was a winter morning in Richmond, Virginia, and Mrs. Johnson was seated on an indigo couch on the second floor of the governor's mansion, there to visit her son-in-law Governor Chuck Robb, her daughter Lynda, and the grandchildren. Her hair was a bit grayer; she was erect, yet unassuming; she was dressed in a navy skirt and creamy satin blouse, weary from greeting various groups touring the mansion. She was troublesome to interview because she was more interested in asking questions about Ruth than she was in answering them; she said she had unsuccessfully tried for years to learn more about her friend. The problem was that because of their husbands, the two women could rarely get a word in edgewise.

"It's not easy to get her to talk about herself," Mrs. Johnson observed. "The conversation around Billy is always very substantive and exciting. And I like to hear him talk too about the places he has been and all these crusades he has conducted—and his feelings about a country, its culture, its economy, its stability. And pretty soon I've lost the thread about her childhood and I've found we're listening to these other things."

Ruth was accustomed to being her husband's second priority. His ministry came first and she wanted it that way. There were, however, a few times when she would come in third, for when a world leader needed her husband, he felt it was his patriotic duty to be there. Johnson certainly saw the logic of this reasoning and demonstrated as much on August 13, 1972, the Grahams' twenty-ninth wedding anniversary, when Billy and Grady Wilson were on the ranch with him. That night Billy telephoned Ruth to wish her a happy anniversary and Johnson picked up another extension:

"I sure do want to thank you for letting us have Billy today. But I needed him more than you did. We've been having a time riding around. Grady's here doing a good job keeping the dogs in the backseat, but he's a damn poor substitute for you."

Shortly before four in the afternoon on Sunday, January 22, 1973, two days after Nixon's second inauguration and the day before a cease-fire was announced in Vietnam, Johnson, alone in his bedroom, suffered a fatal heart attack.

For years he had expressed his hope that Billy would preach at his funeral. The last time the evangelist was with him on his ranch Johnson had taken him to the family cemetery, about a mile from the house, and showed him the exact spot where he wanted to be buried; he had given him specific instructions about the service.

"Don't use any notes," he told him. "The wind will blow them away. And I don't want a lot of fancy eulogizing, but be sure to mention my name."

On January 24, a raw, overcast Tuesday, Johnson's body was flown to Washington in *Air Force One*. The next day the flag-draped casket moved slowly up the steps of the Capitol, where Billy led in prayer. Then the Grahams flew to San Antonio and waited in a private lounge for the presidential jet to arrive with the body. While there, Ruth talked with one of Johnson's sisters.

"He was the best brother anyone ever had," the woman said numbly. "He was a much better Christian than most believed. He really believed. We had been taught that way. When Daddy was sick he used to get up in the night and go to see him, he was so good to him. And after Daddy died, he was so good to Mother. How he loved Mother!"

Air Force One arrived and they moved from the lounge, positioning themselves outside. Anonymous onlookers lined the fence around the runway, faces pale, shoulders hunched in the cold. The jet taxied into place near a waiting hearse. Friends, officials, military officers, lined up behind Billy as he stood bareheaded in the icy rain, a black robe over his winter coat. An elevator platform was rolled into place at the plane's rear exit and the casket was lifted; he stepped forward to meet the Johnson family as they deplaned from the front; they stood together, somberly facing the crowd while a band played hymns and white-gloved hands smoothly slid the casket inside the hearse.

People dispersed to private cars or limousines to make the hour's drive to the ranch. Protocol directed that Billy was to ride alone behind the hearse, but Mrs. Johnson requested that he stay with the family. Ruth rode with the John Connallys. People lined the road on both sides for miles; traffic stopped, cars pulled off the road to let the procession pass. Each small town and farm along the way had its own cluster of spectators, some of them holding signs that read "We love you, Mr. President" and "Forgive us, Mr. President."

It was a small cemetery, girdled by a low stone wall, shaded by massive oaks, peopled at that moment with generations of family, both living and dead. Thousands gathered outside it, standing in the rain and mud. Ruth was to follow the Connallys through a barrier of Secret Service agents and stand inside. Instead, she stood just outside the gate while her husband read John 14:1–3, and briefly eulogized Johnson. He pronounced the benediction and the honor guard folded the American flag, then presented it to Mrs. Johnson. She kissed it.

Hundreds of friends had been invited to the ranch afterward for coffee. Mrs. Johnson had asked the Grahams to spend the night, but "we felt the kindest thing we could do was to leave as quickly as possible," Ruth wrote at the time. Inside, the carpeting had been covered with heavy plastic and the furniture had been pushed back. Yuki was curled up on the couch.

"I wanted so much to say something to let Mrs. Johnson know how we loved and admired her—how our hearts went out to her," Ruth recorded. "Instead she hugged me and said something about reading everything I wrote or that had been written about me. And we hugged again and I slipped away. I, who had come to love, had been loved. I, who had come to give, had been given to. Such is the stuff of which she is made. Nor was I the exception. There was a word, a hug, a cordial greeting, or a warm smile for each." She wrote:

Of this historic moment
two things I kept:
that earth was gray
and cold,
and heaven wept.[1]

---

1. Ruth Bell Graham, *sitting by my laughing fire . . .* (Waco, Texas: Words Books, 1977), p. 175.

The Grahams, T. W. Wilson, Grady Wilson, and Calvin Thielman left the ranch late that afternoon by car, heading for San Antonio as the setting sun broke through the black clouds, splashing red and gold over the wet pavement. The next morning, when no cameras or microphones were there to record events, they sat in the San Antonio airport eating breakfast. A woman across the room eyed Billy for several minutes, her face bleak as though the wretchedness of all the world were held in a tiny knot in her heart. Finally, she mustered enough courage to approach him.

"May I talk to you for just a minute?" she asked shakily.

Billy nodded for Calvin to move aside. He listened to her. Then, heads bowed, he prayed with her. When she left, tears in her eyes, Calvin apologized to Billy for not shielding him so he could finish his breakfast before his eggs were cold.

"No," Billy said. "You did the right thing. Her mother is dying from cancer and her heart is very heavy. She wanted me to pray for her."

When President Richard Nixon moved into the White House in January of 1969 one of the first things he did was establish church services in the East Room.

"In those years President Nixon, whether rightly or wrongly, thought that church was so important that you should emphasize it by having it in the White House," recalled Barbara Bush as she sipped coffee in a sitting room of the vice-presidential mansion, on a raw morning in February of 1982. "And of course it also, in all honesty, kept an awful lot of people from going to an awful lot of trouble. If you had church at the White House you didn't have to have the church sniffed and security all checked, and eighty people have to do all of that when the President moves. So he had church at the White House for security reasons. And then he asked leaders in the church to come and preach—Jewish, Catholic, whatever."

Billy Graham was one of these leaders that Nixon occasionally invited to preach, and Ruth usually accompanied him. They had a deep affection and admiration for Nixon. In the same way that Nixon admired Billy's Christian integrity and fortitude, Billy, who had always been interested in world affairs, admired Nixon's genius. Though Ruth never became close to Nixon, she was later grateful for his breakthrough in China, believing him to be unmatched in his skill at foreign policy. She did, however, strike up a warm friendship with Julie Nixon Eisenhower and, in fact, had a significant influence on her. One early Sunday morning before Billy was to speak at the White House Julie asked Ruth about her faith, about prayer, and if God really listened. Together they talked until church time with Julie asking questions in her high-strung, perceptive manner, and Ruth calmly replying, her leatherbound, copiously marked King James Bible open in her lap.

"She's been an inspiration to me," Julie said. "She's so real. She's one of the few persons I've known who really lives her faith."

Ruth inspired Julie enough to become the subject of a chapter in Julie's book *Special People*.[2] She shares page space with Prince Charles, Golda Meir, and Anne Morrow Lindbergh, among other notables.

Nixon had first heard about Billy in the forties when his mother, Hannah Nixon, had attended a Graham crusade in Southern California and had written her son about how impressed she was. Senator Clyde Hoey introduced the two men in 1950 and, through Billy's friendship with President Eisenhower, they became well acquainted.

The days of Ruth's kicking her husband under the table for discussing politics were long gone. "Bill was supposed to limit his advice to spiritual and moral matters," she said. "Knowing Bill, knowing myself and how prone we are to give free advice even when unasked for, I wouldn't be at all surprised if when he was with the President, if the President asked his opinions, he would tell him what he thought, and give him advice that wasn't limited to spiritual, moral things. He wouldn't say, 'I'm sorry, Mr. President, that's out of my field.' And frankly, I don't see what's wrong in asking the advice of a clergyman if he's got a good clear head on him. The media's taking exception to what they are afraid Bill might be saying doesn't make sense to me. I would think they would be happy to have as many good, decent, clear-thinking men as Bill as possible at the White House.

"Do we want a president in the White House who is not free to call on a clergyman if he feels the need of one? Well, that's what it will boil down to if clergymen are driven to the position some members of the press have tried to drive Bill to. Christianity is above ideology. It's for Democrats and Republicans alike. It's for sinners and I think the press would be the first to admit there are sinners in politics."

William F. Buckley, Jr., puts it well: "It seems to me plain that

---

2. (New York: Simon & Schuster, 1977).

presidents should have access to religious figures; plain, also, that there will be attempted abuses, in both directions, in many cases."

Whatever Nixon's intentions towards her husband were, Ruth said in retrospect, he impressed the Grahams as being a "religious man who did not wear his religion on his sleeve."

Nixon, said Billy during an interview in Montreat on a raw, blustery November afternoon in 1982, "is a very serious person and a very deep person and a very intellectual person." And yet, the evangelist added, he was surprisingly sensitive and thoughtful. For example, "he would never forget a birthday."

"I was playing golf in France," Billy recalled, "and I had an old set of clubs that I had rented. And I played one of the best games I've ever played and I wanted to buy those clubs. The golf pro would not sell them to me. So when I got home and was playing golf with Mr. Nixon in California one day, I told him about this and I didn't think anything more of it. And did you know I got those golf clubs for Christmas? He had sent over there and gotten them. He was just always kind, courteous and thoughtful. . . . I never felt he was using me—*ever*."

In May of 1970, Nixon appeared on the platform of the Knoxville crusade at Neyland Stadium, University of Tennessee. It was the first time in history that a president had spoken on an evangelist's platform and the first time Nixon had appeared on a university campus since he'd ordered troops into Cambodia the month before.[3] Seventy-five thousand people jammed Neyland Stadium and another twenty-five thousand spilled into the parking lot and the grassy area around it. Three hundred antiwar demonstrators pooled toward the rear of the stadium, unfurling banners and flags. Members of the University of Tennessee football team wanted to force the protesters back outside, but Secret Service agents shook their heads. It was wise, they said in agreement with Billy, "to avoid a confrontation."

Pat Nixon and the President waited with the Grahams until all the platform guests had been seated. Then Nixon and Billy, followed by Mrs. Nixon and Ruth, filed up the platform steps to deafening applause and a standing ovation; the obscenities and boos of the dissenters were, for a moment, barely discernible.

"The rudeness, immaturity, and stupidity of the demonstrators was unbelievable," Ruth recorded. "Whatever they think of Mr. Nixon they should respect the office of the presidency." During Nixon's

3. John Pollock, *Billy Graham: Evangelist to the World* (San Francisco: Harper & Row, 1979), p. 106.

speech the protesters stood time and time again, shouting and waving their banners. "It was a strange mixture of feelings I had—mounting anger that the President of the United States cannot speak at a religious rally without being shouted down," Ruth wrote, "pride in Mr. Nixon's dignity and graciousness . . . and profound gratification that the vast majority were solidly behind him and let him know it."

After Nixon's brief speech the late Ethel Waters, the black singer and former actress who had been a frequent guest at Billy Graham crusades, was helped to the pulpit to sing.

"I've known my precious boy 'Dickie'—President Nixon—and his precious Pat for many years," she said. "I expect the next time we meet, Mr. President," she added, turning toward Nixon, "will be in Heaven."

Then, directing her attention to the protesters, she said, "If you knew them you'd really like them. They're just nice, fine people. And now you precious children, I love you but if I could get close enough, I'd smack you!"

After the service Nixon asked the Grahams to ride out to *Air Force One* with them in the long, black, bulletproof limousine. For miles the road was lined with people.

Beside *Air Force One* Nixon was surrounded by dozens of reporters. Obviously in a good mood, he quipped that he'd had to borrow money from Billy for the offering and that he would repay him later with golf balls. The reporters attempted to interview the evangelist, but their questions were swallowed up in the roar of the jet's engines as the silver door shut behind the President.

The Grahams discovered that Nixon had left orders for the limousine to drive them back through Knoxville to their hotel. Flanked by motorcycles with flashing blue lights, they cruised slowly through town, "feeling ridiculous," as Ruth remembered it.

The event was disturbing to Dan Rather, who was there with a press pool. Rather, an admirer of Billy's, could understand an evangelist's desire "for the opportunity to talk to and perhaps influence the country's leadership and world leadership." But, he recalled, "the Knoxville scene was personally troubling to me. I remember walking into the stadium and saying to myself, 'You know, this is just really not right. I mean, Billy Graham shouldn't be doing this, or someone in Reverend Graham's position shouldn't be doing this, President Nixon shouldn't be doing this.' I would think both of them would have a little embarrassment about that scene today. It had the appearance at least of being a little too calculated on both sides and a little too blatant on both sides—using one another to each's advantage.

"There was a tremendous crowd and it was a little piece of Americana—great football crowd, all that big U.T. stuff hanging around the stadium and Reverend Graham running a crusade and Richard Nixon running his own crusade; two crusaders meet—it was a bit much."

Ruth, too, felt ambivalence about Nixon's appearance on her husband's platform, and she was disappointed that Nixon had not given a spiritual message to the people. "I think to have [presidents] come and sit in the audience is one thing," she remarked years later. "To have them speak from the platform is another."

In the spring of 1971 Nixon, with the argument of "national security," demanded that his campaign aides step up their political intelligence. In June, one year later, five men were arrested in the Democratic National Committee Headquarters at the Watergate complex. Three days later Nixon and his top aide H. R. Haldeman met to discuss the arrests. (The tape of this conversation is the one with the notorious eighteen-and-a-half-minute gap.) The scandals collectively known as Watergate were beginning to escalate, but in the public eye Nixon was untainted.

On October 15, a year before the presidential election, Nixon paid Billy an amazing tribute by appearing on the platform with him for Billy Graham Day in Charlotte. The prominent media executive and president of the Charlotte Chamber of Commerce Charles Crutchfield conceived the idea of having the city publicly honor its most celebrated son. When Crutchfield telephoned Billy about it he refused, saying he'd been honored enough by the people of his birthplace.[4]

Crutchfield wouldn't take no for an answer. After Nixon appeared with Billy in Knoxville, Crutchfield had decided both that Billy Graham Day was a grand idea and that what would really make it spectacular—indeed historic—would be the appearance of Richard Nixon in Charlotte to honor his evangelist friend. Crutchfield contacted the White House; soon afterward Nixon telephoned Billy. He wanted Billy to accept the honor, he said. And Nixon wanted to be there with him to honor their years of friendship.

"If that is your wish, Mr. President," Billy replied, "then of course I'll accept."[5]

4. Ibid., pp. 174–75.
5. Ibid.

October 15 was designated a holiday in Charlotte. The children had a day off from school. Tremendous crowds of cheering citizens lined East Independence Boulevard as dignitaries like North Carolina Senators Sam Ervin[6] and B. Everett Jordan, South Carolina Senator Strom Thurmond and the John Connallys rumbled past in a motorcade. There was a public rally at the coliseum during which Billy spoke, followed by Nixon, who used no notes. He made comments such as, "What I know about the law I owe to this state"; and "Greece, Rome, Ancient Persia, their civilizations died . . . because as they became wealthy, they became soft, as they became educated without principle they became weak . . . it is the character of a nation that determines whether it survives.

"Let me just say this," he continued, "we all think of Billy Graham as a strong man. But as I look at the Graham family, if I am asked, 'who are the stronger, Billy Graham or the women in his family?' I'll say the women every time. . . . God made man out of the soft earth but he made woman out of a hard rib—the woman is the stronger of the two.

"I think of his wife Ruth who has been by his side, born in China of missionary parents, lived there three hundred miles from Shanghai for seventeen years and now giving him the support, the strength, that any man who is in the arena needs, needs when he goes home."[7]

On Sunday, January 22, 1973, Nixon began his second term by having Billy speak at the White House church service. That morning people convened in the spacious East Room with its parquet floors, gold draperies, mirrors, and crystal chandeliers. Nixon stood at the podium, flanked by portraits of George and Martha Washington, and talked of his mother, her deep Christian faith and how she loved to hear any new preacher in her area. When Nixon was a student at Duke Law School, he went on to say, he received a letter from his mother saying she'd heard a young preacher by the name of Billy Graham.

"'I think he is going to go places,'" Nixon quoted. "I still have this letter."

"They are a wonderful family," Ruth wrote at the time, "and America is fortunate to have them for another four years."

---

6. Ironically, Senator Sam Ervin would later head the Watergate investigation on Capitol Hill.
7. "Records of Blue Ridge Broadcasting Corp" (15 October 1971), Tape 35, Collection 45, Archives of the Billy Graham Center, Wheaton, Illinois.

A short time later, when Israeli Prime Minister Golda Meir was to appear at the White House for a dinner honoring her, she requested that Billy Graham be included in the guest list. On March 1, just before the 8:00 P.M. dinner, the Grahams mingled with the other guests in the East Room. When Billy greeted the prime minister in the receiving line, she reached up and kissed him.

At dinner, Golda Meir sat between Nixon and Billy at table 12. Ruth sat at table 9 next to Speaker of the House Carl Albert, where she watched the proceedings with a bit of amusement. A Jewish woman sitting at Ruth's table stared at Billy and Golda Meir suspiciously, not realizing that the evangelist's wife was sitting inches away from her.

"What is Billy Graham doing sitting next to Madame Golda?" the woman asked no one in particular as she picked at her poached red snapper and wild rice. "Do you suppose he is proselytizing her?"

"I would put my money on Madame Golda Meir," Ruth replied with a laugh. "But never fear, when we get home tonight, I'll straighten him out."

On August 9, Nixon resigned the presidency. The man revealed on the Watergate tapes was a man the Grahams had never met. They felt sick with disappointment and disbelief. The only Graham friend who seemed undaunted was Ethel Waters, who one day remarked to Grady Wilson, "If my baby Dick said damn, he damn well needed to say damn!"

The scandal, however, did not change the Grahams' affection for Nixon. After listening to his resignation speech Ruth wrote, "He spoke from his heart, quietly, movingly, eloquently. This was the man we [saw] on other private occasions. Warm, human. . . . I still wonder, what did he do to warrant this?"

Billy attempted repeatedly to reach Nixon but his telephone calls were never returned. It was as though an iron curtain had dropped between the Grahams and the Nixons. "I tried many times to get through to him, to just have prayer with him, to encourage him," Billy said. "He wouldn't have anything to do with me." Later, he learned that Nixon had told his aides, "Don't let Billy Graham near me, I don't want him tarred with Watergate."

That fall, while Nixon was hospitalized with thrombophlebitis, a rather bold idea occurred to Ruth one night. Why not fly an airplane carrying a message up and down the beach in front of Nixon's hospital? At her request, a friend arranged for an airplane to be rented in

California. It pulled a banner that read: "NIXON, WE LOVE YOU—SO DOES GOD." Photographs of this spectacle appeared in newspapers and magazines throughout the country, but its perpetrator remained a mystery.

The Grahams' reaction to Watergate showed two things. First, they were not likely to voice criticisms publicly, especially if their opinions risked breaking the pastoral promise of confidentiality. Both seemed to have an inexhaustible supply of forgiveness. Secondly, neither of them turned his back on a friend.

As Barbara Bush observed, "They're close friends to the Nixons. I mean they really are, still. They're that kind of friend. They don't think we're perfect. And they don't think the Nixons are perfect. But that doesn't mean you drop a friend."

17

A New Season

Oh, time! be slow!
it was a dawn ago
I was a child
dreaming of being grown;
a noon ago
I was
with children of my own;
and now
it's afternoon
—and late,
and they are grown
and gone.
Time, wait![1]

Ruth Bell Graham, 1971

For her, it was autumn: the season when beauty rises with the sinking of the sap, igniting the hills in a final purgation; the season when the moon, ponderous and yellow, floats to the surface of night and sifts light over the cool features of the earth, illuminating what has been dark; the season in a woman's life when she begins to look like herself, in the end transfigured by the spirit inside her.

Ruth had become more lovely. Her face was older now, and it seemed that all she had ever been or done was etched there. It was the face of one who often smiled: Her brow was smooth and lines

---

1. Ruth Bell Graham, *sitting by my laughing fire*... (Waco, Texas: Word Books, 1977), p. 225.

radiated from her eyes; two fine creases ran from the wings of her nose to the corners of her mouth, lifting her cheeks in tucks when she smiled, her teeth bright between them like the sun shining through sashed curtains. Her eyes were wide and expressive: sparkling like water when she laughed, winking like light on a windowpane when she teased. At pensive moments, when she was alone with her thoughts, weariness and wisdom wavered through them like the shadow of a fish swimming through a pond. Her bones were more sharply defined, exquisite: the straight nose, the high cheeks, the strong jaw. Her skin was taut, her veins prominent as a leaf's.

She was trim and firm, weighing less than she had in college. More dapper and conservative in dress, she preferred tweedy suits with pocketed long skirts and short jackets; she enjoyed unadorned leather boots and slippers, turtleneck sweaters, and long-sleeved blouses. Frequently, she wore a strand of pearls. The only jewelry she wore on her fingers was a wide gold band Ned had found on a playground, and her wedding band and a guard ring. She wore simple pearl or gold earrings, sometimes a thin gold bracelet or necklace. She disliked wristwatches. She pinned her gray-streaked hair in a French twist when her husband was away, occasionally tucking a fresh rose in the back; she wore it down, flipped up and brushing her shoulders, when he was home.

Her children were almost grown. Her parents and the missionaries from her childhood were dying or already gone. By 1970 her father had suffered four heart attacks; her mother was losing her eyesight, her body wracked with pain. In 1963 GiGi had married Stephan Tchividjian, a Swiss psychologist. In 1966 Anne had married Danny Lotz, a dentist and former University of North Carolina basketball star. Three years later Bunny had married Ted Dienert, an advertising executive.

By 1983 Bunny and Anne would have three children each, and GiGi would have seven. They implemented many of the child-rearing techniques that had once been used with them. Like their mother, they prodigiously studied and marked their Bibles. GiGi and Bunny had inherited a love of writing, publishing several books between them. Anne had inherited a zeal for teaching others about Christ and would start a Bible class in Raleigh, North Carolina, with a weekly attendance of five hundred women.

The three daughters' admiration for their parents was obvious: They set home and family as their top priority—as had their mother;

and they chose husbands who were devout Christians, respected in their professions and devoted to their families—as were Nelson Bell and Billy Graham.

With her daughters happily married, Ruth was free to travel more and devote her full attention to Franklin and Ned. Their friends became her friends, several of them visiting her when her sons weren't home. She took an active interest in their hobbies, like rock climbing and automobiles; and she attempted a few new ones of her own, such as riding motorcycles, hang gliding, and parasailing behind motorboats.

Ruth's family and friends had always known she was fearless, if not a bit foolish. She was known for killing rattlesnakes and copperheads on her mountain with the long, hand-wrought fork that in its lighter moments was used to roast marshmallows in the fireplace. Upon spotting a snake, she would pursue it, pin its head with this instrument, then beat it to death with whatever was at hand—usually a rock or a stick, once a lug wrench from the Jeep when she saw a rattlesnake luxuriating on her road. "If any of us seen a snake," recalled Beatrice Long, "we'd just holler 'Miz Graham! Come kill the snake!' She'd get that fork and stick the prong right down on its head. I wouldn't get that close to one for *nothing.*"

In the early seventies, Franklin acquired his first motorcycle. It was plenty loud and he enjoyed waking up the college students on early weekend mornings by roaring beneath the dormitory windows until showers of soda pop bottles sent him on his way. It was easy to figure where Franklin got his temerity: from his mother, who was last becoming the resident Motorcycle Mama. Three times she swung into the black leather seat, determined to master the sport: The first try she zoomed along Old U.S. 70 in Black Mountain, knowing how to do just about everything except stop. She plunged over a steep embankment, to the alarm of the burly, tattooed driver of the Mack truck behind her. The man stopped, peered down at her from the road, more than a little surprised to discover that this trim woman dressed in black and riding a Harley-Davidson wasn't exactly a teenager.

"Lady," he asked, "can I help you?"

"Thank you," Ruth replied. "If you could just get it on the pavement headed in the other direction, I've a friend at the end of the road who'll help me stop."

The second try landed her in a lake. The third try she accelerated instead of braking and burst through the split-rail fence, severing a vein in her leg.

Ruth wasn't exactly a benign influence in an automobile either. Just as the coolies had scattered when Dr. Bell roared into sight in his Austin Healey, so the Montreaters hugged the edge of the mountain roads for fear of meeting Ruth head-on around a curve. New drivers were warned to "watch out for Mrs. Graham."

While her husband served on the National Safety Council, preaching on film, "Drive unto others as you would have them drive unto you," his wife was behind the wheel practicing situational ethics. When in a hurry she would careen around the narrow, winding roads or roar along a highway. "Father, I'm sorry," she would pray while breaking the speed limit, "but You understand." Perhaps He did understand, for in all her years of driving she was cited only twice for speeding. The first time, the patrolman, realizing who she was, urged her to pay her ticket when the station opened early the next morning "so no one will see you."

The second citation came after Ruth had driven fifty miles from Montreat to Waynesville to visit friends. At three o'clock that afternoon Billy telephoned her and said he was with a German businessman and wondered if she could serve them tea at four.

"Sure, honey," she said cheerfully.

She sped along Old U.S. 70, the red needle wagging at eighty, when suddenly the ominous blue light flashed in her rearview mirror.

"Could you please hurry with that?" she asked the patrolman as he filled out her ticket. "And when you finish, please don't follow me, because I'm going to have to do it again."

She was home in time to greet her guest.

When Franklin bought a used early model green Triumph Spitfire, it was clear he had inherited his mother's racetrack talents and would outperform her. Not only did he drive fast, but he had a dangerous habit of zipping through the Montreat gate, entering through the exit arch or exiting through the entrance. Usually he resorted to this in the summer when he'd find himself locked into a long caravan of tourists, creeping like a centipede through the perilously narrow stone walls. He would simply bypass the traffic jam.

Police Chief Pete Post finally caught Franklin in the act one afternoon. With blue light flashing he chased him up the road toward the Graham mountain. At the lower remote-controlled gate, Franklin touched a button, roared through, and then slammed it shut in Post's face.

The children and their spouses, 1980: back row (left to right): Ted Dienert, Danny Lotz, Ned, Stephan Tchividjian, Franklin; middle row: Bunny Graham Dienert, Anne Graham Lotz, Carol Kolden Graham, GiGi Graham Tchividjian, Jane Cunningham Graham; front row: Ruth and Billy.

Anne, Bunny, GiGi and Ruth (left to right), 1981.

Ned, Billy and Franklin, 1981.

Ned at 4 years of age.

Ned, age 3, in the courtyard of Little Piney Cove.

Franklin, age 5, on the banister inside Little Piney Cove.

From left to right: GiGi, Anne and Bunny, ages 13, 10 and 7½ respectively.

Billy and Ruth holding their grandchildren Jonathan and Morrow Lotz, 1974.

Buying a cabin with one of her workmen, 1955.

The building of the Graham house, 1955.

Little Piney Cove.

Four generations of Bells—back row (left to right): Ruth; front row: Virginia Bell, Anne Graham Lotz holding daughter Morrow, 1973.

Ruth's Bible study desk in her bedroom.

Rosa, Ruth, Virginia and Clayton (left to right) in front of their former Tsingkiang home, 1980.

Visiting Guatemala after the devastating earthquake of 1976.

Cliff Barrows, George Beverly Shea, film producer Dick Ross, Billie Barrows, Ruth and Billy (left to right) in Hollywood, California, 1949.

The Grahams greet President Jimmy Carter, 1979.

With their close friends June Carter and Johnny Cash, 1978.

Shortly before sailing to Korea for High School, 1933.

Ruth in her black dress and strand of dimestore pearls, c.1940.

Ruth, 1949.

Shortly before she rode off the
embankment on Old U.S. 70.

Just married, c.1944.

Ruth on the mountain, c.1954.

At Vero Beach,
Florida.

Ruth, 1982.

By virtue of his late arrival, Ned was more a second family than a fifth sibling. He was a sensitive, affectionate child with more than his share of charm and wild blood.

A carbon copy of the young Billy Graham, he abounded in nervous energy and was tall and thin as bamboo. He was persuasive and articulate, capable of talking his way in and out of anything. He was perhaps the brightest child, with a keenly analytical, inventive mind. He was handsome, with strong, yet chiseled, features. His eyes were deep-set like his father's but mercurial like his mother's. By age ten he was teasing the little girls in school; by twelve he was a dandy, admiring Italian boots, leather jackets, and designer-label clothes.

Despite his talents he did poorly in school. His mind froze when he took examinations, a symptom that had begun in the primary grades when a teacher repeatedly punished him harshly for minor infractions. In the spring of 1972, when he was fourteen, his parents decided to send him to Felsted School in Sussex, England. A stately but stern public school, it was located on seventy-three acres of playing fields near the North Sea.

That September, mother and son flew to London. She checked into a dreary hotel near Hyde Park, where Donald Soper was again haranguing and a group of doomsayers were proclaiming that the end of the world was at hand. In some measure, it felt like the end of the world to Ruth, who did not want to leave her son. On September 11, their last night together, they watched television in her hotel room and he briefly laid his hand over hers. "And it came as a shock to feel the weight of it," she recorded, "and realize it was larger than mine. . . . It was thirty-nine years ago this fall in Shanghai, China, when a thirteen-year-old girl cried herself to sleep and prayed to die before morning. But morning came and she sailed for Japan and Korea. Today I'm glad. Only now—it's tonight. And boys don't cry."

The next day they unpacked his belongings in the dormitory. It was a tiny room, scrubbed and Spartan with study desks, chairs and space for little more. Honeysuckle grew on the wall outside his window, its sweet fragrance permeating the air. Nearby was a large room with rows of gray-blanketed iron cots where he would sleep with some twenty other boys. Later, Ruth stared through the taxicab window, watching him wave to her from the drive, clad in his navy blazer and gray slacks, lank and smiling.

It was to be a rather brutal experience for Ned, more wretched than his mother had imagined. He soon discovered that academically he was three years behind the other boys his age, deepening the very discouragement his family had sent him there to overcome. He was also unaccustomed to the hazing by older boys traditional in English preparatory schools. They were tyrannical, prone to mete out harsh punishments for obscure infractions. Ruth was horrified when she later learned that more than a dozen times during the bitter winter months Ned was forced to sit in a bathtub while it was slowly filled with icy water. When the water reached his chin, one of the older boys would dunk his head.

More than ever before, she was alone on her mountaintop. Even when her children were home for brief stints, she knew they were already gone. The world she had known was changing. Sometimes she wasn't sure if it was for the better; but she knew the evolution was inevitable, a rhythmic function of time.

By now the BGEA had grown into a worldwide organization with more than five hundred full-time employees; it included the movie studio World Wide Pictures and the weekly radio program "Hour of Decision." The vastness of the organization made the Grahams' lives more pressured.

The ministry was now taking her husband to remote, troubled areas of the world, such as Nagaland, the sparsely populated state between Assam and Burma, where headhunters and cannibals had once roamed the densely forested hills. Two nights before he was to leave, October 29, 1972, he commented to Ruth as they were drifting off to sleep: "Well, a month from now you may be a widow."

"Life being what it is," she replied, "I might beat you to it."

His increased travels to totalitarian countries also kept her alert, if not a bit uneasy. Accompanying him on one trip, for example, she decided she would locate the "bugs" in their hotel room—not cockroaches and silverfish but surveillance devices. She had read enough spy novels to conclude that there must be bugs in everything from the ice cubes to the telephone. The latter, of course, was where she looked first. Unscrewing the mouthpiece, she held it up to the light, then close to one eye, squinting as though she were threading a needle or peering through a telescope. She shook it a bit. No bug. Then the earpiece. Same procedure, and no bug there either. Her husband, lounging on the bed with his hands behind his head, watched her with a somewhat dubious expression.

"They know exactly what you're doing," he said.

"There's no way *they* can tell," she replied saucily, holding up the telephone to show how she had cleverly taped down the cradle so *they* couldn't detect that it was off the hook.

Satisfied that the telephone was bug-free, she peeled off the tape, pressed the receiver to her ear and, to her dismay, discovered the distinct and portentous absence of a dial tone.

"I think it's dead," she remarked, matter-of-factly.

Well, there was nothing that would make her husband sit up and take notice more quickly. In fact, he panicked. Ordinarily he hated the telephone. But now that he was without one, he became obsessed with the thought of it: There were calls to make; there were calls expected; there were itineraries to discuss. What if there were an emergency? He paced the length of the floor, muttering, while she unscrewed, shook, banged, and rescrewed the mouth and earpieces, unable to figure out what she had done wrong.

She would have to be his gofer, he announced. So she slung her black raincoat over her nightgown and dashed out the door to begin delivering the messages to people he had suddenly decided had to be reached right that minute. After running around the large hotel for a considerable length of time, she returned to the room, where she found him attempting to fix the telephone. He was having no more luck than she had. And if there were any invisible ears (she should have checked the lamp) listening to the dialogue and disgust generated that evening, they were generously entertained—although they certainly learned no national secrets. At last, in the flash of brilliance one is willing to read four hundred pages of a detective novel for, she followed the cord behind a couch to the wall socket. It was unplugged.

Perhaps more than anything else, it grieved Ruth to watch her parents slipping from life. They were failing rapidly.

In 1972, her mother was eighty and almost blind with inoperable cataracts. An unsuccessful hip replacement had left her virtually crippled; a stroke had left her speech tortured. It was as if she had several short circuits in her mind that would substitute letters and words for the ones she wished to use. In her diaries she measured her days by the amount of pain and frustration she had suffered. Though she rarely complained to others, her anguish showed when she would scrawl comments such as: "Oh woe . . . It took me more than ten minutes to spell 'Ruth.'" Or "I can't read, and I can't talk."[2]

Ruth's father was seventy-nine, and wracked with pain from an ulcer that had developed between two toes after he bought a three-

---

2. 25 January 1969, The Private Papers of Virginia Leftwich Bell, Montreat, North Carolina.

dollar pair of imitation leather shoes. Because he was diabetic, the ulcer would not heal. The pain became so acute that he could not sleep. Finally, in the summer of 1973, he visited the Mayo Clinic and begged the doctors to amputate the infected toe. They replied that because his circulation was so poor they would have to amputate his leg at the hip. He refused. Despite his suffering, he treated his wife "like a queen," as she put it; and he led an unusually active life. In 1972, he had been elected moderator of the Presbyterian Church in the U.S., the highest office that could be held in the denomination, an office that had eluded him twice since he'd left the mission field.

"I don't know if your moderatorship will be able to stem the tide in our church today," Ruth told him at the time. "But at least for one year our church will get a glimpse of godliness."

After serving his one-year term he continued traveling throughout the South to address what he considered to be the growing ills of the Southern Presbyterian Church. A formidable proponent of the Presbyterian tradition of his youth, he was grieved by what he deemed the modern church's leanings toward humanism. In addition to his stumping, he taught the adult Sunday school class in Montreat, which was broadcast over seven states. And several times each month he flew to Washington, D.C., for *Christianity Today* board meetings.

On Sunday, July 8, 1973, he preached at the Swannanoa Presbyterian Church, the church he and his wife had first attended when they had moved to Montreat thirty years earlier.

Ruth sat beside a window that stretched from the eaves to the floor. Beyond was the cemetery, lined with the granite markers and monuments of generations. Montreat had no place to bury her dead. Some residents, especially many of the retired missionaries, like her parents, had purchased plots here. "I knew as I sat there listening," Ruth wrote at the time, "watching his loved figure, his white hair, his kindly face, that the next time he came to this church would be in his coffin."

Her prediction would soon come to pass.

On Wednesday, August 1, she telephoned her parents, offering to bring them supper. They weren't hungry, they said. She did not see them that day.

The next morning Mrs. Bell awoke at 7:30. She strained, listening for the familiar buzz of the television playing in the living room, for it was ritual for her husband to rise before she did and turn on the news. The house was silent. She called out to him, lowering herself from her bed to her aluminum walker. Stumbling, almost falling, she made her way across the carpet to his bed. He lay motionless, resting on his left side, his face cradled in his bowed left arm, his right arm comfortably tucked beside his neck. His face was smooth, devoid of the tension of life. She groped for the telephone, stabbing at numbers she was too blind to see, dialing randomly. By chance she reached a neighbor and stammered the words, "Nelson, dead."

She lowered herself into her wheelchair and rolled herself into the kitchen. T. W. Wilson was the first person to arrive. To his amazement, Mrs. Bell, who had not stood unassisted in three years, was standing beside her wheelchair. She unlocked the kitchen door for him.

"Nelson . . . dead," she whispered.

Wilson gently helped her back into her bed; then Ruth arrived, still in her bathrobe. She kissed her mother, then she went to her father and kissed him gently.

She sat beside her mother, held her hands and said, "He's in Heaven now—with Nelson, Jr."

Next arrived the family doctor, Eugene Knoefel, and his wife; then Calvin Thielman and Billy. It appeared, Knoefel told Billy, that Dr. Bell had died at dawn.

"That was when he usually got up," Billy replied.

"And he did," added Ruth.

Throughout that day members of the family flew in from all over the country and gathered at the Bell home to reminisce. Mrs. Bell sat regally in her wheelchair, listening, a solitary tear sliding down her cheek when she thought no one was looking. Late that night when all was still, Ruth wrote: "There's been a lot of laughter. . . . How can one remember Daddy and not laugh? Humor was as much a part of him as his walk and the tone of his voice. And tears spring unbidden too. I sat briefly on the porch, remembering: his hard work, never complaining, enjoying life, his faithfulness; spiritually, his thoughts were more theological than devotional and so he fed on meat rather than milk; his wonderful sense of fun."

He was dressed in the navy blazer and gray slacks his children had bought for him when he had been elected moderator; his wire-framed glasses were tucked in a pocket—the one thing, Ruth later recalled with a sad smile, "he certainly would no longer need." He was buried the next day at 3:00 P.M. on a gentle slope facing east, as thunder rumbled behind the mountains and rain began to fall. "Sitting on the porch tonight listening to the katydids, watching the almost full moon emerge thru' the clouds above Rainbow," Ruth wrote a week later, "it is hard to realize he is gone."

Billy and Ruth asked Mrs. Bell to move in with them. At first she refused. Like an old woman lightly fingering some parched memento of her wedding day, like a mother wandering through her grown children's photograph albums, so she was with the house. It held memories. It held objects he had touched. It held objects they had carried home from China. She wanted to linger. For a while friends spent the night there with her; sometimes Ruth did, sleeping on her father's old bed, listening to the various clocks striking out of sync, on the half hour, throughout the house. She listened to the sounds he had heard. She thought of her mother's pain. "I think losing a loved one," she wrote in late August, "must be a little like losing a leg. First there is the shock, then the anesthetic, and the pain killers; the attention of doctors and nurses, flowers and cards and visits from friends. But sooner or later you have to learn to walk without it."

One day, while Ruth was sorting books and papers in her father's study, she stumbled across a leatherbound concordance she had given him years before. Tenderly, she thumbed through it and found jotted inside, in his unmistakable and unreadable scrawl, a prayer list. "Franklin—school," the last item read.

Had he lived a little longer he would have begun to see his prayers answered, not just about Franklin but about Ned too. Rather than returning to Felsted, Ned was attending a private school in New York, where he excelled in the martial arts and made a name for himself as a swimmer. His curiosity was voracious, vacillating from literature to philosophy to science. In 1979 he married a Mayo Clinic nurse named Carol Kolden. By 1983, he was studying at a university on the West Coast.

The turning point for Franklin came in the summer of 1974, when he was twenty-two and was asked to help with the preliminary set-up for the International Congress on World Evangelization in Lausanne, Switzerland. It had been planned by various international committees, but his father was the force behind it. Every nation had been invited to send its Christian leaders as delegates. Franklin flew to Switzerland and soon found, for the first time, that he was virtually alone. There was no television in his small apartment, no nightlife nearby, no automobile, no motorcycle. He began picking up the Bible and reading in the Psalms, Galatians, Ephesians, and Proverbs, developing an unexplainable hunger for the words.

The congress began July 16 with more than four thousand people from more than 150 nations gathering in the Palais de Beaulieu. Billy arrived, and one night he sat down with Franklin for a father-to-son talk.

"Franklin," he said, "I don't know when it will be but I know that at some point the Lord is going to get ahold of you. I love you very much, but you are going to have to make a decision. I believe the Lord has something for you to do, but you are going to have to choose Him, and you are going to have to go all the way out for Him. You won't be able to ride the fence or rock back and forth."

Franklin listened to him, an incipient yearning inside. Several weeks after the conference ended, he traveled to the Middle East with BGEA team member Roy Gustafson, a kindly man with a rapier wit who had known Billy since his college days. Since his late teens, Franklin had assisted him in guiding tour groups through the Holy Land. Gustafson treated him as though he were a son, sure of his talents, even more certain that the young man was destined to contribute something of significance to the world if he would stop running. Gustafson's friendship and example left their mark. One day, in his hotel room in Jerusalem, Franklin felt the urge to throw away his cigarettes. Wadding up the package, he tossed it into the trash and knelt beside the bed.

"I want You to be Lord of my life," he prayed. "I am willing to give up any area that is not pleasing to You. And I'm sick and tired of being sick and tired."

That August, he married an appealing young woman named Jane Austin Cunningham, who had been his friend and confidante for years. In 1977, almost four years to the day after his grandfather's death, Franklin would graduate from Appalachian State University in Boone, North Carolina, with a degree in business administration. By 1979 he was president of the Boone-based World Medical Missions Inc. and Samaritan's Purse. World Medical Missions recruits Christian doctors for short-term service in Third World countries; its relief agency, Samaritan's Purse, sends aid to devastated peoples throughout the world. In 1981 he was ordained as a minister.

By 1983, Ruth would have sixteen grandchildren. To them, she was "Tai Tai" (Chinese for "Great One"), and going to her house on the mountain, Bunny described, was "like going to Disneyland." She was the ideal grandmother—attentive and, best of all, indulgent. In the same way Billy had let his children break all the rules when he had come home, so Ruth let the grandchildren break all the rules when they came for a visit: Taught at home that they mustn't write on themselves, they arrive on the mountain and are soon covered with "happy faces"—drawn by their grandmother; taught at home that they mustn't get dirty, they are virtually unrecognizable after a day of streaking down the mudslide built by their grandmother— who's usually the first one to try it out.

In early October, 1974, her playfulness with the grandchildren almost ended in tragedy. She was visiting GiGi, who had recently moved to Milwaukee where her husband was doing graduate work in psychology. One afternoon Ruth took her grandchildren outside and began rigging up a pipe-slide—a sturdy length of wire threaded through an eight-inch section of pipe. She fastened the wire between two trees at a sharp angle. The object was to climb the tree at the highest end of the wire, grip the pipe and slide at breakneck speed over the yard. Wanting to make sure that the contraption was safe, she decided to test it first. The wire snapped and she plummeted fifteen feet, her heel striking the earth first, then her head. She lay motionless on the grass, and GiGi and the grandchildren thought she was playing 'possum until their dog licked her face and she didn't react.

In the emergency room in Mequon, the doctors could not find her pulse at first. Her left heel was split in five places, and she had a broken rib, a crushed vertebra, and a severe brain concussion. Billy, who had just arrived in Brasilia, received a garbled message that prompted him to conclude that his wife had been critically injured in an automobile accident. He telephoned GiGi, who assured him that Ruth was receiving excellent care, and she urged him not to cancel his five-day crusade in Rio's Maracaña Stadium. He preached to more than half a million people, sick at heart, not knowing if his wife would survive.

She was unconscious for a week. When she finally awoke, her memory was wiped clean of, among other things, all the Bible verses she had memorized since childhood. Her progress was slow. In October, she wrote from GiGi's home, where she was convalescing: "I have had difficulty reading anything—my Bible included—as my mind just wanders or won't absorb. I prayed, 'Lord, take anything from me, but *please* give me back my Bible verses.' Out of the clear blue this verse came to me: 'I have loved thee with an everlasting love; therefore with lovingkindness have I drawn thee.'" Days later came another, rising mutely to the surface like a bubble in dark water: "And all of thy children shall be taught of the Lord: and great shall be the peace of thy children." Others came, unfamiliar verses she had no recollection of ever having read, much less memorized. They came when she needed them most.

While she was yet recovering, her mother suffered another stroke. Ruth flew home in a private jet, to find her in the hospital, miserable and furious. Tubes protruded from her nose and mouth and she was surrounded by attendants who could not decipher her speech. When a nurse glided in to remove her dentures, Mrs. Bell tried to bite her.

"Couldn't we take her home?" Ruth asked Dr. Samuel Crow, a cardiologist who had known the family for years.

"If the whole family agrees, it's all right with me," he said.

At dawn, November 8, she died quietly in her own bed, surrounded by her family. Ruth attended the funeral, dizzy, swinging perilously down the aisle on crutches. Later, she could not recall the service. The deaths of both parents blended into a single blurred event, making it seem that she had endured one interminable suffering.

According to Mayo Clinic doctors, the fall left Ruth with a mild impairment of the short-term memory. It was also probable that the trauma precipitated the various problems she later experienced with the left side of her body, culminating in the replacement of the hip and a portion of the joint in the wrist.

The loss of her parents left a void. Often she would awake early in the morning, the usual thoughts rising through the sleepy gray film as they had for decades, thoughts of them and of what she could do for them that day. Then, with the feeling one has after waking from a pleasant dream to realize it was just a dream, her heart chilled. "I awoke this morning after Bill left," she wrote four months after her mother's death, "and lying there I realized Bill was gone, but the comfortable feeling came over me, 'Mother and Daddy are home.' Then I remembered. It comes at unexpected moments—time to fix a bite for their supper, meals they had up here—the back of someone's head that looks like Daddy's, Mother's old wheelchair in the coat closet, Daddy's battered hat on my bookshelf."

Reminders were thoughtfully scattered throughout Ruth's house: her mother's black cane leaning against the hearth in her bedroom, her father's favorite suit hanging in the hall closet; a Chinese bowl on the mantle, her mother's ruffled pillow. In private, she was poignantly sentimental. Matter-of-fact with people when she was with them, she transmuted them into symbols when they were gone: like the packet of love letters Billy had written her in their youth, worn and fragile now after hundreds of perusals in his absences; like his tweed jacket, the one she had slept with from time to time in the early years, when she was home alone; like the stuffed animals in the children's empty bedrooms, toys she intended to pack but somehow never had the heart to.

The next year, when she was in Taiwan for a crusade, she bought slabs of marble and had them carved into headstones. It was appropriate, she decided, for her parents' grave markers to come from China.

She resorted to the remedy she had used in the old days, when she was home, the children all there and her husband gone: She kept busy. She became energized, eluding loneliness through movement. She was fifty-five now, her children were gone, her parents were gone, her husband was busier than ever. She rose in a whirlwind of motion. For starters, she got arrested.

It was a sunny afternoon, May 20, 1975. Spring stabbed the heart with its sweetness as the sun twinkled on the small lake in Charlotte's Freedom Park. Ducks waddled on the shore and paddled through the murky water. Like a Monet painting, the trees were a pastiche of countless dabs of green; yellow flowers bordered benches and dotted the shore. Pooled around the bandshell was a sea of colorful suits, shirts, dresses—some seventy-five thousand people, all there to celebrate Mecklenburg Independence Day. President Gerald Ford was to deliver a short speech; Senator Jesse Helms was there, and so was Billy Graham. Peppering the crowd were the inevitable protesters and their signs.

Graham and Ford.

God and Country My Ass!

Ford Has a Better Idea.

Ford's a Tory.

On the rise behind the shell, the demonstrators booed, making loud asides and blowing a bugle when anyone rose to speak.

Ruth sat in the front row, next to the center aisle in a restricted area that had been roped off for security. Midway through Ford's speech she noticed heads turning. Just beside her in the aisle was a scraggly young man, barefooted, shirtless, short, and wiry. He had slipped under the ropes moments earlier, a cardboard sign tucked by his side. Now, almost to the front and no more than a foot away from Ruth, he faced the crowd, his placard held over his head. It read "Eat the Rich" on one side and "Don't Tread on Me" on the other.

It was as spontaneous and matter-of-fact as swatting a fly against a window when Ruth rose from her seat and snatched the sign from his hands. She sat back down and firmly planted her white pumps on it. Startled, baffled, he whipped around like a man whose pocket has just been picked. Seemingly oblivious of what she had just done, she was calmly listening to the President when the young man spotted his property. He squatted beside her, and asked her to return it. Patting his shoulder in a motherly fashion, she shook her head and smiled. Police officers briskly escorted him to the other side of the ropes.

"I have been informed that you are Mrs. Billy Graham," an Associated Press reporter leaned over Ruth's shoulder and said. "Will you confirm this?"

She nodded. After the speech, she was further questioned by the press. It was no great matter, she remarked, it was simply that the sign was "rather stupid." She had acted "instinctively" in taking it. "The man had every right to his opinion," she said. "But when the President of the United States is speaking it is definitely not the place to express his opinion. I am the mother of five children and disrespect has never been tolerated."[3]

That night the major television networks covered Ruth's sign-snatching and former president Richard Nixon telephoned her.

"Good for you!" he said cheerfully.

The next morning the story was in newspapers throughout the United States. The protester, Dan Pollock, was a twenty-eight-year-old member of the antiwar Red Hornet Mayday Tribe, which had recently lost a civil suit in federal court charging that they had been illegally excluded from Billy Graham Day in 1971 when Billy and Nixon had appeared together in Charlotte.[4]

When Pollock realized who his "assailant" was, he immediately signed a warrant for Ruth's arrest, charging her with assault and battery. He told the magistrate that she had shoved him.[5]

"A lawbreaker," Ruth wrote. "Me. Taught from childhood to keep the law. Well, I was taught respect too. Respect for my elders, respect for those in authority. And manners. One didn't interrupt

---

3. Fran Schumer, "Mrs. Billy Graham Grabs, Keeps Protester's Sign," *The Charlotte Observer*, May 21, 1975.
4. Ibid.
5. Ibid.

when another was speaking. That is why I have chafed so when demonstrators and hecklers have increasingly disrupted public speeches—particularly when the President of the United States is speaking. I get irritated when thousands turn out to hear the President and the cameras pan in on the handful of demonstrators. It is like being at a banquet and someone burps and the press zeros in on the burp."

The Buncombe County sheriff telephoned Ruth at her Montreat home, sheepishly telling her that it was his task to serve the warrant. He asked to meet her at the BGEA's Montreat office. She vetoed that and the following suggestion that they meet at the courthouse. The press was on her trail, cameras ready to immortalize the sheriff's handing her the warrant. Transferring messages over the two-way radio in her car, she arranged to meet the deputies between two fashion shops in an obscure area of Asheville.

"Now what do I do with it?" she asked her Charlotte lawyer, Joseph Grier, Jr., moments after receiving her summons.

"Just mail it back to me," he said. "And don't talk to reporters."

So the world was cheated out of the press statement she had already written. It read in part: "The only difference is: if it had been my son, instead of a reassuring pat on the shoulder I'd have given him a resounding whack on the bottom!"

If convicted, she would face a fifty-dollar fine or thirty days in jail.

"I've already made up my mind," she told her lawyer. "If there's a question of a fine or jail sentence, I'll choose the jail sentence. I feel very strongly that what I did was right and paying a fine would be to me an admission of guilt."

She had rolled up her sleeves and was ready to fight, her demeanor one of calm stubbornness. "I could get a lot done in thirty days in jail, I think," she wrote. "I'd relish the encounter—challenging a law that protects demonstrators of radicalism and immorality instead of patriotic citizens."

The morning of the trial, Friday, August 29, she wrote Pollock a letter, telling him how much God loved him, explaining how he could come to know Christ. She tucked it inside the handsome brown leather edition of The Living Bible she planned to give him after the trial.

Shortly before 1:00 P.M. she and her lawyer parked beside the Mecklenburg County courthouse. The courtroom was virtually empty when they entered, but it soon filled, a mass of reporters lining the walls. A group of admirers from nearby Shelby slipped her a note, telling her that they had come to pay her fine, should she be convicted.

Pollock was sworn in and questioned. When the defense asked him if Ruth Graham had shoved him or in any way touched his person—other than patting his shoulder—he said that she had not. After forty-five minutes the case was dismissed for lack of evidence.

She caught up with Pollock as he headed toward the courtroom door. "I've been praying for you," she said warmly. "Will you accept something from me?"

"That depends on what it is," he replied suspiciously.

She slipped the Bible from her pocketbook and held it out to him, almost shyly. He drew back in disgust.

"No, I'd rather not," he said as he hurried away.

Reporters and photographers surrounded her.

"How would you like it if someone snatched a sign away from you?" one reporter asked, shoving a microphone in her face.

"I wouldn't be carrying a sign," she replied.

"Would you do it again?" asked another.

"Yes, I would."

"Why did you object to Pollock's carrying the sign?"

"Because thousands of people were being deprived of their civil rights."

"Did you offer Dan Pollock a Bible?"

"No comment," she said.

Just then Joe Grier drew her back into the safety of the courtroom and the Judge swooped to the door like an angry blackbird. "Now get out!" he barked at the press.

That night Nixon called to congratulate her. "It gives me a renewed faith in the American judicial system," he said.

President Ford telephoned her two nights later.

"Don't you want to hire me full time as a sign-snatcher?" she asked him.

"I'll place you on the front row," he replied.

Though Ruth's strong opinions covered more than just demonstrators, it was not her nature to draw attention to herself. The arrest was a fluke. She usually let her husband make the public statements while she worked behind the scenes.

In the spring of 1975, Billy released a statement to the press that read in part: "Americans have a responsibility to provide humanitarian aid to Indochina and call for urgent negotiations to assure the safety of South Vietnamese whose lives are endangered. ... With compassionate hearts for the very needy individual and family we Americans have a responsibility to make available medical assistance and food required to heal and sustain life for all Indochina's homeless, needy, and afflicted people."

Shortly afterward, Elizabeth Wilson, a friend of Ruth's, told her that sixteen members of a Vietnamese family were in danger and needed someone willing to sponsor them if they were to be safely evacuated from Vietnam. Nghia, a member of the family, had graduated from Montreat-Anderson College the previous year. Miss Wilson had helped him financially, as much as her meager resources would allow, making it possible for him to finish college. After leaving Montreat he wrote her an anxious letter, confiding that he feared his relatives would be executed. He wanted Elizabeth Wilson to sponsor them—all sixteen of them. It was something her small pocketbook could not manage.

"Hold on a minute," Ruth told her after hearing the story.

She put down the phone and walked into her husband's office, stopping at the edge of his desk. "Did you mean what you said?"

"What do you mean?" he asked, puzzled.

She referred to his press statement and told him Nghia's story.

"BGEA will sponsor the family," he replied simply.

Days later a man telephoned Billy, saying he had a list of one hundred and fifty refugees that the Christian and Missionary Alliance was willing to sponsor. He needed to get the list to the White House, but with his every attempt, it seemed, he was connected to the wrong secretary. Billy called President Ford and within several weeks, the Christian and Missionary Alliance group and Nghia's family were transported by aircraft carrier to Guam and the Philippines.

"We have, each one of us," Ruth wrote at the time, "felt like we were a small part of a miracle, and though we have been sitting on pins and needles, it has been thrilling to watch God at work."

Through it all, she seemed unperturbed. Without flinching, she bore the loss of her parents and separation from her children, the arrest, the escalating pressures of not only her husband's ministry but now her own. There was always someone who needed her, it seemed, and in addition she was grappling with the deadline for her first book of poetry.[6] She was traveling more than ever; the interruptions and responsibilities were always there. And through it all, she

---

6. *sitting by my laughing fire...* (Waco, Texas: Word Books, 1977).

made it seem easy. To others she seemed mythical, somehow above it all as though she rose each day at dawn, rosy and placid like the mist on her mountain; as though she were a spinner who could talk and sing and perform a hundred different tasks while her hands moved like hummingbird wings at the wheel; as though she were a hawk that could ride the air without fluttering a feather. It was a fact that her face was usually relaxed, her limbs still, her hands gracefully folded in her lap. Her movements were never abrupt. Her disposition was never raw or snappish. She would not break in front of friend or family. Her own daughter GiGi recalled seeing her mother cry only once—when Virginia Bell died.

She was like an ocean, placid on the surface, with strong currents down deep. The first visible manifestation of stress had occurred some twenty years before when she had developed a chronic cough. It was an affliction that doctors had never successfully diagnosed, much less cured, for they could find no physical reason for it. For years she suffered severe headaches. By the late seventies, she began experiencing numbness in her legs and feet, sometimes in her hands—again, the cause seemed to be stress.

In January of 1976, she experienced what she thought was a heart attack when a breath-taking tightness gripped her chest and her fingers began tingling. A friend rushed her to an Asheville hospital where she was kept in the coronary unit for several days; Billy returned home to be at her side. Though the press reported she had suffered a heart attack, the doctors found no cause for her symptoms. Still in pain as she was released, she flew with Billy to Mexico for a rest. Within a week the symptoms were gone.

Obviously, vacations were a matter of necessity, and it was ritual for the Grahams to take at least one lengthy rest each year. Usually they left the country, traveling to places where he was less likely to be bothered. Most often they stayed either in Mexico in a condominium owned by Dallas businessman Bill Mead and his wife, Vivian, or they traveled to Europe with good friends Millie and Fred Dienert. Sometimes they stayed in Jamaica with singers June Carter and Johnny Cash.

The Grahams met the Cashes in the late sixties when Billy asked Cash to write a Christian song for young people and the singer composed "What Is Truth." June and Ruth met shortly afterward and became fast friends. "It was as though I'd always known her—it was as though she had always known me," June reminisced on a rainy morning in her office just outside Nashville. She was girlish and lithe in a loose pink sweater, black slacks, and knee-high boots. "Honest, we're buddies," she said. It was typical of the Cashes to intervene when the Grahams were exhausted and whisk them off to a secluded spot where they could rest. They had furnished a special wing for them in their Jamaican home—a handmade seven-foot-long mahogany bed and various antiques included.

On February 1, 1976, the Grahams' vacation in Mexico was interrupted when they were jolted awake at 5:20 A.M. by an earthquake. It was mild, inflicting no more damage than cracked plaster and windows. Three days later, some five hundred miles south of them, Guatemala suffered the worst earthquake in the history of Central America. More than twenty thousand people were killed and seventy-five thousand injured. Thousands of the homeless were sleeping on the pavement; thousands more had moved into lean-tos made of cardboard, plastic, and fragments from leveled buildings. Eight inches of silt blanketed the cities. Adobe houses were flattened, and bodies were being bulldozed into mass graves as the threat of epidemic loomed. Billy was informed that supplies had been donated for relief, but no money for transport. He replied that the BGEA would guarantee the necessary funds. Next, he began telephoning his influential friends: Bill Mead volunteered to donate several plane loads of high-protein bread; Johnson & Johnson donated antiseptic. Billy agreed to meet with Guatemalan church leaders to discuss the rebuilding of the country.

On February 13, the Grahams boarded Mead's company's Lockheed Jetstar and followed the coastline, passing over volcanoes and rugged mountains, into Central America. President Kjell Laugerud Garcia was at the airport when they arrived and asked to see them immediately. They were driven across the airfield to a small building where they found him, dressed in fatigues and surrounded by armed soldiers, newsmen, and government leaders. He greeted them warmly and placed two military helicopters at their disposal. His twenty-seven-year-old son Luis would fly them to fifteen of the three hundred cities that had been most devastated.

The helicopter landed in a cow pasture in San Martin where several small boys leaned against the barbed wire fence, their grimy faces furrowed with tears. Beyond them lay the ruins where four thousand people had died. Those left needed food, salt, and medical supplies. People wandered about aimlessly, numb with shock. Ruth stopped several of them and through her interpreter heard stories of entire families wiped out. Old graves had been split open, few new ones had been dug. The incipient stench of death was rising from the rubble around them.

Scores of small tremors occurred while the Grahams were there, one coming in the midst of a talk he was delivering in a church in Guatemala City. Oblivious to the trembling lights and walls, he was startled when members of the congregation jumped to their feet. Assuming they were reacting to something he said, he toned down his message. Assuming that he knew what he was doing, the congregation didn't move for the remainder of the service. Afterward, he looked up to find the ceiling literally dangling over their heads.

The visit to Guatemala ended just as abruptly as it had begun, and the Grahams again boarded the Jetstar, hearts heavy. They felt inadequate, and older than their years. Ruth was numb, wanting to help and unable to. She was sickened by the suffering she could not heal. The aid the BGEA had financed seemed insignificant among so many homeless people. It was times like this when she and her husband so strongly sensed the vanity of flesh and the importance of souls. Midway into the flight, their pilot began talking to another pilot flying several hundred yards below them. He mentioned that Billy Graham was on his plane, returning from Guatemala.

"Tell him," crackled the reply over the radio, "that I was converted at one of his crusades."

18

Lighting the Darker Places

There is little love in prison and Ruth had been an angel of mercy, lighting the darker places where no light, hope, or love had been.

Marvin King

The front door was heavy wood, dark and lustrous with a stained glass window at the top. From the tree-shaded street, the townhouse was no different from many others in Detroit's Palmer Woods residential section near Sherwood Forest. It was a breezy early evening, Friday, June 27, 1976. Two police officers paused on the porch, summoned there by a distraught man who had dialed 911 twenty minutes earlier to report that he had committed a murder. They drew their pistols and entered.

They found Marvin King kneeling on the living room carpet, his head bent, his eyes vacuous. He was a handsome black man in his early twenties, six foot two with a lean, athletic build.

His brain was stunned, paralyzed by shock. All he had ever worked for, all that he was, had been obliterated in a moment. Throughout his life he had been a train, running down a track, striving through mind and muscle to escape his past. He was an accomplished pianist with a taste for Beethoven and Bach; he devoured classics like Dickens, Yeats, and Shakespeare. A college graduate, he was brilliant and sensitive like the music he loved; he was vulnerable and shy, prone to stutter. His accomplishments were prodigious for a dirt-poor black born out of wedlock in rural North Carolina. But with each mile in the track, he had been unwittingly heading for a break in the rails, an instability in his foundation, yawning ahead all along.

On this day, he finally hit it, wrecking himself in an explosion of bewildered rage. He tumbled to ruin.

He did not look up when the uniformed legs flanked him as he slumped over the bloody blue carpet. At his knees lay his best friend, Jim, killed by the repeated and frenzied blows of a kitchen knife.

"I am the murderer," he stammered, reeling with nausea.

They slipped their guns back into their holsters, cuffed his hands behind his back, and led him out into the night.

He was born in a one-story clapboard house, just south of Fort Bragg. His father had left before he was born. His mother was a sharecropper's daughter. Too poor to feed him, she was forced to put him up for adoption when he was five. His grandmother interceded and raised him in Red Springs, twelve miles from the place of his birth. After high school, he applied to Montreat-Anderson College and was enrolled in the fall of 1969. He began attending Ruth's Sunday school class and was struck with her personality, her essence. "It is scintillating," he said, "almost contagious." She liked him, sensing his gentility and the quickness of his mind. She reflected his worth to him. "She was able to give me what my mother couldn't," he recalled. His graduation was delayed a year when both uncles were killed in an automobile accident and he returned home to take care of his grandmother. Vice-president of the honor society, he graduated in 1972 with a 3.5 grade point average.

In 1974, he moved to Detroit where he lived with a family he had met at a Baptist church there. A year later, holding jobs at both a hospital emergency room and General Motors, he moved into the townhouse. That's when his troubles began. He became involved with Jim, the blue-eyed, dark-haired son of a General Motors lawyer. A heroin addict, Jim moved in with King and began his predation, manipulating his emotions, borrowing money which he rarely repaid. The combination of the drug influence and the intensity of the men's friendship increased King's instability and paranoia.

In the spring of 1976 King lent Jim two thousand dollars, ostensibly so he could travel to Holland. He was to meet a woman, his Dutch fiancée, he explained calmly. He wanted to marry her. It was a cruel lie, a scam to rob King of more money. When by chance he saw Jim on the street weeks later, King was wild with pain and anger. They argued in the apartment.

"I never cared about you," Jim told him coldly. "I've just been using you all along."

The agony and anger of all King's years exploded like water through a crumbling dam.

Convicted of second-degree murder, he was sentenced to seven and a half to fifteen years. "I was suicidal," King recalled. "I was suicidal until she came to see me."

In mid-October, Billy Graham was holding a crusade in Detroit. A friend flew Ruth in a private plane to the State Prison of Southern Michigan at Jackson. She was led into a large, glass-walled visiting room where she saw a man sitting in a far corner, his face hidden by a heavy beard. She recognized the eyes, watching her fearfully as she approached.

"Marvin," she said, hugging him. Since late June he had not been touched except by the hands that restrained him.

This was the paradox of her existence: She dealt with the concept of suicide, immorality, dishonesty, or anything else the Bible labels as sin with an Old Testament severity of judgment. But when a sin became embodied by an individual—when she actually came face to face with the adulterer, the thief, or the murderer—her austerity condensed into a downpour of compassion. She was often the first one to visit the prisoner or appear at the scene of the crime; like her father's, her impulse was not to judge, but to heal. Years later, a Montreat woman sneaked into a neighbor's home, placed the barrel of a shotgun in her own mouth, and pulled the trigger. Arriving with towels and cleansers, Ruth helped mop up; she whisked the neighbors to her house for the night; she paid to have the room repainted and refurnished, obliterating reminders of what had happened there.

"What does God say to a Christian who's committed suicide?" a member of the woman's family asked.

"I once heard someone say," Ruth replied tenderly, " 'God did not call her home, but He welcomed her.' "

Guards in black slacks and Kelly green jackets stood sentry, bored and cynical. They eyed Marvin King and his guest with mild curiosity.

"Isn't that Billy Graham's wife?" one whispered loud enough for King to hear.

"Why should this black convict be having such famous company?" the other asked in a singsong of sarcasm.

She sat in an upholstered chair; King sat across from her on a bench.

"You were wrong," she told him. "But you still have a chance. The Lord can forgive you. You can be a witness."

"I have been living disobediently," he told her quietly. "But I have truly repented, and though I cannot undo this horrible deed I am grateful I can at least pay my debt to society. I can accept God's forgiveness but it's hard for me to forgive myself."

"There is nothing that God cannot forgive except for the rejection of Christ," she said. "No matter how black the sin, how hideous the sin, if we but confess it to Him in true repentance and faith, He will forgive. He will accept and forgive. Marvin, let me tell you a story:

"Some fishermen in the highlands of Scotland came back to an inn for tea. Just as the waitress was serving them one of the men began describing the day's catch in the typical fisherman's gestures, and his right hand collided with a teacup. The contents splashed all over the whitewashed wall and an ugly brown stain emerged.

" 'I'm so terribly sorry,' the fisherman apologized repeatedly.

" 'Never mind,' said a man who jumped up from a nearby table.

"Pulling a crayon from his pocket, he began to sketch around the tea stain, and there emerged a magnificent royal stag with his antlers spread. The artist was Sir Edwin Henry Landseer, England's foremost painter of animals. If an artist can do that with an ugly brown stain, what can God do with my sins and my mistakes if I but turn them over to Him?"

Later, he watched her leave, walking gracefully. She carried her black leather Bible, its cover dull and soft from use, its pages swollen and so fragile that she now girdled the book with a black leather belt—her "Bible belt," she jokingly called it. And he felt a tightness in his chest as though he wanted to cry. He recalled her words continually, month after month, fingering them like rosary beads. Periodically he received letters from her and classical music tapes. Two and a half years later he was transferred to Muskegon Correctional Facility in Michigan, and two and a half years after that he was granted an early parole. "I sometimes find it hard to forgive myself," he reflected. "But Ruth was a woman whom God chose to use in keeping the candle of hope and love burning when fate had plunged me into the abyss of guilt and despair."

In the fall of 1976 the administrators at Montreat-Anderson College and Calvin Thielman planned what they called "The Fall Festival of Faith." The guest singers were two Armenian brothers named Dennis and Danny Agajanian. Ruth drafted them, forming a roving band that began appearing throughout western North Carolina, visiting such places as the Juvenile Evaluation Center, the Veterans Hospital, the Alcoholic Rehabilitation Center, local high schools, the Orthopedic Hospital, and the county jail.

Unencumbered and at her peak of energy, she immersed herself in the suffering of others, carrying with her the message of Christ's love and forgiveness. In the Orthopedic Hospital, she stopped by the bed of Cindy, a five-year-old girl who had once been pretty, with delicate features and curly brown hair. Two years earlier her mobile home had caught fire one evening while her family and friends were playing cards in the living room. She was asleep when they evacuated, coughing, stumbling blindly in a cloud of smoke. In a moment of horror, her uncle remembered her, dived into her bedroom and threw her out the window. He died from smoke inhalation. She received third-degree burns over most of her body, her features melted away as though she were a wax figurine that had been held in a flame. She was hideous to look upon, her head like a jack-o-lantern carved from a cabbage. Inside was an intelligence that detected the flicker of repulsion in the eyes of those who saw her, that knew she was now an untouchable. Life to her was broken in half like a line on a time chart: There was the time "before I was burned," as she would whisper; and there was forever afterward. Sometimes she tried to force the two to merge, as though believing hard enough would undo her ruination. She tried this when the hospital attendants passed out little presents. She always chose the costume rings, though she had no fingers.

Through two tiny holes she glanced shyly at this woman hovering over her. A hand lightly touched her shoulder, the face was soft and smiling as though she saw only the life inside the scar.

"Honey," Ruth said to her, "what would you like this man to sing to you?"

"Jesus . . . ," she whispered. She began to cry mutely, tiny drops trickling down her scarred face, as Dennis Agajanian bent down to her eye-level and played "Jesus Loves Me" on his guitar.

At the city jail an inmate began to weep as the Agajanians sang. Ruth talked to her, touching her through the bars. "Perhaps the Lord Jesus allowed you to come to a place like this so you could learn of Him."

She befriended a twenty-year-old convicted murderer named Carol, a bright, green-eyed blonde from Kingsport, Tennessee. By her fifteenth birthday she had been arrested on drug charges and sent to a rehabilitation center in Asheville. By twenty, her drug habit was costing her five hundred dollars a day. On December 28, 1976, she borrowed her boyfriend's .357 magnum revolver, tucked her hair beneath a dark blue ski mask and attempted to rob an Asheville beauty salon. The gun accidentally discharged, killing the shop's seventy-four-year-old receptionist. Three months later, Ruth visited Carol in the county jail. She sent her letters and called her when she began serving a sixty-year sentence in Raleigh's Correction Center for Women.

"I had a lot of people that tried to get into the jail to see me—the more or less want-to-save-your-soul type people," Carol recalled in 1982. "Most of them were trying to cram a whole Bible down my throat in fifteen minutes—typical for this section of the country anyway.... I was hearing so much of how I was being damned and going to Hell. But Ruth wasn't like that. She wasn't judgmental. She didn't try to push me."

This ministry of hers was not always warmly poignant. There were days when the world snapped at her and her partners like a fenced-in dog. One day they visited war veterans in a local hospital. As soon as Danny Agajanian began playing his guitar, an old man jammed a finger in each ear and rolled his wheelchair out of the room, disgust written over his face. On another afternoon as Ruth, Calvin, and the Agajanians headed back to Montreat, Danny stopped the car at Pack Square in downtown Asheville to run an errand. The others, waiting in the car, suddenly realized that they were parked in front of a pornographic bookstore. Without a word, Dennis left the car and sauntered inside.

"Dennis," remarked Ruth with a grin, "has no idea what kind of shop that is."

Moments later he burst out the door like a bronco, shouting, "Jesus is the way! Go to Heaven! Stay out of Hell!"

Scrambling on the car hood, he had just begun to strum his guitar when a short, portly police officer waddled up, "looking a bit like an overdone Christmas pudding," as Ruth described him, "and rather angry."

He ordered Dennis to stop his singing. "I always obey the law," he replied as he climbed off the hood. Then the officer ordered him not to move until he radioed for his superior.

Enough was enough, and Ruth and Calvin boiled from the car like water out of a pot. "This amounts to false arrest!" they objected hotly.

Another officer arrived, informing them matter-of-factly that if they wanted to have a "street meeting," they'd have to get a permit.

"All right," Ruth said. They promptly drove to City Hall where, much to her amusement, she was issued a slip of paper that read: "Mrs. Billy Graham has permission to sing at Pack Square. . . ."

The next day Ruth, the Agajanians, and a busload of Montreat-Anderson students poured into Pack Square. They held their street meeting, abruptly awakening the "Christmas pudding" officer who had been sitting inside his three-wheel police vehicle beneath the obelisk. When he stepped outside to investigate, walking with uncertainty as though one leg was asleep, a six foot seven, three-hundred-pound college student with bushy brown hair billowing over his shoulders lumbered toward him.

"God bless you," the fellow said as he handed the befuddled officer a tract.

The student, who most of his life had been known as "Moose," was one of the Agajanian brothers' converts and one of Ruth's newly acquired young friends.

His name was Malcolm Winger and he was born in Spartanburg, South Carolina. His father was a mill executive. His mother had died of cancer two days before Christmas when he was twelve. "And I pretty much made up my mind then that I was going to be my own man," he recalled. "I never agreed with my father and I was going to be totally different from him." He succeeded.

A talented guitarist, he succumbed to the enticements of rock and roll and the self-destructive lifestyle that often goes with it. After high school he washed up on the shores of Montreat-Anderson College.

On a fall night in 1976, Winger and several friends were walking in the rain, popping a mixture of speed and heroin called MDA. Drenched and dazed, they slogged through the puddled sidewalk flanking Anderson Auditorium, a massive native stone building between the lake and the post office. The auditorium's windows glowed and the applause inside sounded like the rain just beyond. The concert ended and Billy and Ruth Graham moved into a receiving line in the lobby to greet the guests. Winger and his friends peered in from a side door, eyes glazed with chemicals and mischief.

"I dare you to go in there and shake hands with Billy Graham," one of the fellows nudged Winger and laughed.

"Just watch," he replied. Clad in a holey T-shirt, patched blue jeans and a twenty-year-old Pendleton jacket, his long wet hair plastered to his meaty back, he pushed through the door. Strolling through a sea of tuxedos and evening gowns, he boldly made his way to the line. He shook the Grahams' hands simultaneously. Ruth smiled as though the absurdity of it all didn't register.

"I was there to shock everybody. But she wasn't upset. She wasn't shocked," Winger recalled, incredulous. "She was radiant and friendly—It was like *I* was in a tuxedo."

Weeks later, he met the Agajanians, and Dennis brought him to Ruth's house. "When I walked in," Winger said, "I expected this very staunch prude. But you can't get past her laughing eyes. You immediately become attracted to her."

They became friends. She wrote and telephoned, sharing the Scriptures with him, advising him as though he were a son, and sometimes playing pranks at his expense—such as giving him an extra-extra-large white T-shirt with "Believe It Or Not Jesus Loves Me" in bold red letters on the back. He wore it when he took up the collection in Anderson Auditorium during the summer conferences. She had his friends to her home for pizzas and discussions with such people as the Agajanian brothers and Nicky Cruz. But what meant most to Winger was that she took an interest in his music.

He and a friend named Rodney "Flash" Ferrell had formed a band. Ferrell, from Johnson City, Tennessee, was five foot ten and weighed a hundred and thirty pounds, a rowboat to Winger's *Titanic*. He had earned the name "Flash" during his high school football days when he would wind and weave practically around the block to avoid being tackled. Also a guitarist, Ferrell had been entrusted with a set of keys to the college choir room where the public address system and various amplifiers were kept. The equipment, which rested neatly on the Montreat Presbyterian Church platform on Sunday mornings, made the rounds on the weekends when Ferrell and Winger would sneak it out of the choir room and use it for their barroom acts.

Their music was ear-shattering, nerve-fraying rock and roll, complete with original Christian lyrics like "Jesus help me quickly, I'm sinking in the sewer." In the spring of 1978, just before they graduated, they invited Ruth to one of their concerts, certain she wouldn't come. But she surprised them, arriving at the opening song and sitting through it all, smiling and wishing miserably that she had remembered to take aspirin before leaving the house. After the last note had died away, she approached them.

"How would you like to attend this Bible school in Colorado?" she asked, referring to Ravencrest Chalet in Estes Park.

"Well," Winger shrugged good-naturedly, "why not?"

She sent both of them there.

But it would be inaccurate to imply that most of the people she tried to rescue were transformed overnight. In fact, most stories were open-ended. After Bible school Winger began playing the bar circuit; Ferrell drifted. After Tony Mendez graduated from Bible college, he disappeared, leaving his battered gray Oldsmobile rusting on the Graham mountain until weeds pushed through the floorboard and Ruth had it towed away. When he appeared in the spring of 1982, it was in a red Cadillac with white leather seats; he owned an arcade of slot machines and video games in Barbados, he told her. But, he added brightly, he was merely saving his money until he could afford to become a minister and join the mission field.

"Tony," Ruth said sadly, "in one gambling city, our security guard told us that those big hotels with the casinos in them have separate elevators to carry out the corpses. There's nothing wrong with making money, Tony. It's how you make it and what you do with it."

They stood on the driveway, pausing before he left again.

"I guess one of the first things I need to do is sell that car and get a small one," he said, his face pained as he looked lovingly at the red Cadillac.

"I think it would be a very good idea, because, Tony, you don't want to drive up outside of a little country church in that long, bright red Cadillac."

"You know, Ruth," he laughed, chagrined, "that's my ghetto mentality."

19

Darkness over the
Face of the Earth

*At last, you have come, and you have brought the sunshine
with you.*

Polish girl to Ruth, 1978

B etween 1977 and 1980, Ruth traveled around the world twice, following her husband throughout the United States, to Hungary, Poland, Sweden, and the Philippines. When it was over, she was weary beyond remedy, it seemed, and determined to stay on her mountain as much as possible in the future. His taking her along, she had decided, was "rather much like a general taking his wife to battle."

In early February of 1978, they traveled to Las Vegas for a five-day crusade, their arrival coinciding with a macabre event that was being bruited about in the press. A beautiful young Spanish-American woman named Maria Torres had hacked off her left hand with a machete, claiming that Jesus had told her to do it. Reporters seemed interested in linking the story with the Billy Graham crusade. "What would Satan love better," Ruth commented at the time, "than to have her do something hideous like that and blame it on Jesus?"

At the first press conference a reporter asked Billy if he planned to visit Maria in the hospital.

"I've just gotten here and don't know a thing about it," he replied. "If I have time, I'll be glad to see her."

But Ruth wouldn't hear of it. She knew he didn't have the time, and even if he did, she reminded him, "It's sure to be turned into a media event, which would defeat the purpose of the visit." That afternoon she went in his stead. A nurse told her that Maria was sleeping and promised to telephone her when the young woman was ready to see her.

The call came the next day. In the hospital room she was greeted by a lovely face with wide, brown eyes. Ruth sat beside her and gently touched the reattached left hand, bound at the wrist and resting on a pillow. It was black and cold as death. For the first time since the young woman's self-inflicted injury, she began to talk. After an hour of rambling about Old Testament massacres, a previous drug addiction, and her recent live-in boyfriend, she told Ruth why she had cut off her hand.

She was reading the Old Testament, she said, poring over the massacres, when suddenly, "I realized I was not living the way I should and I heard a voice saying—'Because you are not living the way you should I want you to take a knife and cut off your left hand.'" The voice kept saying, "Cut it off! Cut it off! Cut it off!" She tried a carving knife and then the machete. "I screamed and I screamed. But I hacked and I hacked and I finally got the thing off." At that moment, a doctor arrived to wheel Maria to the operating room, where the hand was to be reamputated. Before leaving, Ruth bent over her and said, "Jesus never told you to cut off your hand. It was the Devil. He can quote the Bible, too. Jesus loves you. Whenever you need Him, call. He'll be right there."

Later Ruth asked some doctors, "Could Maria possibly have experienced a drug flashback?"

"No," they said.

Two days later Maria was transferred to a psychiatric ward in another hospital. Again, Ruth went to see her, carrying an inscribed New Testament to substitute for Maria's Gideon Bible. "I wanted to get her out of the Old Testament," she later explained, "especially the Old Testament massacres, because there was no way she would understand them." She found her sitting cross-legged in the center of her bed, her open Bible on her lap, cradled between her right hand and the freshly bandaged stump.

"Maria," Ruth said, "look, I brought you another Bible."

Her eyes remained riveted to an Old Testament passage, her body rigid, slightly swaying like a cobra. Slowly, she lifted her head, staring at her with dull, unblinking hatred.

"Maria," Ruth repeated, "I've brought you a new Bible."

Lightly placing her fingers on Maria's forearms, she attempted to lift them and replace the Bible with the New Testament. They were like iron pipes—she could not budge them. Conceding, she placed the New Testament next to Maria and talked for an hour while the unblinking eyes bored into hers, as though there were a monster inside the girl, staring out at her. Ruth quoted Scripture, praying silently for protection.

"I can't help you," Ruth said, "but God can."

Maria began panting and then slowly fell backward. Ruth caught her before she tumbled over the edge of the bed. She eased her around until her head rested on the pillow.

"Remember, Maria," she said as she left, "Jesus *loves* you and if you call for Jesus He will be here and He will help you."

The eyes closed and a single tear slipped down her cheek.

Ruth took the Gideon Bible and left, meeting the ward supervisor outside the room. Ruth wondered aloud if this could be a case of demon possession.

"Well," the woman said coldly, "I just don't happen to believe in demons."

"Well," Ruth said, "my father was a medical missionary for twenty-five years in China and had personal experience with them. The Chinese had separate words for having a devil and being crazy. Once he was called out to see a woman who was demon-possessed. It was winter. He had on his long johns and overcoat. He told the woman when he went into her room that he couldn't help her but Christ could—and *only* Christ could. And at the mention of His name, she went absolutely livid and grabbed his arm and bit him and broke the skin through all that clothing. It was superhuman power."

Years later a chaplain from Las Vegas, who was working as an usher at a crusade Ruth was attending, approached her. "I have the New Testament you gave Maria Torres," he said.

"Where did you find it?" Ruth asked, surprised.

"In the trash at the hospital."

Eight months after the Las Vegas crusade, Ruth traveled to Eastern Europe, stopping first in Sweden, then Poland, where four years later General Wojciech Jaruzelski would impose martial law, interning thousands of citizens as the government attempted to crush the trade union movement called Solidarity. On September 25, she boarded a plane in Charlotte and flew to Stockholm. She waited there two days while her husband preached to a crowd of twenty thousand people in Oslo and endured the assaults of one hundred and fifty members of "The Heathen Society," who were determined to upset the services. A young woman struck him with a ball of a red doughy substance and then shinnied up a pole and unfurled a banner which read, "When Christians Get Power They Kill People." A young man climbed up after her and ripped it down to the wild applause of the crowd. Billy preached without pause.

From September 27 to October 1 he visited Stockholm, conducting services which were broadcast in Norway, Sweden, Denmark, and Iceland. On Monday, the night of the first meeting, Ruth was asked to address the wives of the men helping with the crusade. She sat between two interpreters from the Salvation Army. One was a woman named Gunvar Paulsson, who had been badly injured the summer before when terrorists attacked a mission station in Rhodesia. Two missionaries had been murdered; she was assumed to be dead and left face down in the dirt. Now, dressed in a black dress and bonnet, her left arm permanently crippled from bullets, she sat quietly on the platform, translating Swedish to English for Ruth.

"How honored I am to sit beside you," Ruth quietly said to her. "I have never had to suffer for my Lord the way you have."

"Believe me," Miss Paulsson replied with a smile, "it was a joy. You know, I had never had to suffer for my Lord before this happened. And in spite of the horrors going on all around me at the time, there was such a sense of the presence of the Lord Jesus Himself that it was a pure joy."

The Grahams rested three days in a hotel in Copenhagen. A quilt of red-tile and oxidized copper roofs stretched from their balcony to the Baltic Sea. On the raw, drizzly morning of October 6 they boarded a DC-9 and flew to Poland, passing low over the wet black earth and fields of cabbages. They landed in Warsaw just as the plane carrying Cardinal Karol Wojtyla was taxiing down the runway, heading for Rome. Pope John Paul I had died the week before after serving only thirty-four days. Cardinal Wojtyla would soon be named his successor. It was one of those historic moments that slip by unnoticed: A Polish Cardinal is en route to becoming the first non-Italian head of the Catholic Church in more than four centuries; an American Protestant, with the permission of the Communist government, is en route to proclaim the Gospel in a land that is more than ninety percent Catholic.

They would travel through Poland for ten days. On their way to their hotel, Billy laid wreaths on two monuments. Ruth, wearing a black coat, followed several paces behind him, the rain steadily falling on her bare head until a young Pole loped out of the crowd and held an umbrella over her. On Saturday, October 7, the sun broke through the overcast sky, dispelling the dark, wet weather for the first time in well over a week. Billy conferred with an ecumenical group of clergy in a Baptist church while Ruth and an interpreter met with a group of women. She was expected to lecture. But as she often did on such occasions, she opened the floor to questions.

"How can we be sure our children will grow up believers?" one woman asked. It was a pertinent question. In Poland, both parents worked, in order to survive. Their children were placed in state day care centers each day.

"Samuel's and Moses' mothers kept them until they were weaned and we know that in primitive societies today, this can be three or four years," Ruth replied. "I would think that Pharaoh's court could hardly be described as an ideal place for a child to be raised. And Eli's temple was even worse since, under the guise of religion, his sons had turned it into a cesspool of iniquity. And yet both Moses and Samuel grew up to be men of God. We know that the sovereign hand of God was upon them. But I cannot help but feel it was more than that—it was God honoring the godly influence of their mothers."

As she left the meeting a young woman with plump cheeks, a babushka and steel teeth approached her and said she had come from Russia. "And Christians from my town knew that I was coming and why," she said, tears streaming down her face, "and they asked me to deliver a request: Will you pray for us?"

"We have not ceased praying for Russian believers," Ruth assured her.

On a foggy Sunday, October 8, the Grahams, their associates, and Dr. Denton Lotz (brother of Danny Lotz) departed for Bialystok, northeast of Warsaw and just short of the Russian border. Billy was to preach there in an outdoor service at a Baptist church. He rode in a sedan, with Ruth behind him in a bus loaded with BGEA team members and American pressmen. She had been told that in Poland when the bus made a "comfort stop" it meant the passengers were let out in the woods and left to their own devices. She didn't understand what this meant, nor did it make sense to her when a handsome young preacher-photographer named George Boltniev grinned at her and remarked, "I can't wait for the rest stops so I can get a picture of Ruth Graham picking mushrooms."

When the bus finally braked, the passengers were set loose at the edge of a wooded area, thick with trees but sadly lacking in underbrush. The others were ambling off in different directions, looking neither left nor right, each furtively in search of a fat tree, preferably with low, foliated branches. She headed for a ramshackle privy, changing her mind six feet downwind of it. She was saved by her voluminous black raincoat: Unbelted, it settled around her like a tent. She picked a handful of mushrooms on her way back and, with mock solemnity, placed them in George's lap as she returned to her seat.

There had been no advertising for the Graham crusades. Nonetheless, the news spread as Christians on foot and on bicycles passed the information by word of mouth. Eight hundred people attended the service that afternoon, standing stolidly in the chilly wind and listening intently to the message. "Each face," Ruth observed at the time, "was a sermon in itself, especially the older faces on which seemed to be etched centuries of suffering." Billy asked those who wanted to commit their lives to Christ to raise their hands. One third of the audience did so.

After the closing prayer a distinct click-click-click-click rippled through the audience.

"What was all that tongue clucking?" Billy asked Ruth later, when they were back in their hotel room. "Did I say something that offended them?"

"No, you nut," she laughed. "Those were tape recorders being switched off."

Polish Christians duplicated his sermons and spread them throughout Eastern Europe.

Late that day as dusk fell and pockets of fog scudded over the bus's windshield, the small caravan headed toward Treblinka, a concentration camp where more than half a million Jews had been exterminated during World War II. Billy had an appointment there with a West German film crew.

"Doesn't it seem ironic," Ruth asked an Associated Press reporter, "that it should be a German film crew that had insisted on Bill's coming to this particular extermination camp?"

"Some elements of the liberal German press," the man replied, "are doing all they can to keep the memory of these extermination camps fresh in people's minds and to play them up whenever possible."

That, Ruth wrote at the time, "made me do some thinking. These places should never be forgotten, nor the horrors committed there. But, at the same time, I wonder if they could be used as a sort of diversionary tactic to keep our attention off what is happening in the world today."

The evening of October 9, Billy addressed four thousand people in a Roman Catholic church in Poznan. The next morning, a rosy mist veiled the old city and cawing crows peppered the sky as the Grahams and team members boarded the buses for Wroclaw. It was the harvest season for sugar beets and potatoes, and they passed cart after cart, each heavily laden and fishtailing behind a straining horse. Ruth had awakened that morning exhausted, sick with a cold and looking it. Her friend Harold Lindsell, who since his Wheaton days had edited the Lindsell and Harper Study Bibles, was traveling with the BGEA this trip. He studied her closely.

"Ruth, I have a confession to make," he remarked. "I have been praying for Bill on this trip, but as I sit here looking at you I realize it's you I need to pray for."

"Thank you, Harold," she replied dryly. "It's all right to tell a woman you're praying for her but you don't have to say she looks like she needs it."

The service that night was in the Old Catholic Church, a formidable cathedral with flying buttresses and a great vaulted ceiling. It overflowed with people; thousands had arrived four hours before the service in hopes of making it inside. After Billy's message he gave the invitation and there was, as there had been at the other services, a quick response. Priests and nuns were among those who raised their hands, signaling that they wished to recommit their lives to Christ.

The next day in Katowice, just before the evening service, Ruth was approached by three Russian women who had come from the Moldavian Soviet Socialist Republic, on the Black Sea. They told Ruth about their eight-hundred-member church, joyfully showing her photographs of the congregation and of a service where forty people were being baptized in a river. They had come to Katowice especially to ask if, someday perhaps, Billy would go to Moldavia to preach. Later, Ruth told her husband about the women. It was such encounters and the hundreds of letters voicing similar requests that intensified his desire to preach one day in Russia. His wish would be fulfilled in May of 1982 when he was invited to preach in two churches and address an international peace conference sponsored by the Russian Orthodox church. He accepted. The trip generated some of the worst press he had ever received, reporters and clergymen alike accusing him not only of insensitivity but idiocy.

"He was fully aware that there would be attempts to 'use' him and exploit his presence," said Senator Jesse Helms, who conferred with the evangelist after the invitation was issued and urged him to accept. "But Billy saw an opportunity to serve the Lord, and he was willing to risk the criticism and misrepresentation that were almost certain to be aimed at him. I was not surprised by the subsequent controversy; Billy is often criticized and misrepresented."[1]

On the Grahams' first day in Poland they had attended a workers' luncheon at the headquarters of the Polish Ecumenical Council where the heads of different churches rose to make lengthy extemporaneous speeches. Each expressed the same concern—a very real and deep fear of a World War III.

"When the United States dropped the atomic bomb," one man said, "they looked for a flat place where it could do the most harm. Poland is a flat place."

"One could not but have deep sympathy for these who have suffered so much in the past and have a very real fear of going through it all again," Ruth wrote at the time.

On Thursday, October 12, she was granted a gut-wrenching view of what the Polish people had suffered, the symbols of their pain and fear encysted in a grisly archive called Auschwitz. Her bus turned off a main road onto a circuitous dirt lane. Uncoiling through stately trees, it deposited them in a parking lot packed with tour buses. Beyond were railroad tracks, a depot, and a simple archway with the German words for "Work Liberates" in wrought iron letters. Inside were the red brick barracks which had been built decades ago by the very people who later died there.

Their tour began with old, authentic films of the prisoners' arrival, grainy, ghostly, and soundless except for the steady clicking of the reels.

Darkly clad figures with pale faces pinched with pain, hollow-eyed

---

1. Senator Helms's assessment of Graham's trip to Moscow and a copy of the evangelist's address at the World Conference are found in the *Congressional Record* (16 August 1982, vol. 128, no. 112).

men and women clutched their bags and filed into the camp. Some leaned on friends, others held babies. Suitcases, many bound in rope, were painstakingly marked with former addresses. They were merely relocating, they had been told. One day they would be reunited with their belongings, with their families and friends. The men who had invaded their homes weeks earlier had emphasized the importance of clearly marking the bags.

Nazis, mouthing silent commands and gesturing mechanically, separated the men from the women. They hurried each line into the bleak, barren showers and ordered them to disrobe. After their ablutions, they were told, they would find fresh outfits awaiting them, new clothes for their trips to their new locations. Naked and naive they herded beneath the nozzles that were connected to poison gas lines.

Forty minutes later, no more than that, perhaps less, all were dead. Bodies were carried on conveyor belts to the next floor. Hair was shaved for mattress and furniture stuffing; some of it would be woven into cloth. Gold fillings were extracted from teeth. Bodies, unadorned and pillaged, were again loaded on conveyor belts and fed into the raging maws of the ovens. There and in the distance, the black smoke billowed from stacks flagging the darkest evil of the human heart.

Chilled and shaken, the Grahams were shown three bolts of the human hair cloth, rough like homespun wool. They were taken to a cell where some prisoners, awaiting death, had been detained. On one of the walls, preserved behind a glass plate, was the outline of Christ's head, which a prisoner had etched with his thumbnail. They moved from building to building, each containing mammoth glassed-in showcases filled with clothing, shoes in adult and child sizes, eyeglasses, the carefully addressed suitcases, photographs, and hair, now bleached and gray with age.

Finally, they were led into the courtyard between two barracks where prisoners had been lined up in front of a brick wall and shot. Twenty thousand men and women had been executed there. With Ruth by his side, Billy placed a wreath before the wall, his throat tight with tears. Together they knelt in the soil that had once been so drenched with blood that the Germans had tried to replace it bucket by bucket before the Allies arrived. They prayed silently, dozens of camera shutters clicking behind them, above them, eerily sounding like the cocking of guns.

Ruth rose, queasy and in a cold sweat. Her husband sent her ahead to Krakow to rest. He went on to tour Birkenau, some three miles away, where wooden barracks and chimneys stretched for as far as he could see.

Later that day Ruth visited a home in Krakow run by the Catholic Order of Caritas for children with speech defects. She was led to the second floor where the children sat around small tables in a sun-washed room. When she appeared at the door, they jumped to their feet.

"Good day!" they said in unison.

Smiling, she seated herself and asked through the interpreter if they would like to hear a story. They eagerly pooled around her feet, gazing up with wide eyes.

"A little boy and girl had gone to the country to visit their grandmother," she began. "The first day they were there the little boy was throwing some rocks and accidentally hit his grandmother's pet duck, killing it. He looked all around to see if anyone was watching. He saw no one. So he quickly buried the duck.

"That night after supper when the grandmother suggested he and his sister clear the table and wash the dishes, his sister said, 'I don't feel like washing the dishes but my brother would love to.'

"Angrily the little boy whispered, 'What do you mean you won't wash the dishes but I would love to?'

"Whereupon the sister whispered in his ear, 'I saw what happened with the duck. I was looking out the window. If you don't do what I say, I will tell Grandmother.'

"So the little boy had to clear the table and wash the dishes. The next morning when the grandmother called them to breakfast, the same thing happened again and the little boy found himself doing the dishes while his sister played.

"At lunchtime, the grandmother called them to come in and set the table and help with lunch. Again, the little girl said she didn't want to but that she knew her brother would love to. When he started to object she whispered, 'Remember the duck.'

"At dinner time it was the same way. This went on for several days, and his vacation was being ruined. Finally he went to his grandmother and told her exactly what had happened and how sorry he was for it. She listened to him kindly, then with a smile she said, 'I was wondering how long it would take you to tell me. You see, I was looking out the kitchen window and saw just what happened. I was wondering how long you were going to let your sister make your life miserable for you. Now that you have told me what happened and how sorry you are, of course I forgive you!'

"God," she concluded, "sees everything we've ever done and He's willing to forgive. But we must confess to him."

The next day she visited the British and Foreign Bible Society run by Madam Narzynski, wife of Bishop Janusz Narzynski of the Polish Lutheran Church.

"Does it not have an effect on those who have to proofread the text?" Ruth asked her, knowing that the Bibles and New Testaments were published by the state printing house.

"But of course!" she replied.

When the Germans began bombing Warsaw, she reminisced to Ruth, her mother had dashed back into the store, then located on Jerusalem Street, and single handedly carried five thousand Bibles into the basement. Trapped in heavy fighting, the woman hid in the rubble of bombed buildings for two weeks before she was captured and sent to a concentration camp. She escaped, was captured again and badly beaten. She escaped a final time when another inmate wrapped her face and arms with bandages and claimed she had an infectious disease.

For months, Madam Narzynski, a young girl then, and the rest of her family knew nothing of the mother's whereabouts. Then a message was delivered to their home, thirty miles outside Warsaw, saying that their mother had been killed. Their hearts were cold with grief and bitterness. One day, they heard a faint knocking on the front door. There on the porch stood a wizened old woman, hollow-eyed and smiling weakly like an apparition. They stared without recognition for an instant. Then with cries of joy they embraced their mother.

"How did your mother manage to walk those thirty miles in such weakened condition?" Ruth asked.

"It was a mother's heart going to her children," she replied simply.

After the war Madam Narzynski's family distributed the five thousand Bibles. Later, they returned to Warsaw to see what was left of the British and Foreign Bible Society. It was leveled with the exception of one wall. On it were painted the words "Heaven and Earth shall pass away: But My Word shall not pass away."

20

Return to China

Beyond those hills
lie yesterday
the silenced now,
—and a tomorrow.
The clouds
that wrap those hills
like shrouds
are free to come and go
at will:
no guns can frighten them away
nor stop the moon
and stars, nor say
the sun must shine.
No manifesto tells the rain
where it must fall,
how much
and when. . . .[1]

Ruth Bell Graham, 1973

It was June 8, 1973, a Friday afternoon, cool and clean like a pane of glass. She sat in a restaurant on a rise above the Hong Kong harbor, staring hypnotically out the window. The charred hull of the *Queen Elizabeth* lay on its side like a dead whale, dwarfing the scores of multicolored boats quietly rocking around it. It had been

---

1. Ruth Bell Graham, *sitting by my laughing fire* . . . (Waco, Texas: Word Books, 1977), p. 226.

there forever, it seemed. Why no one hauled it away, she didn't know.

She could see Deep Bay bridging mainland China and the Portuguese province of Macao. Thousands of Chinese had swum across its waters to freedom since 1949, or died in the attempt. Far beyond, the mountains of China's Kwangtung province formed a chalky blue smudge across the bright sky. It was the closest she had been to the land of her birth since she had sailed from Tsingtao thirty-six years ago.

The month before, she and her husband had traveled to the Orient where he was to hold several crusades. The sights and sounds stirred her, dislodging memories of her childhood and creating a yearning that overpowered her one night in a room in Tokyo's Imperial Hotel. She lay awake until dawn, the thought of returning to China clattering through her brain like a solitary marble.

The next day she placed telephone calls, then drafted a letter to the Chinese Travel Service in Peking, requesting permission to visit Tsingkiang, or Qingjiang, as it was now spelled. In part, she was just as afraid of being told yes as she was of being refused.

Two weeks had passed since then and now she sat in this Hong Kong restaurant surveying the Kowloon peninsula and listening to two Australian tourists sitting behind her argue over whether or not the body of water below them was Pearl Harbor. She had heard no reply to her request to return. The desire began to fade. "It is too far to go back," she decided at the time.

It was too far in years and memories, not miles. The land of her birth was a lost civilization, a kingdom devoid of her parents and the missionaries she had loved, perhaps destitute of the faith they sacrificed their lives to carry there. It was possible, however, she might find remnants, shells whispering with the sounds of her past. She wasn't sure she could face either.

The next day, June 9, she boarded a plane to Bangkok, passing over Vietnam shortly after takeoff. Tears in the thick layer of clouds revealed a land pockmarked by shell craters and charred tree trunks. Life had not changed so much from the days of the bandits and the Long March: The human heart enlightened by history was yet dark and immutable. Two and a half hours after takeoff she landed and caught a Swissair flight to Geneva, where she was to speak to a group of women in Lausanne. Donald Hoke, a retired missionary Ruth had known since her college days, and his wife, Martha, were there setting up the International Congress on World Evangelization. He persuaded Ruth to visit the Chinese consul in Geneva and again ask permission to travel to Qingjiang. The morning of June 12, Hoke drove her there.

The Chinese consul lived in a large old house in a quiet section of the city. Trees bordered the narrow winding streets, and most of the homes were surrounded by walls or hedges. Crumpled paper and other bits of trash fluttered over the gravel drive around the consulate like tumbleweeds in a forgotten town. They were greeted at the door by a short, unsmiling houseboy who eyed Ruth with suspicion when she told him she had an appointment with the consul. He shut the door in their faces and conferred with people inside. Several minutes later the door was again opened, this time by an older Chinese man dressed in cloth shoes, ill-fitting dark gray cotton trousers and a pale gray rumpled shirt that bulged over his corpulent middle. His unshaven face was impassive as Ruth briefly explained her mission.

With a slight nod he turned and led them through the entrance hall, around a corner and into a reception room with pale gray walls, several tapestries and a few Chinese objets d'art. Draped across one wall was a scroll bearing Chairman Mao's sayings. The savory odor of cooked cabbage and garlic permeated the airless rooms. Ruth and Hoke seated themselves in Chinese chairs with plush red cushions. They were soon joined by a young Chinese woman, dressed in the familiar comrade's garb of loose gray trousers and jacket. The pink collar of a western-style blouse peeked out at her neck, and her short black hair was parted low on one side and fastened with a barrette. She was silent throughout the conversation, her eyes passing back and forth between the consul and Hoke, never focusing on Ruth.

"My father had the honor of serving the people of China for twenty-five years as a doctor of medicine," Ruth explained. "He is in his seventy-ninth year and not well, and if possible, we would like to return home for a visit. This would be a strictly private and personal pilgrimage, not to Shanghai or Peking but to Tsingkiang, Kiangsu."

"How long ago did you leave China?" he asked Ruth.

"Thirty-six years ago," she replied.

"There should be no difficulty," he said. "When do you wish to go?"

"Perhaps sometime within the year?" she queried.

He left the room and returned with forms which he advised, with a faint smile, that Ruth and her father should complete and mail to a committee in New York.

On June 18, Ruth flew home and asked her father to return with her to China. Despite his wife's frantic disapproval and his own failing health, he eagerly embraced the plan. Ruth gave him the form, which he never completed because soon afterward it mysteriously disappeared. Two months later he died. After his wife died the following year the form was found among her belongings, where she had hidden it.

Two years passed, years of silence in response to her requests, years of loss and change. With renewed interest she read histories of China and analyses of what had happened to the culture, the people, and their faith since the 1949 Communist takeover. Her concern for the Chinese people became an avocation, a subject she frequently impressed upon those she talked with: "It's the oldest continuous civilization in the world," she would say. "It's the third largest country in the world. And it has by far the world's biggest population. We cannot ignore it." And, in later years, she often mentioned a symbol that was of great importance to her: the Chinese character for ten superimposed over the Chinese character for four. It means "the tenth for the fourth," an encouragement to people to set aside the tenth day of each month to pray for a fourth of the earth's people.

In the fall of 1975 she and her husband returned to Hong Kong and Taiwan for crusades. The urge to return to her birthplace grew.

She was asked to address a large group of women in the Great Hall in Taipei, Taiwan, October 29. "While I was growing up," she wrote at the time, "I planned to return to China to preach and to teach the Gospel. God had other plans. Now the committee has me scheduled to address a group of women (they hope many unbelievers) and I, accustomed to raising children and teaching an American college Sunday school class, am faced with a slight fulfillment of my childhood dream. And I am asking God to give the right message, anoint it that someone might be converted to Christ who may someday go back to China and carry the Gospel of Christ as I have longed to do."

The Wednesday of the talk arrived. Dressed in tweed, she entered an auditorium filled with brightly dressed Chinese women. For a week she had labored fruitlessly on the speech, wanting it to be the best one ever, paralyzed by the symbolism of the occasion. The harder she had tried, the less productive she became. Days passed and she produced nothing. Amid tiers of expectant faces she now mounted the podium. She had no notes, no prepared talk; her dream had evolved into a nightmare. Silently praying, she asked for the words she did not have.

Through an interpreter, Ruth ad-libbed about her parents' mission work and her own childhood in China, closing with a description of Wang Nai Nai, her Chinese nanny.

"Her Christian life had such an impact on us children," she said. "She taught herself how to read the Bible after becoming a Christian, and she loved the old hymn 'There Is a Fountain Filled with Blood.' Only after we were grown were we told the evil life she had lived before becoming a Christian. She and her husband were engaged in the Chinese version of 'white slave traffic'—procuring young girls for sale in Shanghai.

"Then I understood why she so loved that old hymn, especially the last verse: 'The dying thief rejoiced to see/That fountain in his day/And there may I, though vile as he,/Wash all my sins away.' "

A wizened, elderly woman hurried to her afterward and hugged her. "I too Tsingkiang person," she said, her eyes glowing.

Holding her hand as they walked along an aisle, Ruth kissed her at the exit. "Such a small link," she wrote that night, "and it leaves one speechless."

The first week in November she flew to Hong Kong. On Sunday, November 9, she addressed another group of women, reliving the horror of mounting the platform with no prepared speech. Afterward she wrote: "A year ago today Mother was buried. Perhaps it was significant that today at 3:00 I spoke to two thousand mostly Chinese women in the largest Baptist church in Hong Kong. I never had a harder time speaking. It was as if I had spiritual laryngitis."

Three days later she was out of bed at 6:30 A.M. to catch the hydrofoil to Macao. There was a bleak unassuming memorial somewhere on that six-square-mile province. It called to her. She found what she was looking for in a tiny, Spartan cemetery filled with plain stone markers, weathered and covered with moss. Amid them was the grave of Robert Morrison, the father of Protestant mission work in China. A Presbyterian minister, he had arrived in Canton in 1809 and died there twenty-seven years later. His accomplishments were the translation of the New Testament into Chinese, a Chinese-American dictionary, and the baptism of ten converts. His wife was buried beside him. Shortly after they had arrived she had died in childbirth. Their baby was buried at her head.

One man had sacrificed so much for what seemed so little. Ten converts. One would have been enough, at least to Ruth. "The popular thing today is to criticize the early missionaries who went to China and point out their many mistakes," she wrote that night.

"Even Robert Morrison. I thought about this as I stood beside his grave. At least they went. They went, carrying with them the Living Word and the written Word. And the gates of Hell have not prevailed against it."

Her last evening in Hong Kong, November 16, shortly before midnight, she sat in her hotel room alone. Her husband had left for the United States earlier that day. She would fly to Korea the next day to visit her sister Virginia, a missionary. Like the shadow of the Kwangtung mountains on the mainland, the past was a blur, within reach but untouchable. She was drawn there, drawn to the patch of earth where her parents had worked, and where she had played as a child. Those seventeen years in Tsingkiang had shaped her more than anything that had happened to her since; they were her fabric. She could take the regular tours to China, as thousands of sightseers had, but that would bring her no closer to the place of her birth. It was not on a tourist route. Even if it were, she reminded herself, she could not be sure the house or anything remained. "This is perhaps the closest I will ever get to the land of my childhood," she decided.

Through the cool darkness of her room, she moved to the window and drew back the draperies for a last look at the Hong Kong harbor. Boat shadows gently bobbed in the milky glow of lamps along the dock. A seaworn junk glided past slowly, noiselessly, its wide sails round with breeze.

MONTREAT, JANUARY 1980. Billy pushed the lighted button on his telephone and picked up the receiver. He was greeted by the familiar voice of Richard Nixon. The former president was preparing to leave for another visit to the People's Republic of China.

"Is there anything I can do for you?" Nixon asked him at the end of the conversation.

"Yes," Billy replied, "I think Ruth should go back to her old birthplace."

"It's no problem," Nixon replied. "I'll arrange for it when I'm in China."

True to his promise, Nixon did arrange it, and without delay Ruth received word that the Chinese-American Friendship Association would officially receive her and the other immediate members of the Nelson Bell family. Theirs would be a special tour of their old home.

Aside from the tediousness of completing numerous applications and writing letters, the plans for the trip went smoothly until the day before Ruth was to leave in the spring of 1980. Her husband decided he wanted movie producer Irwin S. Yeaworth to travel with the party and film the event. Yeaworth, who had produced many secular films, including actor Steve McQueen's first movie *The Blob,* had worked for Billy in the past. Again, Nixon's name was needed to gain clearance, but he was somewhere in Germany and even his daughter Julie Eisenhower didn't know how to reach him. Finally, several days before the party was scheduled to meet in Tokyo, Yeaworth, aided by Julie, managed to obtain permission to travel with the group.

Ruth, her two sisters, and her brother left from different locations for the long pilgrimage home. Yeaworth hastily packed his bags and rushed to join them as their chronicler. On April 29, 1980, Ruth met her older sister Rosa Bell Montgomery in Los Angeles. Rosa was married to Don Montgomery, an engineer at the Atomic Research Laboratory in Los Alamos, a small, isolated city on the Pajarito Plateau of New Mexico. She had lived in the arid climate of New Mexico since first arriving there with tuberculosis almost forty years earlier. The next day, the two sisters flew to Honolulu and were reunited with their brother Clayton Bell, senior minister of the Highland Park Presbyterian Church in Dallas, Texas, one of the largest Presbyterian churches in the country. At forty-eight, he bore a striking resemblance to the young Nelson Bell, though he was much taller and heavier. On May 6, the three arrived in Tokyo, where they were joined by their younger sister, Virginia Bell Sommerville. She was married to John Sommerville, a university professor in Korea, where they had been Presbyterian missionaries for more than twenty years.

It was a rare and joyous family reunion made even more unusual by its purpose. The next day, May 7, the family landed in Peking at 2:10 in the afternoon. They were greeted by members of the Chinese-American Friendship Association and introduced to their government companion, Yao Jin Rong, a brilliant linguist who had been in charge of the U.S. Press Corps during Richard Nixon's 1972 visit. Their companion would be with them for the next fourteen days—a subtle reminder that they were semi-official guests of the government, not pilgrims. They were to travel in tan limousines with filmy curtained windows. They were treated to excellent food and accommodations. "Things were scrubbed as they'd never been before because of Nixon," Yeaworth recalled.

Their first afternoon in Peking, May 8, they had tea with Madame Soong Ch'ing-ling, the widow of Sun Yat-sen, the father of the Republic of China. It was a bit of historical irony that Madame Soong and her sister Soong Mei-ling had spent a summer in Montreat in 1912 while they were in America attending school. They stayed at a lodge next door to the house the Bells would live in some thirty years later. When the Communists drove the Nationalists off the mainland in 1949, Soong Mei-ling, who had married Nationalist leader Chiang Kai-shek, followed her husband to Taiwan; Soong Ch'ing-ling stayed behind.

Madame Soong, eighty-three, without a wrinkle on her porcelain skin, spoke impeccable English. They visited for an hour in the old one-story gray brick house enclosed in rings of courtyards. She talked about her sister and their American friends, and about the social organizations she aided, such as the Children's Palace, which trained exceptional children.

Ruth and her family stayed in Peking two days, touring the usual places: a primary school, the imperial palaces in the Forbidden City which had been converted into museums, a cotton textile mill and a factory commune. Then it was on to the Ming Tombs and the Great Wall where Ruth, whose arthritic left hip caused her pain when she walked, cheerfully slid down the steel railing, heedless of the masses swarming along the wide thoroughfare. Over her navy turtleneck sweater, she wore a gold cross. It attracted attention.

"Do you wear this cross as a symbol or a decoration?" one young man stopped on the Great Wall and asked her in his broken English.

"As a symbol," she replied, smiling.

"Of Christian?" he asked. "Do you believe in Christian?"

"Yes," she said. "We are Christians. We believe God sent His Son Jesus to die for the sins of mankind. But he didn't stay dead. He is risen!"

"So, you are believers in Christ!" he exclaimed.

Other than the necklace, the only symbols of her faith she carried with her were the few New Testaments and devotional books in her luggage that the government would allow.

At last, after six days of touring, they were to see what they had traveled halfway around the world for. On Monday, May 13, early in the morning, they were driven toward Tsingkiang. It was a clear day and the limousines thrummed along a two-lane road, the chauffeurs honking frequently, swerving through crowds of bicyclists, pedicabs, pedestrians and horse-drawn wagons. Beekeepers had set up shop beneath the blooming locust trees on either side of the packed-clay thoroughfares. Bamboo cages swung by the sides of the old men walking their birds. They paused to chat with shopkeepers. Scattered throughout the noisy throng were guards wearing green caps with the familiar red star above the bill.

They passed through small villages, and the sights became more familiar: mud-walled cottages with thatched roofs, a lone water buffalo loitering over a murky pond; the drab walls, shops and landscapes splashed at intervals with the brilliant red, pink, and yellow of azaleas and roses. Eyes followed the limousines, the people wondering who the passengers were. When the cars stopped at one point, the party was immediately surrounded. The Chinese laughed in delight when Rosa spoke Mandarin, and they beamed when Ruth soothed a frightened little girl by producing a tiny stuffed koala bear from her luggage and presenting it to her.

Approaching Tsingkiang from the west, Ruth knew they were almost home when they crossed a bridge over the Grand Canal. The water and the junks and sampans looked as they had when she was a girl. But there were no children frolicking in it, no women washing their rice on the banks. Years ago, the first sight upon entering the city had been the chimney of the Tsingkiang mint. It was gone. Next, one would have seen the corrugated red tin roofs of the mission compound arched above the skyline like a dragon's back. They too were gone. Instead, there were smokestacks, there were billboards advertising Coca-Cola, and the sidewalks were as wide as the streets used to be.

The ancient city gate and the wall where the heads of criminals had once been impaled were gone. The limousines passed through an arch of sycamore trees and parked at the Tsingkiang Guest House, a two-story building with private rooms, hot water, electricity, and flush toilets. After a sumptuous lunch, they returned to the cars. A black limousine joined them and led them toward their old home. "This," Ruth recorded at the time, "was really an embarrassing way to arrive home as we would so have loved to walk in like ordinary folks."

The ancient mud wall that she had once walked atop to school each morning was gone, replaced by a wide road; gone also was the foreign cemetery where her baby brother had been buried. Next they passed a gray brick wall to Ruth's right and then a building. After a hard right turn through wide gates, the car halted. The house they had been raised in stood before them, ravaged and sad like the face of a forgotten old woman. A red banner had been draped above its front porch: "American Friends, You Are Warmly Welcomed by the People Living in Your Birthplace."

It seemed so much smaller. The yard which had once been spacious enough to contain a tennis court was no more than a balding scar between the house and the lot next door where the James Woodses had lived. It was shutterless and chimneyless, and the old tin roof had been replaced with artificial gray tile. The drainpipes were orange with rust and the brick wrought-work balustrade that had once girdled the downstairs porch littered the backyard.

It wore the death mask of old, neglected homes: Inside paint-peeled frames the windows gaped like empty eye sockets. The door to the central gable which had once led to the sleeping porch was gone, leaving a gaping orifice frozen into a yawn. It symbolized much more than the demise of their parents and the passing of time in their own lives. The scene before them was like a dismal monument to an age that had been completely obliterated. There were no more missionaries. Most Chinese were too young even to remember the courageous foreigners who had carried Christianity's promise of salvation and their culture across the world to share with them. One wondered if the missionaries, many of whom had died there, had left no more than this.

Getting out, they were greeted by a welcoming committee on the porch. Then they explored. In the backyard Virginia discovered the crumbled balustrade and inquired if they could each have two bricks from it to take back with them. Ruth headed straight toward the eight-foot-high gray brick wall at the edge of the yard.

"I wonder if it's the same wall," she muttered to herself. "I wonder. Right along here. . . ."

"What was there?" Yeaworth asked her.

"My little pet dog," Ruth said, referring to Tar Baby, the mongrel she'd buried among the irises half a century before.

"My first one and the one I loved most," she said as she took slow steps, absorbed in an unsuccessful search.

Inside, the whitewashed walls were mottled like greasy butcher's paper; naked light bulbs dangled from twisted cords. It was time for tea, and they were led upstairs into a room dominated by a large table. It had once been their parents' bedroom.

"I'm sure our father would be very, very happy to know that we his children have come back here," Rosa told their hosts. "He always loved the people in Tsingkiang. He dreamed about them many, many times."

"People here," a Chinese man replied in English, "still have very good memory of your father and they knew that many of them were treated by your father and they knew that your father had done good things."

After their tea, they again explored, reminiscing out loud and squabbling cheerfully about the previous locations of furniture and whose bedroom had been where.

The nook in the house Ruth wanted to see most was her favorite attic bedroom over the kitchen wing. But it was impossible, their Chinese host told her, for the occupants had locked the door and he did not have a key. The party was told it was time to leave. Reluctantly, they headed for the cars, having found only one visible sign that they had ever lived there—two hooks in the porch ceiling where the swing had once hung.

In touring the compound they found that all of the buildings they had known as children were standing except for the Woodses' home, the boys' school and the men's hospital. The women's hospital and administration building were missing entire floors and had been converted into classroom buildings. The hospital where their father had practiced surgery was now a technical school, his former house apparently one of its dormitories. The Chinese-style house where Ruth had been born still stood, as did the schoolhouse where Lucy Fletcher taught Rosa, Ruth, Sandy Yates, and the Talbot boys each morning. The walk to school, as Ruth remembered it, had been long. But now she was surprised at how close it was to the house. It seemed that time shrank distance and buildings as well as people. The schoolhouse had been newly whitewashed and each room was filled with industrious young students, their heads bent intently over their books while a portrait of Chairman Mao watched from above the blackboard.

They toured several former missionary homes. All were overcrowded. Porches had been bricked in to make extra space, and entire families lived in one room. The Chinese guides could not contain their amazement that this American family had once had an entire two-story house to themselves.

"What," the interpreter asked Rosa, "did you do with all that room?"

By afternoon it was time to leave the compound. They took more photographs of their old house and climbed back into the limousines, preparing to drive to a nearby garment factory for another tour. When they emerged from the brick gate, they found the street lined with hundreds of Chinese who were applauding and waving. An elderly man rushed toward the car and grabbed Clayton's hand through the open window, shaking it warmly as though he recognized him. When Nelson Bell had left China he had been the same age his son was now. The family wondered who among the crowd along the roadside remembered their parents. They would never know.

That night, in the Tsingkiang Guest House, they had three unexpected visitors: a Chinese woman named Miriam Chen and her younger brother and sister. Miriam's sister Mah-li'ah had been a nurse in Nelson Bell's hospital. Later, during the Gang of Four's rise to power, she had committed suicide, leaving behind a husband and children. Miriam Chen chatted rapidly and unabashedly, gesturing with each remark.

"The seed your father sowed is still bearing fruit," she said quietly. "The older ones have mostly died but the younger ones are carrying on." She asked Clayton to lead them in prayer. Then, with tears in her eyes, she walked toward the front door. "God bless you," she said. "We are still Christians."

The next morning the group loaded their suitcases into the limousines. Their next stop in Tsingkiang was the new three-hundred-and-sixty-bed People's Hospital, where they observed surgery performed on patients whose only anesthesia was acupuncture. Issued white cotton boots, gowns and caps, they were invited into the operating room to witness a stomach resection and goiter removal. Later, they were driven to see the former home of Jim and Sophie Graham, the missionary couple who had met the Bells in 1916 when they first arrived in Shanghai, and had evacuated to Tsingtao with them twenty-one years later. The house had been converted into a wholesale grocery and vegetable outlet. The giant ginkgo trees and the rose garden were gone; the front steps and brick balustrade remained. Inside, the floors were grimy and worn smooth as stones in a creek bed, the steps sway-backed like an old horse. The corner room on the left where business was conducted had once been the living room where the missionaries had met Wednesday nights for prayer meetings. Ruth was flooded with memories: of "Aunt Sophie" playing hymns on the piano, vigorously nodding her head in time to the music; of the sun dipping below the tile roofs and the servant girl

Gwei Ying gliding about noiselessly to light the oil lamps; of "Uncle Jimmy" rising, his worn leather Bible in hand. Ruth often forgot to listen to his sermon as she watched him, fascinated by his bushy handlebar mustache and the waggling flap of skin under his jaw.

It had been in an upstairs bedroom that Ruth and Sandy Yates had spent a frosty December night in 1932 when Virginia Bell was in labor and the girls had been banished from the house.

> Ruth and Sandy climbed the stairs to the second floor, shyly entering the first bedroom to the right. The beds were piled with quilts and a welcoming fire crackled in the trash burner. Undressing as rapidly as possible, they scurried into their beds, grateful to feel the rubber hot water bottles tucked beneath the covers; the warmth at Ruth's feet traveled slowly up her legs like mercury in a thermometer. Whenever she shifted, the bitterly cold air seeped under the edge of her covers.
>
> Early the next morning Uncle Jimmy slipped into the bedroom with bundles of soybean stalks under an arm. Through one barely opened eye, Ruth watched him stoke the trash burner, light the fire and then steal away, quietly shutting the door behind him. She drifted back to sleep as the crackling, popping fire began slowly to thaw the air. An hour later she and Sandy reluctantly dashed out of bed, scooping up their clothing, dressing before the fire as the icy floor bit into the soles of their bare feet.
>
> That morning they returned home for breakfast and Ruth's father told them that Benjamin Clayton Bell had been born during the night.

As the group left the Graham house a Chinese guide told them that they would quickly swing by their former home—a key to the attic had been found. They drove the short distance, re-entering the building both strange and familiar, and they climbed the steep, narrow steps to the attic. At the top of the landing, immediately to the left, had been Rosa's room with its dormer window overlooking the hospital. To the right, up several more steps, was the room with its tiny window under the eaves. It was here Ruth had so often stood as a girl, wistfully staring beyond the wall, beyond the acres of grave mounds to the magnificent sunset on the horizon, imagining she was getting "a glimpse into heaven."

The Chinese guide fumbled with the key and clicked the lock open. The room was dark and crammed full of furniture, mattresses, and other miscellaneous items. Obviously, the door had been locked the day before because the residents had packed their clutter behind it, tidying up the house for their American guests. A light rain had begun to fall as they drove away for the last time.

On May 15, at a sandalwood factory in Suzhou, Ruth bought a fan for ten dollars because its spicy fragrance stirred up memories of her mother fanning herself and perhaps a nearby child during church services and prayer meetings in the stifling hot Tsingkiang summers. Then in an open market downtown she spotted an old Chinese peasant loitering beside his cart. She began bartering with him over the *bien dan* propped beside him, holding up one, two, and finally five yuan. He took the money and handed her the split bamboo pole which the Chinese have used for centuries to carry their burdens across their shoulders. As she picked up her new purchase, the crowd began to yell at the old man, claiming he had cheated her.

"You charged her too much," a young soldier shouted. "You should give her some back."

The man sheepishly handed one yuan back to Ruth.

"She could have gotten it for sixty cents in the country," a peasant woman muttered as Ruth walked away.

When she returned to her group she found the interpreter laughing. He explained that the money she had paid the old man was special money issued by the government to tourists and worthless to the natives.

"Well, anyone crooked enough to charge me so much will find a way to spend it," Ruth replied with a saucy smile.

That night they took an hour's train ride to Shanghai, where they were met by their hostess Madame Shi and two female interpreters named Da Hsiao and Shao Hsiao (Big Summer and Little Summer). The next morning, May 18, they attended a Sunday service at the Mo An Church. The sanctuary was filled and they were told that people had begun lining up at three o'clock that morning to get seats. Entering the old Gothic building they were greeted by the tinny piano rendition of "This Is My Father's World." Other traditional hymns and a sermon based on John 1:1–18 followed. That night, a retired Chinese schoolteacher approached Ruth. He was the son-in-law of the former pastor of the Chinese church the Bells had attended so many years ago in Tsingkiang. The man told Ruth that he had once visited her father, his foot badly infected.

"Your father not only healed my foot," he said, "he led me to Jesus Christ and I am a Christian today. I am your father's fruit."

That afternoon Ruth asked their government companion if she could visit a Chinese man and his wife, a couple known and loved by friends of Ruth's in the States. The man, a former pastor, had been released the previous March after twenty-two years at hard labor. His wife had spent fifteen years in another camp. Permission was granted and she took a taxi to the quiet street, finding the cramped, two-story house where the couple lived. The doorman told Ruth that they were not in. In her broken Chinese she left the message that she would be back at five o'clock that afternoon. She returned to her hotel, disappointed and frustrated.

"You know I needed to see them," she prayed silently. "I need to learn from them. We who have never been through what they have been through need to hear how You supported them—it may help prepare us for what lies ahead." The words floated through her mind: "Look to the Rock from whence ye were hewn." Later, she wrote, "We are so prone to look to one another for the help which we can only get from Him. When our time comes, He will sustain us, not with what He used to sustain these dear Christians necessarily, but He will sustain us Himself in whatever way He sees we need the most." When she returned to the apartment several hours later, her desire, she recalled, was to go "not in order to get, but to give."

The doorman led her upstairs and, without knocking, opened the couples' apartment door for her. She found herself facing a thin, balding man who squinted at her curiously, his eyes almost blind with cataracts. Then she met his wife. She was younger, almost as blind but at least, as she often pointed out, she had more teeth than he did. "He has five teeth," it was her wont to tease, "only two of which meet."

Ruth introduced herself and his mouth spread into a wide grin. Weeks earlier, several Chinese friends in the United States had asked Ruth to visit the elderly couple. One woman had suffered in a labor camp with the wife. She asked Ruth to deliver a letter and photographs to them. The pastor held the photographs close to his nose and chattered excitedly when he recognized the figures. Ruth produced the letter and, mindful of the couple's deafness, read it at the top of her voice, though she was sure that anyone outside the apartment could hear every word.

"Once," said the pastor toward the end of the visit, "your father invited me to Tsingkiang to hold meetings for the hospital staff and the patients who could walk and the families of the patients. But," he paused apologetically, "I was too busy."

"That's understandable," Ruth assured him.

She left them, somehow learning what she had wanted to know. There was no bitterness or complaining, no hatred for the perpetrators of their suffering. They were at peace. They were grateful to God, not because He had shielded them from pain, not because He had prevented the loss of their human rights and for a while even the loss of each other, but because He had given them the strength to bear it all.

The last day in Shanghai, shortly before they were to fly home, Ruth, her sisters, and her brother walked on the bund along the Huang-p'u River. On Quinsan Road they found an old four-story building with arched windows and ornate dormers along the roof. Ruth stared at the familiar gray bricks and the black number four painted in the doorway, confirming that it was the former Missionary Home. The memories washed over her as she conjured up the image of the young girl on top of the sheets in the stuffy darkness, crying because she did not want to leave home, preferring death to the pain of separation.

Again, today, May 21, 1980, she was leaving. But this time it was with no regrets and with no desire to return. She had seen the gray brick walls, the bleak remnants of her past. She had found them depressing until it had occurred to her: "God's work is not in buildings but in transformed lives."

Epilogue

June 5, 1982
Nickerson Field
Boston University
Boston, Massachusetts

It was almost 7:30 and the faint swells of "He Is Lord" floated up from the field. Linking arms with a friend, another acquaintance behind her to shield her with an umbrella, Ruth ventured out into the rain-spattered dusk.

She slogged through the mud, dragging her trash bag–covered pumps over makeshift boardwalks and puddled artificial grass. Choosing an empty row on the playing field, several hundred yards from the platform and just in front of the back tiers, she tilted a gray metal folding chair to spill the inch of rainwater from it. Demurely, she seated herself, tucking her skirt and bright pink rain cloak around her. Momentarily, she proceeded to loosen one finger at a time, removing her wet black kid gloves and tucking them inside the dry interior of her purse. She wormed her hands up her sleeves, kimono-style.

Regal and unflinching in the bone-chilling downpour, she sat erect, the steady thrumming of rain muffling her husband's voice as it echoed off the stands. Swathed in a heavy khaki trench coat and now hatless, he preached, slightly bent against the blustery wind and rain, the awning flapping wildly above him. He could see little but the hazy white glow of the lights clustered on poles girdling the field high above him. He was oblivious to the bird that had alighted on a nearby lamp and then commenced singing lustily for the duration of the service, as though it were chirping a shrill concert solely for his benefit. From his vantage, the crowd was dark and formless.

To her he was a faraway yet beloved figure, sometimes obscured by umbrellas tilting in her line of vision. Soberly she listened, her eyes riveted straight ahead. She smiled when he leaned close to the microphones and began teasing her about the "bright new rain outfit" she had just purchased, cracking the usual jokes about wives and their outrageous shopping habits, adding that she was sitting "somewhere out there among you, but I don't know exactly where."

The Boston crusade is just one of many she will attend now. For the first time, she is truly free to travel with him, though she does not have the energy to make some of the trips, the ones to Eastern Europe, for example. Shortly after Boston they will leave for Europe. By the fall of 1983, she will have traveled with him to crusades in Spokane, Washington; Chapel Hill, North Carolina; the Bahamas; Orlando, Florida; she will have accompanied him on trips to Mexico; Washington, D.C.; Jamaica; San Francisco; southern France; and Amsterdam, The Netherlands. All she wants in life now, she says, "is to be free to help Bill." By now she has resigned from the various boards she was on. She refuses numerous invitations to speak. She's mulish in her reluctance to appear on talk shows or grant interviews. She regrets that she doesn't have time to write the forewords to the four or five unsolicited manuscripts writers mail to her monthly. When they are home together in Little Piney Cove, she's finding illustrations for his sermons just as she did forty years ago when she was a young bride in Hinsdale, Illinois.

Some fifteen minutes later, with head slightly bowed, she shut her eyes in prayer as strains of "Just as I Am" rose above the rain and the wind. Thirteen hundred people, some bareheaded, others shielding themselves with umbrellas and trash bags, streamed forward, forming a dark pool around the raw plank platform. After Billy's closing prayer, after the counselors had been dispatched to talk with those who had made their walk of surrender, Ruth stood. At the vanguard of the exiting crowd, and yet unnoticed, she made her way back to the field house.

Once inside, an aide quickly and quietly whisked her across the mud-splotched tile floor. In a flash of bright pink she was ushered toward the entrance, where a station wagon waited in the pitch black night, motor idling, wiper blades vigorously swishing water off the windshield. She paused before walking outside, stooping to remove the trash can liners from her shoes. For a brief moment, when the back car door was opened, her face was illuminated by the interior light, her sharp features silhouetted as she ducked and gathered her garments around her. In the muffled sound of a door sucking shut, she vanished, as though the night had parted and then sealed, swallowing her.

Index